BATTLEGROUND BERLIN

DIARIES 1945-1948

EUROPEAN SOURCES

LITERATURE

American Journals
Albert Camus

Diary of An Unknown
Jean Cocteau

Letters to Gala
Paul Eluard

Letters to Merline
Rainer Maria Rilke

Souvenir Portraits
Jean Cocteau

HISTORY

Berlin Underground: 1938–1945
Ruth Andreas-Friedrich

Battleground Berlin: 1945–1948
Ruth Andreas-Friedrich

Series Editors
Russell Epprecht and Sylvère Lotringer

BATTLEGROUND BERLIN

DIARIES 1945-1948

Ruth Andreas-Friedrich

Translated by Anna Boerresen
Afterword by Jörg Drews

Paragon House Publishers
New York

First American edition, 1990
Published in the United States by
Paragon House
90 Fifth Avenue
New York, NY 10011

Originally published in German under the title *Schauplatz Berlin:
Tagebuchaufzeichnungen 1945–1948*.

Copyright © 1984 by Suhrkamp Verlag.

Designed by Deirdre C. Amthor

Library of Congress Cataloging-in-Publication Data
Andreas-Friedrich, Ruth.
[Schauplatz Berlin. English]
Battleground Berlin: diaries, 1945–1948/by Ruth Andreas-Friedrich;
translated by Anna Boerresen.—1st American ed.
p. cm.
Translation of: Schauplatz Berlin.
ISBN 1-55778-191-5
1. Andreas-Friedrich, Ruth—Diaries. 2. Berlin (Germany)—
History—Allied occupation, 1945– 3. Berlin (Germany)—
Biography. I Title.
DD857.A65A3 1990
943.1'55087'092—dc20   89-77176
CIP

Manufactured in the United States of America

The paper used in this publication meets the minimum requirements
of American National Standard for Information Sciences—Permanence
of Paper for Printed Library Materials, ANSI Z39.48-1984.

10 9 8 7 6 5 4 3 2 1

DEDICATED TO HEIKE AND FRANK

BATTLEGROUND BERLIN

DIARIES 1945-1948

"They're still shooting," Frank says into the darkness. I can hear him fumbling for matches. A small flame flickers up, then fades away. Kerosene fumes pervade the cellar.

"What's going on?"

"They're shooting," Frank repeats.

"Who?"

I try to make sense of it. War? No. When we went to bed the war had been over. Yesterday was the final battle for Berlin. The front at our door. We were sitting in the cellar. Jo Thäler, Frank, Andrik and Fabian. Heike Burghoff, Dagmar and I. Two illegals, two semilegals, three quasi-legals. The whole clique.

Strafings, flamethrowers, shellfire. In between, werewolves. Their guns sounding like dogs barking at the storming Russians. Suddenly a boom, then shouts. "They're coming," someone yells. Strangers are pushing their way through the hallway. Andrik runs up to them. "*Drusya*," we hear him call out. *"Drusya, tovarish!* . . . friends!"* Then we are conquered. Eat Russian kasha with Russian soldiers. And upstairs Russian officers take up quarters . . .

"Frank," I whisper, "who's shooting?"

1

"Wake the others," he says instead of an answer.

I get off my mattress. Next to me lies Jo Thäler with the blanket pulled over his head. Two steps away lies Dagmar. Breathing like a sleeping child. "Get up!" I stumble into the hallway. "Heike! Fabian!" At my feet two shadows roll off the folding bed. "But where's Andrik?"

His place in front of the cellar door is empty. The pillow is cold. "Andrik," I shout. No answer.

In the meantime Frank has lit our shelter lamp. A makeshift lamp in a glass jar. Reddish soot rises from the wick made of wool. The six of us stand around the small white table that for three years has held our air shelter paraphernalia. Still drugged with sleep, we stare at the gas masks, the bandages for burns, the biscuits and water bottle, and a dusty pile of goggles.

"What's going on?"

"Can't you hear it?" asks Frank. "Werewolves!"

Heike's childlike face looks terror-stricken.

Frank nods. "It looks as if they haven't buried the hatchet yet. What's the word up there?"

Above our heads the pounding steps of soldiers. We hear a shout. Something like *"Rassypatoya."* It sounds like a command. Again a shot is fired.

"Damn it!" mutters Frank.

Suddenly Andrik is back. "They needed me as an interpreter," he says. "They were quite friendly, but . . . "

Tack, tack . . . tack, tack, tack it goes against the outside wall.

"And that calls itself peace," sighs Fabian while rolling a few cigarettes.

"What time is it?"

"Six o'clock," says Jo Thäler.

Dagmar searches through our supplies. "I suggest we have breakfast." Shoving bandages and goggles aside, she puts a loaf of bread on the table.

From bottles, cups and pots we collect the little water we have left. Heike spreads jam on slices of bread. "One sip of water for each slice of bread," she decides. We eat silently. The water cup is passed around.

2

It turns seven. Then eight. Above us soldiers' boots are pounding. Suddenly the cellar door flies open. "Hey!" someone shouts. Andrik leaps forward.

"What's up?" he asks in Russian.

"Order to vacate." The Mongolian sentry who seemed so friendly yesterday now brandishes his machine gun. "Twenty minutes . . . *dvatset minuty,*" he urges.

"For heaven's sake, why?"

The soldier motions outside. There machine-gun fire is erupting again. "*Skoro . . . skoro . . .*" He tells us to hurry up.

We feel paralyzed. "I'll talk to them," says Andrik and hurries upstairs. He returns looking depressed. "It's because of the were-wolves. They're combing the neighborhood. They lost ten men last night. I can't blame them."

"*Skoro . . . skoro . . . ,*" the sentry reminds us.

In the cellar chaos sets in. Packing . . . searching . . . opening suit-cases . . . closing suitcases. Everybody is in everybody else's way.

"My manuscripts," cries Fabian. "They were right here a minute ago." In a panic, he indiscriminately throws everything around.

In a corner Heike prepares sandwiches of bread and jam which she stuffs into her string bag. Four minutes left, two minutes. Only a breath away from having to leave a life we had grown accustomed to.

"The typewriter! Don't forget the typewriter," Frank shouts. I let go of a suitcase full of summer dresses, and rummaging among boxes and bags and scattered closet contents, I grab the typewriter. Air raid losses, at least, spared one the task of having to decide oneself what could be done without for the future.

"Are you ready?" Staggering under our heavy loads, one after an-other we climb the cellar stairs.

"*Aiye ucknyem . . .* haul away . . . ," whistles Fabian.

We don't look back. In single file we plod across the market garden that separates our housing complex at the water tower from the cem-etery. Andrik is walking next to me. Two suitcases in his right hand, two in his left. Sweat is pouring from his forehead.

"Where to?" I ask.

"Wherever. We shall see." He smiles encouragingly. "Hand in hand," he quietly quotes the theme of our love.

3

The morning is clear and beautiful. At least spring can't be taken away from us.

"Across the cemetery," shouts Frank, who by natural disposition has become our scout. "Bismarckstrasse is cordoned off."

We turn into the cemetery. On the path lies a dead soldier. His arms outspread, his face turned toward the sky. He is not the only one. They are lying about, left and right. Squeezed between the graves like sheaves of grain after the cut. Around them bright spring. "Faithful unto death . . . " I read on one of the fallen tombstones. Faithful to whom? The Nazis? The Fatherland? The oath of allegiance? The silent dead are the silent answer. "To yourself . . . only to yourself . . . "

"Listen to that blackbird!" Heike gives me a push. For a moment I let go of my bags. "Indeed . . . there still are blackbirds."

A shadow appears in the sky. "Watch out for strafers," Jo shouts. In a split second we are all lying flat. Our faces pressed against the grave mounds, close to the dead below and around us. Machine-gun fire whizzes above us, so low it nearly touches us. We almost crawl into the ground, we become as flat as stamps. Then all is quiet. Carefully Frank looks up.

"We can continue now." He gets up and brushes the sand off his knees.

"Aiye ucknyem," whistles Fabian.

Beyond Bergstrasse sentries stop us. Andrik negotiates. He keeps trying to make them understand. Our eyes are glued to his face. Now he finishes.

"Into town." Resignedly he picks up his bags. More and more slowly we drag ourselves through the streets. No one is about. Once in a while a Russian soldier passes us, looks at us with suspicion and reaches for his machine gun. In the distance the sound of shooting.

"Stop!" Frank says suddenly.

We are in front of a bombed-out building. Bombs have stripped its roof and compressed the top floors. Next to the ripped-out front door a heap of rubble. The sound of engines . . .

"Inside," shouts Frank. With our bags and bundles we stumble across the debris, down some stairs, up some stairs, and then find ourselves in an empty coal cellar. Above us bombs are crashing.

4

"Our new home, how cozy." Heike throws her knapsack onto the floor and searchingly looks around. "Hmm . . ."

Fifteen minutes later the attack is over. "What now?" Quietly I wonder how we will manage to turn our twenty-nine pieces of luggage into seven passably comfortable beds.

"We have to look around," says Frank. "No house consists of coal cellars alone."

An hour later we try for the second time to get to the janitor's basement apartment. One room with a kitchen. Furnished even, at least insofar as anything remains after the bombs.

"If we go on this way we'll reach the first floor by evening."

We pull our luggage up the cellar stairs. At the door another delay. Five Russians block the entrance. "Clock? Clock?" they demand.

Frank obediently raises his sleeve. "Eight minutes past eleven."

That was not what they meant. In a second his watch disappears into the questioner's pocket.

"Clock? Clock?" The tone is friendly, almost cordial. Five watches change hands. Watchless and timeless we move into the partially bombed-out basement apartment left behind by Erwin Machulke, the janitor.

Four men, three women. The remnants of the resistance group "Uncle Emil."

"We should clean up a little," says Heike, looking at the fallen plaster on furniture and floor. "If we are to stay for a while . . ."

Whirling dust in our noses. Like startled chickens the men flee into the farthest corner. One and a half hours later Herr Machulke's partially bombed-out basement apartment looks almost comfortable. Dagmar inspects the kitchen cabinet.

"Nothing left," she declares. "Completely cleaned out. And I am terribly hungry."

Hungry? Suddenly we too realize we have not eaten anything since morning. One cannot live on air alone. Nor on manuscripts inside an evacuee's suitcase.

"We have to look around," Frank repeats his advice from this morning. He turns to Jo. "You want to come along?"

Jo Thäler nods. Together they try to reach the upper floors.

5

"Don't fall," Heike calls after them. Their chin-ups through the collapsed staircase look quite perilous.

"Catch," we soon hear from above. Two mattresses come flying down. Pillows, two horse blankets, a frying pan, a dressing gown. They return with their pockets full.

"It's hardly worth the effort," says Frank and throws a few small sacks of grits and noodles, two ropes of onions and a pack of ersatz coffee onto the table. "At most enough for one meal. We have to keep looking for more."

Looking at the inconspicuous little sacks, we are troubled by something. What about their owners . . . Our conscience bothers us. Everybody knows the Seventh Commandment: Thou shalt not . . . Thou shalt not . . . Silently we stand around the table.

"Huiiiii," we hear outside. The floor is trembling.

"Crash!" A bomb explodes nearby.

The small sacks fly across the table. We are showered with pieces of plaster falling from the ceiling, and as if by a spell, we have forgotten about the Seventh Commandment.

Where will we be after the next bomb falls? And where those little sacks? Or their owners? Far from here is our home in the housing complex at the water tower. And there is everything we had owned, all that we had grown attached to. The order of things has ceased. Suddenly we feel as if intoxicated. We are talking loudly all at once.

"Come on," Fabian calls. We run outside. Only Andrik stays behind, pensively looking after us.

The streets are deserted. There are no more streets. Just torn-up ditches filled with rubble between rows of ruins. What kind of people used to live here? The war has blown them away. Just as it drove us into Erwin Machulke's basement apartment. The order of things has ceased. To stay alive one must eat. We are alive. As never before we feel we are alive.

"That's the way to the abyss," I think as we plunge like birds of prey into the ruins left and right. We climb across mountains of ruins, rummage through rubble and broken glass, crawl through unknown cellars, tear out other people's boxes and bags. Shellfire above us. We don't pay attention. We hardly bother to take cover. A fever has gotten hold of us.

6

"Look, bouillon cubes! Whole boxes full of bouillon cubes," Fabian shouts out of a hole in a cellar. "And gumdrops! And sherbet powder! Enough to open a store!" Full of excitement his dust-covered face appears from behind a heap of rubble.

Sherbet powder! Why sherbet powder? None of us ever cared for sherbet powder. And now, by the sweat of our brows, we are hauling five boxes of raspberry sherbet powder through the ruins of Berlin. Jubilating as if we had found a treasure. Triumphantly, Frank shows off three fustian shirts, a pair of overalls, a pair of rubber boots and two bleached-out woolen vests.

"You want to wear them?" Andrik asks. We look bewildered, like sleepwalkers who have been awakened. Wordlessly, Jo Thäler shoves his bundle of women's underwear behind the wardrobe.

• • •

MONDAY, APRIL 30, 1945

Four of us are lying in the Machulkes' marital bed. On the mattresses from upstairs. Covered with horse blankets of unknown provenance.

"There is no place like home," it says on a colorful silk embroidery above the bed. The sun shines into the room. No one has the least idea what time it is. In the kitchen Heike is cooking soup from bouillon cubes. Breakfast? Lunch? Dinner?

"Who cares. One eats when there is something to eat and when one is hungry."

We are hungry. We have something to eat. So we eat.

"A piece of bread wouldn't be bad," mutters Fabian.

Dagmar scolds him: "Gourmand. You should be glad . . ." She stops short. We hear footsteps in the hallway. A face appears at the door. Our Mongolian sentry from the housing complex at the water tower.

"*Strastitye*," he greets us and grins. We jump up. Andrik translates.

"He's only come to visit us," he explains. "He's proud that he found us."

"Visit us?"

7

We are relieved. Heike rushes to get a chair and fills a bowl with bouillon soup for our guest. He sniffs it with suspicion and sneers at it.

"No good," he says shaking his head. "Good for pigs." Offended, Heike takes the product of her culinary efforts away. Nobody likes to feel like a second-rate person. For the first time we feel that we have been conquered.

Meanwhile our guest has made himself comfortable. With a broad grin he reaches into his pocket and throws a handful of candies onto the table.

"For the girls," Andrik translates. For three hours the Mongolian sits there and chats. The machine gun on his knees, two hand grenades in his belt, he digs up amazing things from the bottom of his pockets: wristwatches, lighters, gold rings, silver necklaces. Like a child he jingles with his treasures, turns them in his fingers, and playfully holds them up to the light.

"Where did you get all that?" Andrik asks.

"Trophies," he answers simply. So that is what it is called—trophies. The sherbet powder and the bouillon cubes. The fustian shirts and the woolen vests. Not theft—trophies! There is nothing in the Seventh Commandment about trophies.

At last the Mongolian gets chummy. "Come, woman," he says to Dagmar and tries to pull her onto his lap. Dagmar refuses. She is wriggling and squirming. The Mongolian jumps up angrily.

"*Tschort!*" he curses. He grabs his machine gun and looks like an irritated beast. With some difficulty Andrik succeeds in appeasing him. "*Maya dotchka* . . . my daughter."

"Ah, *dotchka!* Family!" the soldier nods and slowly calms down. But the friendship remains ruptured, and we all feel relieved when he leaves shortly thereafter.

"Let's go trophying," Frank suggests in the evening. It is just past sunset. Again the streets lie deserted.

"But where are all the Berliners?" Heike wonders.

"In the bunkers, where else? Not everyone feels like . . . "

"*Huiiiii,*" a hail of gunfire from low-flying airplanes is bursting against the next wall . . . "being a walking target." Jo Thäler finishes his sentence as we get up from lying in the dust. Get up, lie down, lie down, get up. Carefully we move on. Suddenly Heike cries out.

In front of us a white ox comes trotting around the corner. With gentle eyes and heavy horns. Who knows where he has come from. It wasn't the streets of Berlin that gave birth to him. Frank and Jo look at each other. A trophy? Thou shall not steal . . . Strafers, grenades, ruins . . . Should we . . . could we? Cautiously the ox stumbles around a bomb crater. Yes, a trophy; the crater decides. In a moment we have surrounded the animal. Jo grabs its horns. Together we haul it into the courtyard of our refuge apartment. Andrik shakes his head.

"We have to ask the Russians."

We ask the Russians.

"Take it before someone else does," they say, and a soldier is sent along with us to give the ox the coup de grace.

Five minutes later it is done. Five minutes later we all act as if we have gone mad. Brandishing kitchen knives, their sleeves rolled up, Frank and Jo are crouching around the dead animal. Blood drips from their hands, blood runs down their arms and trickles in thin lines across the trodden lawn. And suddenly, as if the underworld had spit them out, a noisy crowd gathers around the dead ox.

They come creeping out of a hundred cellar holes. Women, men, children. Was it the smell of blood that attracted them? They come running with buckets. With tubs and vats. Screaming and gesticulating they tear pieces of meat from each other's hands.

"The liver belongs to me," someone growls.

"The tongue is mine . . . the tongue . . . the tongue!" Five blood-covered fists angrily pull the tongue out of the ox's throat.

Heike starts to cry. "How disgusting!"

"Ah," a woman screams, and rushing away from the crowd, she spins around twice and then hastens away. Above her head she waves the ox's tail.

I sneak away. Never in my life have I felt so miserable. So that is what the hour of liberation amounts to. Is this the moment we have awaited for twelve years? That we might fight over an ox's liver? And grab what we don't need, take what we never wanted to have? No, that is . . .

I don't know what it is. In any case it is something horrifying. It is something so hopeless that I flee into the Machulkes' marital bed, pull the trophied horse blanket over my head, and sink into a leaden sleep.

In the middle of the night I wake up. A flashlight is shining into my face.

"Come, woman," I hear a voice. The smell of cheap liquor assails me.

"Andrik!" I call out. "Frank!" A hand covers my mouth.

"Good woman . . . come," the voice repeats. A heavy body falls upon me.

"No, no," I gargle, half choked, trying to slip deeper into the pillows. The smell of cheap liquor. Close to my ear panting breath. "O God! . . . Dear God!"

At this moment the door is flung open. Andrik comes rushing in, carrying a candle, his face pale and distorted. Behind him noise. The strange soldier lets go of me and gets up. Self-consciously he answers Andrik's authoritative questions.

"What are you doing here?" he snaps at me.

"What am I doing?" Only now I awake completely. "I think . . . nothing!"

"Well then," mumbles Andrik. His voice sounds broken. He looks at the Russian, motions toward the door and turns around to leave. The scare is over. I am alone again in the dark.

Only toward morning the others arrive. Upset, exhausted. Russian guests throughout the night. Bad guests. May Day drunks chasing after love.

"Like stuck pigs their victims were squealing in the cellars," Fabian says with a shudder.

Andrik falls onto the bed. The smell of cheap liquor.

"Have you been drinking?"

"Drrrrink," he babbles. "I drank all night, so they would leave the girls . . ." The rest of the sentence is drowned by sleep.

O Andrik, my dear guardian!

• • •

TUESDAY, MAY 1, 1945

Silently we gather for our breakfast of bouillon-cube soup. All of us are lost in thought. No happy thoughts. Finally Jo breaks the silence.

"Once in a while everybody breaks down."

Frank nods. The trophied overalls prey on his mind.

"The others are no angels either." Heike tries to justify herself.

"Except that that doesn't concern us," Andrik replies dryly.

We all fall silent again. Yesterday's feeling of intoxication has changed into a leaden morning-after feeling. A mood that does not pass, even when toward noon the Mongolian shows up and announces that we may return to our home.

"Partisanski wiped out," he laughs and taps his machine gun.

Lazily, almost indifferently, we get ready to leave. Packing, rummaging, getting our things together. Farewell, Herr Machulke. Farewell, our home of three days. With twenty-nine pieces of luggage, with bouillon cubes and sherbet powder, with gumdrops and three buckets full of freshly slaughtered ox meat, we set out for home.

The shellfire has stopped. The airplanes are quieter too. Only occasionally a fighter plane roams in delicate loops above us. For the second time the war seems over.

From bunkers and cellars living beings hesitantly reappear. People are coming our way. In small groups or pairs. They are wearing white armbands, the women red kerchiefs. Fabian taps my shoulder.

"Fashionable imitation—Nazi flags as Soviet symbols."

I try to figure out the reason for his sarcasm. Indeed: from every kerchief shines unfaded the round centerpiece, betraying evidence of where there used to be a swastika. What is going on in the heads beneath these scarves? Yesterday brown. Today red. Tomorrow perhaps the Star-Spangled Banner, and the Union Jack the day after. Can one's ideology be changed by simply pulling a few threads? Those who need scarves and armbands, buttonhole decorations and insignia, need them for their own sake. Because they do not trust themselves. But can we trust ourselves? I think of the gumdrops. The woolen vests and the slaughtered ox. Perhaps it is all a matter of degree. And none of us is in any position to judge anyone else.

The farther south we get the more we are confronted by the war's terrible destructiveness. We clamber over bomb craters. We squeeze through tangled barbed wire and hastily constructed barricades of furniture. It was with sofas that our army tried to block the Russian advance! With oilcloth sofas, wing chairs and broken armoires. One could laugh if it didn't rather make one feel like crying.

Tanks riddled with holes block the way. A pitiful sight, pointing their muzzles toward the sky. A smell of fatality comes from them. Sweet, heavy, oppressive. "It's the smell of death," it occurs to me. I hastily move on.

The sentries are gone. Only a few scattered cartridge cases mark the deserted post. Burned-out buildings left and right. God be with us, if it goes on this way. Silently we keep walking. The weight of our luggage is crushing us.

"Aiye ucknyem," whistles Fabian.

Behind a projection in a wall sits an old man. A pipe in his right hand, a lighter in his left. He is sitting in the sun, completely motionless. Why is he sitting so still? Why doesn't he move at all? A fly is crawling across his face. Green, fat, shiny. Now it crawls into his eyes. The eyes . . . Oh God have mercy! Something slimy is dripping onto his cheeks. A dead man is sitting here, and it wasn't only yesterday he died . . .

At last the water tower looms up in the distance. We are at the cemetery. The gate to the mortuary is wide open. Again that sweet, oppressive smell.

"Oh no! Look," Fabian stammers.

Apprehensively I glimpse into the dim room.

Bodies, nothing but bodies. Laid out on the floor. Row after row, body after body. Children are among them, adults and some very old people. Brought here from who knows where.

That draws the final line under five years of war. Children filling mortuaries and old men decomposing behind walls . . .

"Has someone planted raspberry jelly here?" Dagmar interrupts my thoughts. I look up. In the grass in front of me are two jars of preserves. Next to them are more. As if the contents of a pantry had been strewn across the green lawn. Pierced cans, half-emptied jars of jam, bottles, jugs, paper bags and boxes. In between a red-striped eiderdown. Dirty, lumpy.

"A bivouac!" Frank lets go of his bags and picks up one of the objects in the grass. "Peas, medium fine," he makes out from the soaked label.

By the time we leave the cemetery we have gathered a complete dinner. Tasting a little sandy, faintly smelling of garbage, but nevertheless a dinner. Gleanings from the leftovers of a Russian victory party.

At last we arrive at the housing complex. It is still standing. They haven't burned it down. They've been more humane than the avengers of Lidice.

"Good old house," Heike says and appreciatively she pats the sooted wall. "It's still standing! It held out!"

We hurry upstairs. An unbearable stench assails us. Torn-open drawers, knocked-over closets, broken chairs, soiled tables. We wade through clothes and kitchen utensils. Phonograph records are breaking under our feet, empty pill containers and broken bottles. Something slimy makes me slip.

"They can't have been sober." Repulsed, I hold my nose. Andrik stands at the bathroom door. Aghast, he stares at the cause of the stench.

"Buffaloes must have done this," he stammers, totally overwhelmed, and tries to flush the toilet.

There is no water. Nor is there gas, electricity or telephone. Only chaos. Total and impenetrable chaos.

Dagmar comes back from the cellar. "It's even worse down there," she reports and distractedly runs her hands through her hair. "It's a deluge, I tell you, a real deluge!"

• • •

WEDNESDAY, MAY 2, 1945

Fabian has built a stove. Out of bricks on the kitchen floor. It smokes terribly. But it works. There are enough broken things to keep the fire going.

I squat in front of the low grate. Everything is sooty and grimy. Every drop of water is precious. After twenty minutes I look as if I've been lying in a pile of coal. Around me everyone is busy rummaging and sorting things out. Doors are being fixed, windows nailed shut. Only now we discover what is missing, and we jubilate at everything that is found again.

In the afternoon Frank organizes an expedition for water. The next pump is three blocks away. There are many people waiting in line. The pump handle is passed to the next in line. We queue up at the end. It's more than two hours till it's our turn.

"Normally we get it from the reservoir," says a woman in front of me. "But since there's a body floating in it . . ."

"Of course," I agree, "you can't drink the water when there are bodies in it."

"It is a civilian," the woman objects hesitantly.

I hold my tongue. I've never before examined the problem of water hygiene from quite this point of view.

Frank is talking to the owner of a storage-cell radio. He pumps him for information as if he were a living newspaper. "Great news," he says, beaming with joy as we set up relays to get our eight buckets of water home. "I tell you, it's incredible."

Back home he gives us the sensational news: Hitler lies dead in the chancellery; Goebbels has taken poison with his wife and children; Himmler is still fighting in Breslau, and Epp has supposedly attempted a coup in Munich.

"What is the source of your information?" Jo asks.

Frank doesn't reply. He looks at us expectantly. "Well, what do you say . . . ?"

"Hmm," mumbles Andrik. The others remain silent.

"I didn't know Hitler was in Berlin," Dagmar says. Suddenly we become aware of the absurdity of this moment. Hitler is dead! And we act as if it didn't concern us. Events have overtaken him. The Third Reich has vanished like a ghost.

Together with the swastikas on his Nazi flags, Herr Hitler has been thrown in the garbage. To hell with you, Führer and Chancellor of the Reich! *Tempi passati!* You're nothing to us now.

• • •

FRIDAY, MAY 4, 1945

Still no water, no electricity, no gas. No means of transportation and no telephone. Hauling water from the well takes hours every day. We work like slaves. Kindle the fire, gather wood, chop wood, sweep up the rubble. Cleaning up, constantly cleaning up.

Occasionally, Russian visitors show up. They go from room to room, looking around and taking whatever they like. They are not unfriendly, but they are not friendly either. They look right through us as if we don't exist. "Clock, clock," they say sometimes. "Schnapps," and "Velocipede."

Our bicycles disappear. Behind the cemetery there is an asphalt road. There the victors learn how to ride a bike. They do it like children. Persistently and eagerly, unconcerned about the wreckage they leave behind. After three days the street is littered with bicycle parts.

"Flotsam," Frank decides. "I am for retrieving it."

At dusk we set out to pick up the pieces of what was once whole and ours. Saddles and handlebars, twisted frames and torn tubes.

"A nice little do-it-yourself job." Resignedly Frank looks at the pile of junk.

• • •

SUNDAY, MAY 6, 1945

Frank and I venture into the neighboring suburbs. Red kerchiefs and white armbands still dominate the streets. But those who wear them are not carrying suitcases today. Indefatigably, with grim persistence, they are clearing the streets.

"Why are you in such a rush?" Frank asks a woman who wields a shovel.

"Because they . . . ," she swallows, "because they'll burn down the houses if we aren't finished by tonight." Her eyes look like those of a dog that has been beaten up.

"It won't be as bad as all that," we console her. But the woman has turned around already and resumed her hasty work.

"Poor slaves," Frank says.

"But what if it's true?" I ask, alarmed, "I mean that they'll burn down the houses."

Frank shrugs his shoulders. "Maybe it's true. But their fear makes it worse. The Russians don't like cowards."

No, they don't like cowards. Like children and wild animals they like calm, secure friendliness. To those who look at them as if they

15

were dangerous they become dangerous. These days they have become dangerous to many. Panic prevails in the city. Dismay and terror. Wherever we go there is pillaging, looting, violence. With unrestrained sexual lust our conqueror's army has flung itself upon the women of Berlin.

We visit Hannelore Thiele, Heike's friend and classmate. She sits huddled on her couch. "One ought to kill oneself," she moans. "This is no way to live." She covers her face with her hands and starts to cry. It is terrible to see her swollen eyes, terrible to look at her disfigured features.

"Was it really that bad?" I ask.

She looks at me pitifully. "Seven," she says. "Seven in a row. Like animals."

Inge Zaun lives in Klein-Machnow. She is eighteen years old and didn't know anything about love. Now she knows everything. Over and over again, sixty times.

"How can you defend yourself?" she says impassively, almost indifferently. "When they pound at the door and fire their guns senselessly. Each night new ones, each night others. The first time when they took me and forced my father to watch, I thought I would die. Later . . ." She makes a feeble gesture. "Since their captain has taken me as his mistress, it is fortunately only one. He listens to me too and helps make sure they leave the girls alone."

I shudder. For four years Goebbels told us that the Russians would rape us. That they would rape and plunder, murder and pillage.

"Atrocity propaganda!" we said as we waited for the Allied liberators.

We don't want to be disappointed now. We couldn't bear it if Goebbels was right. For twelve years we've been adversaries. We hoped for once to be "for something." If that fails us now . . .

"They rape our daughters, they rape our wives," the men lament. "Not just once, but six times, ten times and twenty times." There is no other talk in the city. No other thought either. Suicide is in the air. They hide the girls behind the roof beams, they bury them under piles of coal and bundle them up like old women. Almost none of them sleeps where she belongs.

"Honor lost, all lost," a bewildered father says and hands a rope to his daughter who has been raped twelve times. Obediently she goes and hangs herself from the nearest window sash.

"If you get raped, nothing is left to you but death," a teacher declares to a class of girls two days before the final collapse. More than half the students came to the anticipated conclusion, as expected of them, and drowned themselves and their lost honor in the nearest body of water. Honor lost, all lost. Poison or bullet, rope of knife. They are killing themselves by the hundreds.

"Frank," I ask him, "do you understand any of this?"

He shakes his head. "But we must understand. If we don't understand, the future ends for us before it has even begun."

I nod. "If this is the upshot of our waiting twelve years, it's pretty sad."

Silently we wander through the streets. The later it gets the more hurried the shoveling becomes everywhere. Absentmindedly, Frank looks at the red kerchiefs and the white armbands.

"Perhaps there is a way . . . ," he begins ponderingly, ". . . I mean a way to understand this." I look at him. "You see," he continues, "when we invaded their country, killed their men, carried away their belongings, the muzhiks thought: They must be poorer than we are. They must suffer from hunger and need. That they would have understood because it's simple and natural. But it wasn't simple. And it wasn't natural. And when they came to Germany they saw we had houses and even bathtubs and mirrors and fancy furniture. Do you understand now why they got so mad? The plundering and looting, the smashing and pillaging? It's the mirrors that made them mad, the bathtubs and fancy furniture. One doesn't attack someone if one is so much better off than one's victim."

"That's it," I agree, grateful to Frank for helping me to regain my faith. "But the rapes," I suddenly remember, "you don't rape just because you don't have fancy furniture. And if you do, then certainly not with entire battalions."

"On the contrary, you do it with entire battalions," Frank interrupts me. "That's what it's about. You must see it as species specific to primitive man."

"Being a primitive man doesn't make one a rapist," I object.

"What foolish logic! Of course not. But if you follow your natural

17

inclinations, you instinctively wish to possess. Flesh or soil, soil or flesh. To primitive man they are the same. Victory is a physical process. It's felt physically and it's expressed physically. It's not nice but it's understandable."

"Not nice but . . . understandable," I admit reluctantly. "In other words, the Russians' intoxication with victory manifests itself in the flesh."

Frank nods. "The flesh of our women. In the flesh they take possession of German soil a little at a time—in the flesh they impregnate it night after night."

Evening is drawing on. Possessed by fear, the diggers keep working. Not being one of them, we become almost suspect. A man casts a hateful glance at us.

"Commissars," we hear him hissing. "Bloody stool pigeons!"

The insult is without effect.

At home, in the meantime, guests have arrived. Everyone feels compelled to make contact in order to find out who is still alive. In catchwords the latest news is exchanged: Cease-fire since yesterday, fighting still going on in Prague. Hitler dead due to a cerebral hemorrhage.

We still subsist on rumors. Still obtain information in a roundabout way through someone's storage-cell radio.

"And how was it here with the rapes?" we are asked.

"They never happened," Andrik answers.

"Because you prevented it," I corrected him.

"A lucky thing for you he knows the language," our guests sigh. "Speaking the language makes everything easier."

It is true. The inability to communicate with each other takes the human element out of any encounter between victors and vanquished. Now we have to pay bitterly for the fact that our school deliberately neglected to teach us about our neighbors to the east.

Andrik tries to make amends. Ten minutes' instruction in Russian history. Ten minutes' instruction in Russian language. By the time our guests leave, each of them takes a piece of paper home on which is clearly written *"Ya lyublyu Russya,"* which means "I love Russia." *"Ya tvoye druk"*—"I am your friend" and *"Ya otchen bolen"*—"I am very sick"—as a possible excuse for being spared unwelcome lovemaking.

Just as we are falling asleep a noise startles us. "Russians in the house," someone is shouting in the staircase.

We jump into our clothes. Andrik runs out. Five minutes later he returns. "They came to plunder," he says smilingly. "I got them riled. Told them to go instead and find us bicycles. How can we ride to work after your comrades took away our bikes? *'Pajaluista,'* they said. 'All right.' And turned to go."

To those who look at them as if they were dangerous they become dangerous, I think. Andrik looks at them the right way. Andrik always does it the right way.

• • •

TUESDAY, MAY 8, 1945

With each day our mood becomes gloomier. We walk around as if we've lost something. Andrik stays in bed. Frank repacks his bags all day long. Heike and Fabian are having their first quarrel, and Dagmar stays out of sight completely. What's happening to us? We are free to start. Why don't we get started?

"I think we're lacking an objective," says Jo. "Just cleaning up is not a purpose."

He has hit the nail on the head. None of us has any idea of what's going to happen next. The struggle against the Nazis is over. Nobody needs our protection anymore. We have lost that role without finding a new one. It is difficult to think of new tasks when electricity and water are wanting and any connection to the outside world must be paid for with tiresome marches.

From salvaged bicycle parts Jo and Frank have built two bicycles.

"Let's ride to the commander's office," Andrik suggests, "and see what's happening there."

We don't get very far. At the next corner three Russian soldiers motion us over. We are about to pass them by when they block our way.

"Machina . . . machina," they say, drawing their pistols. Andrik tries to settle it amicably. Impossible. They can't be talked out of it. *"Machina . . . machina!"* After a brief argument we continue on foot.

"We got rid of them," Andrik says.

19

"Which? The Russians or the bicycles?"

"Both," he replies sadly.

At the commander's office a festive atmosphere prevails. Only one sleepy sentry lolls about in front of the door. "Commander?" He shakes his head. Today is a holiday, he tries to make us understand. Since noon. Because of the armistice.

Armistice! The news more than makes up for the loss of our bicycles. Suddenly we are overcome with joy at having been liberated. Liberated from bombs! Liberated from blackouts! Liberated from the Gestapo, liberated from the Nazis! On the wings of our joy we hurry back home. In the evening we celebrate. We celebrate with all we have. *Pax nobiscum!*

• • •

WEDNESDAY, MAY 9, 1945

The world goes wild celebrating victory. Meanwhile Berliners ponder where to find something to eat. There are no stores yet. They are either closed or looted. We weren't the only ones who forgot the Seventh Commandment during the last days of fighting. Most of what's missing from the stores has been taken by Germans. Only the bakers are already at work. Crowds gather in front of their doors. The bread is black and wet. It feels like lead in the stomach. Nevertheless, it is bread. Heike volunteers to wait in line.

In the afternoon Andrik is called outside. Two Russians want to see him. They are our "plunderers" from Sunday. *"Pajaluista,"* they say. Please—and they shove two bicycles through the door. Almost new, their chrome parts shining. They are grinning from ear to ear. *"Pajaluista,"* they say and disappear.

"Strange people," Frank says, shaking his head. "Lovable people," smiles Andrik, feeling moved.

That's how they are! They return with one hand what they have taken with the other. Where did they get them? From whom? We don't feel like racking our brains about who has to go on foot now instead of us. It's a swapping game. And this time we are the winners.

Heike has served dinner. Bouillon-cube soup and wet dark bread.

It fills the stomach but doesn't stimulate the appetite. We might as well be eating a pile of mud.

"And they raised their hands in appreciation of a delicious meal," Frank declaims while kneading his share of bread into a work of art.

Suddenly Jo raises his head. "Be quiet for a moment, don't you hear it?"

"They're shooting," Andrik replies.

At that moment a rattling noise begins, so loud we cannot hear ourselves speak anymore. Frank runs to the window. Flares illuminate the sky. Fireballs explode in the air.

"They are firing salutes," he says solemnly. "A salute to peace!"

With rapt attention we look outside. On the street people are running. Frightened, they are looking for shelter in the nearest ruins.

"They think the war has started again," Frank grumbles. "They are not used to shooting for joy."

Neither are we. We feel overwhelmed by this incredible spectacle. Large calibers, small calibers, tanks, flak, machine guns and pistols. They let go with all they have. Everyone joins in. Soldiers and officers alike. The last bullet—Attention! Fire!—the last bullet ends the war.

"Do you understand it now?" Frank whispers into my ear. "Here too the symbol was made flesh."

• • •

THURSDAY, MAY 10, 1945

Radios confiscated—telephones confiscated—typewriters confiscated. Notices are pasted to all public buildings requesting the surrender of certain valuables.

"Those who won't give them up will be shot," the fearful ones say, trembling. They disconnect their telephones, pack up their radios and personally drag them to the nearest collection point. A former schoolyard serves as one. Rain is dripping onto the mahogany veneer of all the Blaupunkt and Telefunken, the Philips and Siemens Super radios. They are piled, one on top of another, and stacked in corners. The precious sound equipment is not handled with care. Barely a quarter of it will still be usable after confiscation.

21

"What's this all about?" I ask a man who is sweating as he carries a five-tube receiver on his back.

He glances at his radio. "It's going to Russia, they say."

They won't be able to enjoy it much, I think, looking at a mountain of dilapidated radios.

"The thing was too heavy for us," says the owner of a villa in Dahlem. "We put it out on the street. Whoever wants may have it."

Ten minutes later it's being "collected." The lucky finder is gloating. A big Philips is not found on the street every day.

Telephones confiscated—radios confiscated—typewriters confiscated. The notices requesting they be surrendered are no larger than half a sheet of typing paper. They seem like white patches stuck next to the entrances of public offices.

"What do you think we should do?" I ask Andrik.

"I haven't read anything. Neither do I intend to ruin my eyes. Also . . . if you feel like searching for our Blaupunkt amid the chaos in the cellar . . ."

I understand. Fifteen minutes later our two typewriters and the telephone have disappeared "amid the chaos in the cellar."

Those who stay at home aren't able to read orders. Let's wait and see . . .

• • •

FRIDAY, MAY 11, 1945

The wait has paid off. "The order has been rescinded," the word is passed around. One may reclaim one's surrendered radios and telephones at the collection points. People are running there in crowds. Disappointed, they return home. Most of the items have been stolen overnight.

There are lots of lovers of typewriters, radios and telephones. Even if one just keeps them in store until telephone and electric services are restored. The swapping game again! This time the participants seem to have been mainly Germans.

Battleground Berlin

• • •

SATURDAY, MAY 12, 1945

"I think we should start working," Andrik says at breakfast. "It's time we focus our attention on more important issues than nailing windows shut and cleaning toilets. I, for one, will soon give my first concert."

We are flabbergasted. "A concert? But where? With whom?"

"You'll see."

The news affects us as if we have swallowed amphetamines. Suddenly we remember that we each had a civilian life, interrupted by war and bombs, that we must now take up again. The state of emergency is over. Being companions in misfortune and members of the resistance group "Uncle Emil" are no longer our main occupations. We are a conductor and writer, doctor and actress, secretary and editor —currently unemployed specialists in various fields looking for work. For the first time in many weeks the girls are exchanging kerchief and dungarees for more bourgeois attire, while Frank, Andrik and Jo put on neckties.

"See you tonight," we say before we go our separate ways. Frank takes my arm. "I think we're going in the same direction."

The hospital where he used to work and my old publishing company are located in the same district. Together we walk into town. It is a hot day. Ruins and dust. Dust and ruins. The final six days of fighting have destroyed more of Berlin than ten heavy air raids. Only occasionally one spots an intact building.

Hauptstrasse, Koesterufer, Hafenplatz. People with weary faces poke around in the ruins, here and there recovering some battered "trophy" or charred beam. Berliners are scouring the ruins in search of wood to cook their meager meals.

Between Linkstrasse and Margaretenstrasse there stretches a large pond. Bombs have torn up the underground pipes and turned this residential area into a lake. Gasoline cans float on the surface. Rubbish from the war and filthy paper. In between, two girls wearing grass-green bathing suits frolic in the filthy water. Laughing and splashing as if they were at Wannsee Beach.

The ruins of Linkstrasse giving on that questionable lake are undulantly mirrored on its shimmering surface. The girls laugh. Like the chirping of birds their laughter sounds through the dusty air. Frank looks at them tenderly.

"If one could be like that," he says solemnly.

Over there is the Philharmonic Hall. Or rather where it used to be. A white horse is lying dead among the rubble and ruin of the place where Bruno Walter used to perform. Its body bloated, its eyes black and petrified. Like a gruesome still life it lies spread out under the broken arcades, its stiff legs accusingly pointing in the air. Bernburgerstrasse is one huge pile of rubble.

"Don't go that way," two men warn us. "Over there they make you work clearing rubble."

"Thanks a lot!"

In a jiffy we turn back. Let those who caused it clear the rubble. There are more such "work traps." Where they can't find enough residents to clear the ruins downtown, they force passersby to clear traffic-obstructing rubble. Three hours, five hours, ten hours. While at home families are waiting anxiously for the return of their loved ones. Still, this method works. Voluntary recruitment would not clear the streets in such a short time.

Taking a roundabout way, we arrive at Tiergarten Park. Or rather at what's left of it. Aghast, I look at the torn-up trees. Smashed, blasted, mutilated beyond recognition. Poor trees! How were you to blame for anything? I feel choked with sadness.

"This is even worse than the ruins," I say to Frank. "That's . . . ouch!"

I've stumbled over a hard object. From the tangle of branches covering the ground something black is sticking out. I bend down to move the branches aside. In front of me lies the head of an iron horseman. Buried halfway in the ground, wearing the tricorn and queue of Frederick the Great. A grenade has torn it from the torso and flung it here. Ten meters farther on we find the dilapidated remains of the statue. A horse without a tail, a man without a head. Eerily his right hand stretches out holding an iron bugle.

"Tallyho," it seems to be blowing through the trees. Close to the statue is a small mound. Hastily thrown up, rounded off even more hastily. On it two wooden bars. Tied together with string to form a cross. On it is written in blue ink:

Here lie
one   captain
one   lieutenant
two   sergeants and
six   privates

Rain has smeared the writing, like blue tears trickling down the letters. A grave here, another one there. Hastily buried on the spot where they died. May the earth weigh lightly on your nameless dead bodies!

On Charlottenburger Chaussee the smell of decaying bodies. On closer inspection we see it is only the skeletons of horses. People living in the neighborhood have cut the meat off the dead animals' bones piece by piece, cooked it in their pots and devoured it greedily. Only the intestines are left to decay between bare bones.

The sun is getting hotter and hotter. More and more tired, we drag ourselves along. Now we are passing the Brandenburg Gate. Pariser Platz is swarming with people. They are carrying furniture out of the Adlon Hotel. Gold-plated mirrors, plush armchairs and mattresses.

"Trophy hunters," Frank laughs with sympathy. "They are taking what they can get."

No doubt they are. On wheelbarrows and carts, in bundles and bags, they drag away what's left after the bombing.

We turn into Wilhelmstrasse. Ruins and dust. Dust and ruins. Wherever a cellar has remained intact, trophy hunters are at work, struggling up and down the stairs like maggots on cheese.

In front of the Foreign Ministry a pastel painting lies in the dirt. "Lake Starnberg" is written in its lower left corner. Where might it have hung? Who threw it here? I pick it up.

"As a more pleasant souvenir of National Socialist foreign policy," I say to Frank as I stuff it into my briefcase.

There stands the Chancellery. A battered stone colossus. Cavernous and desolate, its windows look out on the ruins of Wilhelmsplatz.

Nothing stirs behind these walls that hold the remains of Adolf Hitler. Before the entrance a Russian soldier is on guard. His gun across his knees, he leans comfortably back in a green silk-covered armchair. In the middle of the Court of Honor, so-called, an image of perfect peace. The sight of it makes us smile. Certainly this is not the sort of guard the Nazis had imagined for their Führer and Chancellor.

If only it wasn't so hot. For more than six hours we have been walking in scorching heat. The burned walls provide no shade. Rather they reflect the heat even more scorchingly. Thank God, a pump! Relieved I grab the iron handle.

"Don't drink it," a passerby calls out. I look at him. "It's been contaminated," he says. "By the dead bodies in the subway tunnel."

"In the subway tunnel?"

He nods. "The Nazis blew up the north-south tunnel. It flooded and all who were in it drowned."

It's not only the subway tunnel. Almost every bridge in Berlin has been destroyed. Almost every overpass, every underpass of any importance was blown up by demolition squads at the very last minute. Posthumous propaganda for Nazi efficiency.

How will the victors manage to supply Berlin, they calculated cunningly, with all the bridges lying in the water? They wanted to provoke a comparison. A supply comparison in their favor. The Nazis could do it! So much disregard of human life makes me feel like spitting.

In the late afternoon we reach our former workplaces. Frank's hospital is still standing. My publishing house looks quite battered. While one of us waits outside with crossed fingers, the other makes first contact again with the civilian life inside.

Walking down Hauptstrasse on our way home we don't talk anymore about ruins and Nazis, but about a doctor's responsibilities and the possibility of a new magazine for young people.

It's ten o'clock at night when we finally get home. A march of thirty kilometers is behind us. Andrik and the others are already home. The tiny kitchen with the brick stove burning in its middle resonates with passionate reports. Organization of music performances. The lack of doctors and their duties. The press, the theater and a new cultural beginning.

We eat our bouillon-cube soup and chew wet dark bread. In the stove the last piece of wood is burning.

"Let's go to bed," Heike suggests, looking anxiously at the empty kerosene lamp. "The embers give off enough light to find our beds." We each grope our way to bed.

"I forgot to mention," we hear Heike call out from her corner, "as of today the blackout requirement has been lifted."

"Does that include the blackout of the spirit too?" one of us retorts. But nobody answers. Perhaps nobody knows the answer.

• • •

TUESDAY, MAY 15, 1945

Are the Americans coming or not? Will Berlin be divided or will it be left to the Russians? So many questions, so many opinions. Surrounded by rumors, we feel more and more urgently the need for clarification. Everywhere feverish political activity. As if there were a rush to make up for twelve years' lost time. "Antifascist" groups are shooting up like mushrooms. Banners and posters. Notices and signs. At every other streetcorner some political group has been formed.

"Campaign Free Germany" . . . "Seydlitz Group" . . . "Antifa" . . . "Alliance of Hitler Opponents." Not all of these anti-Hitler groups can look back upon a long struggle. With some of them resistance began only as Hitler's ended. There's something fishy about these backdated martyrs. In front of entrances adorned with banners, cars stop. Doormen come running, orderlies whiz in and out. We feel amazed watching this pompous display of activity.

"As if a democracy could be started in one day," Frank says disapprovingly.

Fabian laughs. "The Anti*fa*—the Anti*na*. You can identify them by their names. There were no antifascists during the Nazi regime. There were Nazi opponents or anti-Nazis."

He is right, it's the occupation that introduced this new term. Suddenly Berlin is abounding with dozens of antifascist organizations.

"Let's hope it won't be the wrong ones who come into power now. Those who now act so 'anti' are probably not the best."

Right or wrong? In the chaos currently prevailing it is hard to differentiate. There is a rumor that the victors are going to outlaw all political organizations.

"Who is actually governing us?" I ask Andrik.

He shrugs his shoulders. "Whoever's turn it is. Anyway, right now it's the Russians."

Just now it seems that every week it's someone else's "turn." Mayors are removed and appointed, appointed and removed again. Each governs in his own fashion. But not every fashion is for the good of the governed.

One sees many young men on the streets. With long hair and open collars. The same bohemian fellows one used to see at the Romanische Café long ago. Nobody knows who they are. Nobody has called them. Suddenly they seem to have risen from the underground. Whoever thinks he has something to say wears a black beret. Never before have there been so many berets in the city. They are the Phrygian hats of the first postwar weeks in Berlin. Occasionally a Star of David. Adorning the shirt of its bearer like a decoration. "My alibi," its proud owner seems to say. "My painfully earned claim to compassion and compensation."

Will their claim be recognized, will the true believers be found out? The rumor goes that Stars of David currently go for five hundred marks apiece.

"Ya yavreye!"—"I'm a Jew," our Jewish friends learned to say just before the conquest.

"So what?" the victors countered the formula memorized in the hope it would offer protection. Jewish women have been raped too. The plundering didn't stop at places inhabited by Jews.

For the time being chaos prevails. Fear of life and the will to live. Profiteers and position-hunters and also those who truly seek peace and order. Berlin is going through the pains of rebirth. We worry about Berlin.

• • •

THURSDAY, MAY 17, 1945

The first ration cards have been distributed. Real cards with real coupons. Bread is written on them, meat, lard and tea. Salt, flour, potatoes and real coffee. We feel as if we have been showered with presents.

"Do you think they will really buy us anything?" Heike asks in disbelief.

"Why don't you try it?" Frank says. She grabs her string bag. Right after she leaves, we hear a knock at the door. Our former air-raid warden.

"I just wanted . . . ," he stammers, ". . . I thought perhaps you . . . ," he continues stammering and looks at me imploringly.

". . . could certify that you weren't a Nazi," I help him.

He nods, embarrassed. "I have documents . . . I can prove it . . ." Eagerly he searches his pockets.

I am not interested in his documents. Day after day we hear the same stories. In dozens they come for attestations that they weren't Nazis. They each find another excuse. Suddenly each one knows a Jew whom he claims to once have given at least two kilograms of bread or ten pounds of potatoes. Each claims to have listened to foreign radio broadcasts. Each claims to have helped a persecuted person.

"At the risk of my own life," most of these posthumous benefactors add with modest pride.

The entire NSDAP* seems to have consisted of frondeurs. Amazing acts of heroism are brought to light: They claim to have spoken to a mixed-blood person in broad daylight despite the fact that the block warden was watching . . . or not to have denounced Mr. X even though they knew . . . or to have been against it all from the beginning, or to have stopped believing in it a long time ago—the greater their fear the more stupid their excuses.

But the harmless ones, too, are demanding a piece of paper that legitimizes their harmlessness: "Mr. X known to me personally for years . . ." and so forth and so on. A certificate of good character is the most important document these days. Those who have been members of the Party and are unable to show a certificate of good character are subject to forced labor. The shoveling coolies of Berlin. In hordes they report for work each morning. At seven o'clock. They are sitting in front of what used to be the labor offices waiting to be called: Fifteen Party members for clearing rubble. Eight Party members to dig out bodies. Thirty to sweep the streets, to clean the sewers, to break stones.

* Nationalsozialistische Deutsche Arbeiterpartei, the Nazi party.

They break stones. They dig out bodies. They clean the sewers. They have to work hard to earn their daily bread.

We write certificates and serve as character references. As long as we can assume the responsibility, we shouldn't be vindictive. For twelve years we had time to weigh and judge. We know only too well whom we judged too lightly.

At eight o'clock Heike returns. Triumphantly she shows three pounds of grits and half a kilogram of rock salt. "More coming later," she reports, smoothing her creased clothes. "Transportation difficulties! Because of the bridges."

Frank looks at me. "There you go! Because of the bridges! It won't be long before the supply comparison will be decided in favor of the Nazis." Angrily he crumples up the certificate of good character he has just written and throws it into the wastepaper basket. "Those damned scoundrels!" I hear him grumble.

• • •

FRIDAY, MAY 18, 1945

The lights are on in Friedenau. We ride our bikes there to marvel at the miracle. For the first time since April 24 we hear the British station. A sharp voice is speaking against us. More sharply than we ever expected. Do they really want to blame us wholesale for the crimes of our government? Why don't they punish Streicher and Ley? Mr. Ribbentrop and Mr. Himmler?

Hitler is dead. Goebbels committed suicide. Like eels they slip away from the avenger's net. Ultimately, will it only be the little fish that get caught and dissected in front of the world's tribunal?

• • •

MONDAY, MAY 21, 1945

Reinhardt director Herzberg has founded the Chamber of Cultural Affairs. In the former offices of Hinkel, the Nazis' cultural chief.

A "twelve-year-old millenium" gazes down upon the artists who come here to be registered. By order of the commanders, "responsible cultural workers" are among those receiving the largest food allowances. Writers and musicians, singers and actors, come in flocks for registration, present their character references, fill out the forms and under oath assert their innocence. Woe to him who might one day have to verify what he has just sworn! And yet, who wouldn't swear in the desperate struggle to be permitted to work, a struggle of life and death.

Party members are not allowed to be culturally active. They are permitted only to dig up bodies and clean the sewers. People engaged in the arts who are "blameless" are rewarded with grade one food ration cards. With the categories of ration cards presently in effect, this means a ration of six hundred grams of bread per day, thirty grams of lard and one hundred grams of meat—provided there are no transport difficulties. Party members, housewives and those without work get ration card five. That means three hundred grams of bread per day, seven grams of lard and twenty grams of meat. People call it "the hunger card."

• • •

TUESDAY, MAY 22, 1945

More and more order emerges out of the chaos. Starting with minor issues it slowly extends to the larger ones. The political organizations have been prohibited, but in the district town halls, stability is slowly returning. We already have a city council. A government has been formed. The people of Berlin yearn to be governed.

• • •

THURSDAY, MAY 24, 1945

"Tomorrow at ten I have my first rehearsal," Andrik announced last night at dinner. We looked at him as if he were a miracle.

Hardly three weeks ago the last shot was fired in Berlin. Less than four weeks ago we slaughtered the white ox in the courtyard of Herr

Machulke's apartment. During that warm night in May, long past now, hundreds of women were screaming beneath their rapists' embraces. Thousands of German material goods changed their lawful or unlawful owners.

The "manifestation in the flesh" continues. But Andrik is rehearsing. After twelve days of crisscrossing Berlin on his ramshackle bicycle, bargaining for the necessary permits, procuring instruments, getting hold of musicians and searching amid the ruins for a concert hall, as if nothing has happened, he now stands in front of the Philharmonic Orchestra and looking ecstatic, he rehearses Tchaikovsky's Fourth Symphony.

His face is haggard from strain and lack of sleep. Around him workmen are hammering, repairing damage from the air raids. There are no concert halls in Berlin. Neither public transportation nor billboards or other means of advertisement. It is said that the first newspaper came out on Monday. Maybe they will also have fixed the roof by Saturday. Maybe!

Andrik does not seem the least disturbed by all that. His eyes look inward upon a different world. A peaceful world. After rehearsal he rides his bike to the commander's office.

"The musicians need additional food," he says. "Nobody can play a trumpet on an empty stomach." The commander evinces some understanding. Regarding cultural affairs the Russians always lend a ready ear. They love the arts. And they love them truly.

"We'll have to take pains to keep up with you," Frank says in the evening as we sit around the brick stove. Heike is cooking bouillon-cube soup and trying her skills with Russian grits.

Andrik, looking nearly exhausted, smiles. "One has only to start."

"I've already done so," Jo Thäler remarks quietly. "At the hospital in Schöneberg. As of today."

"Wow," Heike marvels. "Says nothing, shows nothing and suddenly he gets going." She hugs our "quiet one" until Fabian intervenes. He doesn't like too much interference with his "rights."

Battleground Berlin

. . .

Frank too has returned to civilian life. Partly proud, partly embarrassed, he shows us the document appointing him medical examiner. After ten months in the underground, readjustment is not that easy. Again there is lots of shoptalk around the brick stove. About Heike and Fabian wanting to start a cabaret, about the Philharmonic Orchestra's first concert tomorrow, about the isolation ward that is being set up at the hospital in Schöneberg, and about my publisher's attempt to get a permit.

For Dagmar alone there is as yet no position. First-degree mixed blood people were not allowed higher education under the Nazis. They were only allowed to sweep the streets and clean the buses. Schools and universities are closed. We are thinking hard now of where she could fit in. For the first time in her twenty-two years she is free to choose an occupation.

"A great time," she says enthusiastically. "I don't understand why everyone is so disappointed."

"Everyone?" Frank looks at her wonderingly. "Only those who weren't thinking. Only those who believed we'd be showered with cake and whipped cream as soon as Herr Hitler had gone to Hell. Where should it come from, I ask you! From the burned-down silos, the cleared-out slaughterhouses, or the Nazis' reserves that have been devoured to the last crumb? There you've got it already, that damned 'supply comparison.' 'Serves you right!' Herr Goebbels is grinning in his grave. 'Now do you realize how much better you had it with us?' " Angrily he pokes the smoldering fire in the stove.

"Let them talk," Andrik tries to calm him. "Those who don't find it worthwhile to help bring about better times won't be worthy of better times." He looks outside where dusk is approaching, and glances at the nearly empty water buckets. "We should go to the well once more."

The seven of us get ready for the daily evening ritual of hauling water. At the well we are told that Himmler has poisoned himself.

Another one gone! One after another, the masters of the Third Reich are slipping out of this world. *Après vous le déluge!* The Allies should see that at least the rest of that vicious bunch will be tried at the world tribunal.

• • •

SATURDAY, MAY 26, 1945

Heike and Fabian have gotten hold of a former storm troopers' local. A real dump. It's filthy and full of junk. But it has a roof, four walls and a floor.

"A week from now you won't recognize it," Fabian assures us.

At six in the evening Andrik's concert begins. At twenty past five we mount our bicycles. Andrik leads the procession. To honor him we let him use his bike alone. He is followed by Fabian with Heike on the crossbar, then Frank and myself, and finally Jo and Dagmar. Will Furtwängler ever have to make his way to the Philharmonic Orchestra in this manner? For the time being he is somewhere in Switzerland waiting for better times. While Andrik, in the meantime, pulls the chestnuts out of the fire for him. The portal to the Titania Palace is black with people.

"See you," I say to Andrik, "and good luck!" He nods at me, takes off his bicycle clips and disappears into the green room. I look after him.

"Your feat!" I think, feeling moved. "Your courageous accomplishment!"

Inside the theater it is getting dark. Nearly a thousand people are sitting there in silent anticipation. They came on foot or on bicycles. Away from their ruined apartments, away from their daily sorrows, their nightly fears. How beautiful this actually is. How beautiful and comforting. Feeling happy I squeeze Frank's arm. "They aren't so bad after all," I whisper.

Then Andrik comes on. He raises the baton. The violins begin to sing. They sound sweet and tender. Playing "Midsummer Night's Dream." This music had been denied the right to exist by the Reich's propaganda minister, had been prohibited as a "Jewish concoction."

34

May God bless this "Jewish concoction"! Today hundreds of sad spirits are finding solace in it. The violins are playing. Playing Tchaikovsky's Fourth Symphony with jubilant pizzicati.

"That something like this is still possible," stammers a man next to me.

We don't see the movie theater. We don't see the ruins. Forgotten are the Nazis, the lost war and the occupation forces. Suddenly everything else has become secondary. Only what the violins are playing—Tchaikovsky, Mozart and Mendelssohn—is of importance.

Late at night Andrik and I are standing on the balcony. Lost in thought, he gazes up at the stars. ". . . that we're allowed to live," he quietly says, ". . . that we were . . ." A gust of wind sweeps over us. He shudders and forgets to finish the sentence.

• • •

TUESDAY, MAY 29, 1945

"A beautiful morning tonight," Heike laughs cheerfully, blinking at the sun.

I know at what she is hinting. Since yesterday we reckon with Moscow time. Everybody who still owns a watch sets the time two hours ahead. There are not many watches left in Berlin. At least not among Germans. Time stands still on the public clocks. As if frozen with horror when the bombs tore up the power supply system. From their dials one can now read the time the bombs struck. What about the watches? "Clock . . . clock!" our liberators say. Well . . . !

Ultimately one gets used to timelessness. In any case, the lack of electric light in the evening still rules our daily routines.

Moscow time! Not only the time but also the spirit is more and more subject to Eastern influences. "The light comes from the East," Spengler claimed. "The decline of the West is the beginning of a new culture." On the other side of the Vistula young peoples live. With their enormous productive power and an abundance of fresh talent. Wouldn't we be resisting unnecessarily if we ignored this truth? East or West—perhaps that means a decision between the future and the past. Some day we will have to decide. No matter how things develop,

35

Germany can never be transplanted to Africa. Or to Bolivia. Or to Mexico. Our borders and the Russian borders will be linked forever. Can we permit ourselves to hate each other if fate has made us so dependent on each other?

But we don't want to hate them. Like Tobias with the angel, we are struggling to be allowed to now finally say yes.

"If only there weren't so much coercion," I say to Andrik. "So much pressure to conform to their ideology."

"Perhaps with time things will go right. They too need a respite and some time to get started."

"I don't feel like jubilating when I am ordered to do so," Heike retorts stubbornly. "I want to jubilate only when I feel like jubilating. I hate it all."

I hate it too. The parades and the flag-waving processions, the shouted choruses and the party discipline. The collectivization of minds and punishment of those who think differently.

Russia is large. Russia is young, powerful and creative. During the last months under the Nazis nearly all of us were pro-Russian. We waited for the light from the East. But it has burned too many. Too much has happened that cannot be understood. The dark streets still resonate every night with the piercing screams of women in distress. The plundering and shooting, the insecurity and violence aren't over yet.

If one day they generously support all efforts to get the economy started, the next day they dismantle dozens of factories, clear out the libraries, pull up the railway tracks and confiscate the subway trains. And behind all this stands the threatening shadow of the GPU.* That they named it the NKVD* doesn't diminish the fear.

"Freedom is life without fear," somebody claims. But we are afraid. Just recently they came to get a man in our neighborhood. At five in the morning. He was a harmless guy. Why did they arrest him? Why do they arrest anyone at all? I keep pondering. I love the Russians. But I don't trust their regime.

The others are struggling with similar problems. They want to love but feel unable. The average person considers his individual experience to be the rule. The majority of the women in Berlin experienced

* Earlier and later abbreviations for the Russian secret police.

36

our conquerors as rapists. They lost their trust. They hate and are afraid. Should they be judged because of that? Can the Russians be judged because of their nature? We must learn to understand each other. Until we understand each other we can't begin to love each other.

. . .

THURSDAY, MAY 31, 1945

"Blue sky so blue," it sounds, accompanied by an accordion, through the glassless windows of the storm troopers' local at 35 Ahornstrasse. For four days now Heike has had the town hall up in arms. A permit is required for every nail. A permit for every paintbrush. Painters and masons, carpenters and plumbers—beyond reach for most in ruined Berlin, but Heike has found them. Heike pulls them out of nowhere.

"Did you think of beer glasses? Sales slips for the bar? Have the announcements been ordered? What about the saxophone player and the dancer?"

Every morning at seven o'clock twenty Party members arrive. Scrub and sweep, take the garbage out, haul in wooden boards.

Amid pots of paint and scaffolding Fabian stands, his sleeves rolled up, his pants stained. A long strand of hair falls across his face.

"Quiet please! Rehearsal!" he shouts, clapping his hands. Between pots of paint and scaffolding, they are reciting and tap-dancing, fiddling and tinkling and singing ballads by Bertolt Brecht.

"Blue sky so blue, the wind so strong fills our sails . . ."

"We'll make it," Fabian beams, shaking the strand of hair out of his face.

. . .

FRIDAY, JUNE 1, 1945

An order to sew flags. Every house must fly flags in the colors of the four victor nations. We search through the encyclopedia. How many stars are on the American banner? Are the hammer and sickle in the center or closer to the edge? We never were good at hoisting flags. And we still aren't.

"What's the occasion for flying the flags?" Dagmar asks, looking indifferently at the numerous scraps of material Heike has scrounged together for this international sewing task.

"No idea. They say Eisenhower is expected. And Zhukov and Montgomery. Perhaps it's also because of the victory parade."

"Whatever the reason," Frank laughs, "we certainly won't be invited."

Dagmar frowns. "I am afraid it's nicer to be one of the undefeated."

"But not more interesting," Frank consoles her.

• • •

SATURDAY, JUNE 2, 1945

Attention! Attention!
KUTTEL DADDELDU
The Satiric Theater
invites you to its premier performance on Saturday, June 2,
at 8 o'clock at the Ahornschlösschen in Steglitz.

Once again the problem of how to transport seven people on four bicycles. This time Fabian has the honor of riding by himself.

Spectators and posters. The smell of wood and makeup, of glue and fresh paint. The storm troopers' local has undergone a metamorphosis. Behind the tiny wooden stage confusion prevails. Fabian is fidgeting like a racehorse about to start. Heike is everywhere and nowhere.

"Blue sky so blue, the wind so strong fills our sails . . . ," resounds from the stage accompanied by accordions. The words of Brecht, Ringelnatz, Werfel and Mehring fill the room. People are clapping and laughing, jubilating and rejoicing. During the intermission people drink some red liquid out of beer glasses.

"Raspberry sherbet," Heike informs me. "Our trophy from the ox days." Proud as a saloonkeeper, she looks at the candy-colored delicacy.

"Blue sky so blue . . . ," we keep humming the beloved refrain. But

38

something prevents us from enjoying ourselves completely. Something doesn't feel right. Something fundamental. It feels as if when changing trains one had gotten on the wrong train. It is moving, for sure. But in the wrong direction. For twelve years we worshiped the bards of the Weimar Republic like prophets. Loved and treasured them, defended them and kept them hidden. Now the twelve years are behind us. Something new begins. One cannot hark back to 1932 when it is 1945.

"You should have written your own lyrics," says Andrik on the way home.

Fabian pulls a face. "Am I a Werfel? Or a Ringelnatz? Lyrics can't be pulled out of nowhere." He has brought up a real problem. We don't yet have a Werfel. We still waver about the meaning of "today." And some are tempted to confound "the day before yesterday" with "tomorrow."

• • •

WEDNESDAY, JUNE 6, 1945

An hour ago the lights went on here too. One who has never been deprived of them cannot possibly understand what it means. Illuminated evenings. Turning away from the brick stove. And connection —reconnection with the world. The time of rumors is over.

For the first time in six years we are gathered around our radio without being considered criminals.

This is England . . . this is England . . .

"Beautiful," laughs Andrik happily turning the dial through all the stations.

The radio stays on late into the night.

• • •

FRIDAY, JUNE 8, 1945

It is hot in Berlin. It gets hotter every day. Summer heat is scorching the city, brooding over its numerous fresh graves. Below the thin layer of dust the dead are stirring. The smell of death fills the air like a

39

toxic cloud. The stench rising from the Landwehr canal is so unbearable that everyone who passes by presses a handkerchief against his nose.

"I hope there won't be any epidemics," Frank worries.

Already people are spreading rumors about the plague caused by decaying corpses. Already the few remaining hospitals are overcrowded with people suffering from dysentery and typhoid. Jo Thäler works night and day. He is in the isolation ward. Whoever wants to visit him must keep a distance of three meters. With awe we look at the red cross on his white coat identifying him as an isolation-ward physician.

"Like out of the danse macabre," whispers Fabian with fear in his eyes. The authorities in charge have ordered the exhuming of all bodies that were buried provisionally, so they may be properly buried in the cemeteries. Thousands of bodies had been buried provisionally. By the roadside or in front yards, on squares and in the streets, between ruins and archways.

"*Memento mori,*" the nameless mounds remind those who pass by.

We don't need to be reminded of death. It forces itself upon us all the time, fouling the air with the cloying odor of putrefaction. The "coolies of Berlin" work overtime. When they transport their sad cargo through the streets one uneasily looks away. Man does not like to see his fellow man decay. On pushcarts and handcarts they are pulling the dead to their graves. Only scantily covered, just as they were when disinterred.

There are no coffins in Berlin. There are no stretchers, no hearses, no undertakers. And above all there is no room left in the cemetery. Those who are buried today will, at best, be given a cardboard box for a final resting place. Pasted over with black blackout paper and a cross made of tinfoil.

I walk across the cemetery. There, over an entire field, they have dug out ditches two meters wide and a meter and a half deep—just like trenches.

An invisible women's chorus sings in a slow soprano: "Jesus lives, I live in Him . . ." Respectfully I stop. Next to me a man is standing. He is crumpling his cap in his hands and smiles sadly.

"I sacrificed my wardrobe," he says. "Grained birch." As I look at him uncomprehendingly he adds: "For the coffin I mean . . . my wife's coffin."

"Of course," I say chokingly, "that's right!" . . . What stupid things I'm saying here, I think at the same moment. First one must learn how to express condolences appropriately at the sight of mass graves and wardrobe coffins. The chorus behind the bushes falls silent. At the left corner of the trench a funeral procession appears.

"They didn't even give him a box," the widower without a wardrobe says resentfully. Sheepishly we look at the pitiful catafalque. Two bearers, two poles, a field-gray tarpaulin. On the tarpaulin the dead body. Wrapped in a horse blanket, a rope tied around his neck, another around his ankles. Naked, yellow and wooden the feet stick out of the tied-up bundle. This is how, during the Middle Ages, plague victims were carried out of the houses. "Not even a box," the man without wardrobe says indignantly.

Five mourners follow the bier. One of them holds flowers in his hand. Silently they climb onto the mounds of piled-up soil that line the trenches like ramparts. Their faces are devoid of grief and solace. Like cavernous windows in a burned-out building. Now they come to a halt.

"Jesus our Savior lives . . . ," the soprano voices are singing. A push . . . a pull . . . As if emptying a wheelbarrow, they dump the tarpaulin. The bundle rolls down. Stiff as a log. ". . . to be with my Savior, there is no dread . . . ," sounds derisively from behind the bushes. In spite of it I feel dread. I feel horror-stricken. Wardrobe or horse blanket. Tarpaulin and mass grave.

The man next to me turns away. "I would have . . . ," I hear him mumble. Then he walks away.

Four coolies are filling the grave. The trench is fifty centimeters shorter now. Three handfuls of soil. With empty faces, devoid of sadness, the mourners climb down the mound and turn to leave. The one with the flowers almost forgets to leave them there.

The soprano singing ladies disperse themselves too. It's not a bad business to which they devote themselves. Those who sing at funerals are registered as singers. Singers are culturally creative. Which means a grade one ration card. Never before have there been as many applicants for funeral choirs in Berlin.

I wait until the last have left. The trench troubles me. The narrowness of this pitiful resting place. Hesitantly I walk toward the shoveling coolies.

"We put him in the corner right away," I hear one of them say. "That way there is some support so the soil won't keep sliding down."

That crowns it all! Poor dead man, who now until the Day of Judgment has to serve as a support. What can be expected from people who try to find usefulness even in death? Perhaps everything? Perhaps nothing?

· · ·

MONDAY, JUNE 11, 1945

All morning I stood in line to buy meat with our ration coupons. We had had to wait nearly a month for our allotment.

"It's because of the transport difficulties," the butcher explains while weighing five kilograms of some wet-looking substance, ladling it into the scale with a wooden spoon. Suspiciously I look at the dirty gray mush.

"Sausage," the shop assistant informs me. "Liver sausage! I'd urgently advise you to eat it soon."

"Yes," I answer, racking my brain for a way to quickly eat five kilograms of tasteless liver sausage mush. Feeling depressed I drag the stuff home.

At home sits Frank, a nonsmoker, smoking a cigarette. Dark shadows under his eyes. "Aren't you feeling well?" I ask.

"As well as anyone would after six hours of digging up decomposed Nazi victims. At thirty degrees centigrade in the shade."

"But you aren't a party member."

"No, just a medical examiner." Angrily he throws the cigarette into the ashtray. "What pigs they are," he growls. "Pigs, I tell you!"

"Who?"

"The Nazis, of course. The district leader, the block warden or whoever else felt a need to kill thirteen innocent people just a few hours before the end. By shooting them in the head. In the schoolyard of St. Marks School."

"How do you know?"

"Neighbors saw it and they watched as they hastily buried them. Thirteen innocent people!" He shudders. "They finished them off in

42

the shed of the students' latrine. Because two days before the collapse they didn't believe in victory anymore. Ninety-six hours before their Führer and Commander-in-Chief pulled the trigger on himself." Again he shudders. "Disgusting!—We dug them out today," he continues. "Police cordon, forensic commission, recording of evidence and so on. The Party members who were supposed to get them out stood aside and vomited. 'I guess getting them seemed easier,' red Benjamin told them off. That's when they collapsed like little rubber pigs."

I too feel nauseated. How disgusting!

Late at night Andrik comes back. From Russian headquarters. It takes three hours to get to Lichtenberg. Three hours there, three hours back. As he carries his bicycle up the stairs he is panting like an asthmatic.

'Why don't you lock it downstairs," says Heike.

Andrik glances at her incredulously. "I might as well leave five pounds of butter on the street. Or do you think . . .?"

He is right. Bicycles are still much in demand. If the Russians don't take them, the Germans steal them. Since the verb "to steal" became "to go trophy hunting" or "zapp-zarapp," it was not only among us that it lost its disgraceful meaning.

"To go zapp-zarapp" means to take what one needs no matter where it comes from. There still is a lot of "zapp-zarapp" going on in postwar Berlin. So far only a few have found their way back to lawfulness. Without a doubt, turning away from the law is easier than returning to it. We too, despite all efforts, keep catching ourselves interpreting the question of mine or yours rather carelessly. As long as there is nothing to buy, as long as all over Berlin goods worth millions are rotting in the streets, the struggle to remain an upright citizen remains unrewarding. Wherever one goes, the temptations are just too enticing. Who owns the remnants of German army supplies? The hundreds of soldiers' boots, of field-gray socks, coats and jackets scattered about.

Between Wannsee and Grunewald some of the troops defending Berlin were well prepared for the return to civilian life. For weeks they had been wearing civilian clothes beneath their uniforms. Like peace phoenixes they rose from the army's ashes there, mingling with the civilian crowd and escaping Russian captivity. Who are the heirs to their carelessly discarded gas masks, canteens, motorcycle gloves, fur jackets and cooking utensils? The tires and gasoline cans, the telephone cables and parachute containers? Empty are the barracks of the Labor Service, the camps of the Todt Organization. Deserted the antiaircraft gun emplacements, the air bases and hideouts of the SS.

We paid for the equipment. Under coercion and in installments, with thousands of KdF-pfennigs. With taxes and contributions to the Labor Front and the Winter Relief Organization. "Cannon instead of butter," Goering called the transaction. "Butter instead of cannon" is the reverse slogan.

Our liberators called it "zapp-zarapp." They didn't mean army supplies but the contents of our air-raid shelter bags. By the hundreds they are lying ripped open next to the combat boots and uniforms. Who owned the contents of these bags, now indiscriminately scattered over the grounds of the Grunewald? The mildewed kitchen towels, the silk panties, the heating pads, the manicure sets and hot plates?

"Zapp-zarapp," said the conquerers and the first choice was theirs of course. "Zapp-zarapp," repeat the Berliners, pocketing, exchanging and dismantling anything they can get their hands on. The more the Russians leave behind, the more the Germans take. Barracks or cars. Air-raid shelter bags, baggage vans and storage sheds. They are cannibalized, they are scrapped. What's the limit of the emergency laws? When does it all become shameful? With the gas masks? The sherbet powder? The bicycle thefts? If one doesn't pull oneself out of the morass, one risks getting bogged down forever. We are trying hard to get out and return to honesty. We don't intend to remain trophy hunters. Still, it is difficult. Much more difficult than we ever would have imagined.

• • •

TUESDAY, JUNE 12, 1945

Flyers are being distributed in the streets. Yesterday it was announced in the newspaper: "The way to democracy is open. As of today Marshal Zhukov has authorized the integration of all antifascist parties within the Soviet Occupied Zone."

On the very same day the printing presses started clattering. The proclamation of the first German party. "To the workers of Germany!" we read. "To men and women! To the German youth!" Eagerly we skim the densely printed text.

"Sounds great," Frank says approvingly. "No repetition of the mistakes of 1918 . . . No more division of the working people . . . No leniency whatsoever toward Nazism and reaction . . . No agitation and hostility against the Soviet Union ever again . . . Four points with which I'm agreeable."

"Read the conclusion aloud," he asks Heike.

"The Central Committee of the Communist Party of Germany believes that the measures proposed above could serve as a basis for the federation of the antifascist democratic parties (of the Communist Party, the Social Democratic Party, the Center Party and others) . . . We declare: Solidarity, determination and persistent work will guarantee the success of our legitimate cause. With firm steps. With heads held high. Set to work with all one's might. Then freedom for the people and a life of dignity will emerge out of hardship and death, out of ruins and disgrace."

"Hmm!" Frank says. "Not bad! I just don't like the 'firm step'— that smacks of the SA.* At least of their slogans. What do the other parties say?"

"Nothing," Andrik laughs. "Because they don't exist yet. Neither on flyers nor as far as the central committee is concerned."

"Let's wait and see," Frank decides. "Once they've all got themselves organized, one may choose, join and become active."

'You really want to become a party member?" Heike stares at him incredulously.

"Don't you?" Frank retorts just as incredulously. "Do you believe we can make it staying out? By standing aside, didactically raising your forefinger?" He gets to his feet. "I beg of you. For twelve years we were all in the same boat. If we don't want to take responsibility now . . ."

Heike shakes her head. "Are you trying to tell me that responsibility requires party membership?"

* Military arm of the Nazi party.

45

"Not always, but now it does. Don't you understand, for God's sake? Coming to terms with the rotten legacy of a national catastrophe isn't simply a right. It's our duty . . . Talking doesn't improve the world. Get active, my dear! Being active makes all the difference!"

"Perhaps you're right," Andrik interposes. "It's just easier to be united *against* something than *for* something. But, after all, the parties are . . ."

"Parties or no parties," Fabian breaks in, "let's not argue about eggs that haven't even been laid yet. When the chicks have hatched there will be enough time to decide. And for the time being "—he raises his teacup—"here's to you, comrade Matthis! Long live the 'same boat'!"

Feeling somewhat depressed, we empty our cups. Can it really be so difficult to agree on something positive? I feel a vague foreboding that our group may split up. We are all still in the same boat. But the destination has changed. And this time there is not solely one way to this new destination.

· · ·

WEDNESDAY, JUNE 13, 1945

Frank is thinking about taking a trip. By bicycle, since the trains are not running yet. It doesn't look as if they will be running in the foreseeable future. Instead of rebuilding, they keep dismantling. The Russians take the railway tracks, the Germans, the fixtures from the railroad cars. Are they making pants out of the brown-gray plush of the second-class seats, I wonder? Or do they make it into scouring pads or slippers? Whether it's ashtrays or window latches, luggage racks, seat covers, foldaway tables or light-bulb sockets, it all disappears, it all seems to be useful and pocketable. Looking at the stripped subway and railroad cars, one gets the impression that all Germany is one big scrapyard.

But what do we know about Germany anyway? There is no mail service yet. Despite the radio and occasional messages delivered by word of mouth, we hardly know more about the people in neighboring regions than we know about the Martians. It's about time to get some idea. Frank has been urging it for a while.

He is worried about a friend. Just before the end of the war he had been trying to get through to the Oderland district. Did he make it? How does one stand worrying for more than two months whether a person one loves and has been close to for twelve years is still alive? "I'm going," Frank decides.

"You're crazy," the others say. "You'll return barefoot and without your bike."

Andrik is concerned too. "One shouldn't tempt fate. And you don't understand a word of Russian . . ."

Frank won't, however, be dissuaded. When he has made up his mind, nobody can change it. His determination affects me.

"Let's go together," I propose. "Traveling together makes it easier." He is delighted.

"All right, when shall we leave?"

"Tomorrow afternoon at five. To avoid difficulties, we'll travel during the night."

"At night?" I object. "What about the curfew? They'll shoot if they catch us out during curfew hours."

"All the more reason not to get caught." Frank tries to dispel my worries.

All day long I rush around packing our things. All the food, drink, bedding and whatever else we might need to keep us going for four days and nights must be carried on our bicycles—including bribes. These include five cigarettes, donated by Andrik, and sixty tablets of Pyrimal, a popular remedy for certain dire consequences of lovemaking. Frank calculates them in as travel expenses.

• • •

THURSDAY, JUNE 14, 1945

The weather promises to remain fair. Loaded like camels, our bicycles stand outside the door at ten to five.

"What about identification papers?" Andrik inquires. Frank proudly pulls two papers out of his pocket.

"It's all taken care of!" He hands them to him. "This is to certify that Dr. Frank Matthis, physician, residing at Street No. X, Berlin, is entitled to use a bicycle. We request that he be permitted to pass without hindrance," it says in German and in Russian. Next to an illegible signature is a stamp.

On the other piece of paper I appear as a social worker entitled to the same privileges. "Where did you get these?" Andrik marvels.

Frank laughs slyly. "That's my secret. But the stamp is authentic. And what's written on the paper is true. When there is no competent authority one has to invent one."

"That we should still have to be our own passport office in the Fourth Reich too," Andrik sighs. "Well then, good luck and most of all, don't get caught." He embraces me and kisses me in the Russian manner three times on the cheeks. Since we have been under Soviet occupation he has reacquired many old habits from his childhood days in Moscow.

We bicycle eastward. The sun still is far from setting. Russian time saves evening light. We keep bicycling. The roads stretch away in endless misery.

Suddenly the first stop. In the middle of the road five coolies are kneeling. Eagerly scraping at something grayish red and sticky that crusts the asphalt. We jump off. What might have been poured out there? Curious we step closer. For God's sake! It is a human being! Tanks have rolled over him. Ironing him into the asphalt as a bloody pattern. And now they are scraping him off. With knives they are scraping him off the ground piece by piece. Perhaps somewhere a mother is crying for him or a child will keep waiting for years for his return.

For a long time we bicycle in silence. By the time we have passed through the last suburb, three hours have gone by. It's eighty kilometers from Berlin-Steglitz to the Oder district. If we want to make it there in a day and a half we will have to push it.

Fields and meadows. Forests and country roads. Strange to meet so few people. The outskirts of Berlin have never appeared to me so deserted. Once in a while a truck passes us. Loaded with household goods, it is rolling toward the new border. Frank looks after it.

"These are the mirrors and the furniture that made us appear too rich to the Russians. Too rich to start a war of aggression. For four years their stuff had been rolling from East to West. Now ours is rolling back. A swapping game that makes sense!"

Again a truck drives by overflowing with bourgeois belongings. On top of it all wobbles an old-fashioned convertible sofa. On it lies a soldier. His machine gun under his head, he lies there as if resting in the bosom of Abraham, sleeping the sleep of the just. At every pothole his chubby body bounces up like a shuttlecock. It makes me laugh. God knows, they really are children.

As dusk is falling we push our bicycles into a grove. Frank carefully probes the area. "I think we can unpack." Between two pine trees he pitches the tent. We sit in front of it and watch the night fall. No sound to be heard. Except an occasional breeze blowing through the treetops.

Night falls quickly. The pine trees darken. I let my eyes wander up the high trees. "Look, the North Star," I whisper. Frank draws nearer to me.

"To be able to enjoy all this," he whispers back.

We both feel it. Never before has nature appeared as lovely to us. So beautiful, so peaceful and so festive.

As I fall asleep, I hear dogs barking and loud voices in the distance. "Sounds like drunks," I want to say but sleep ties my tongue.

• • •

FRIDAY, JUNE 15, 1945

I wake up. Something strange is in the air. Daylight shines through the chinks of the tent. "Psst," Frank whispers next to me. He is sitting up and with his head moved forward he listens attentively. The snap of a branch. Silence. We are listening so attentively that we can hear our hearts beat. Again a branch snaps. With one grasp Frank pulls the tent flaps apart. My God, a Russian! We are staring at the muzzle of his gun.

"*Drusya*," Frank stammers while trying to smile as amiably as possible.

He motions us to get out. He frisks us. When he realizes that we carry no weapons he starts looking more relaxed. Frank pulls out our identification papers. The soldier turns them in his hands, shrugs his shoulders and says something in Russian. We don't understand a word.

"*Drusya*—friends," we try again.

49

Instead of answering he shouts something unintelligible into the woods. Behind the trees another Russian appears. Then a third one and a fourth. Now we are in for it! We try to look as cheerful as possible under the fatal circumstances. "Looking at them as if they were dangerous makes them dangerous," I silently recall.

The first one motions to us. "Pack up and come with us," we interpret his signals. As we strike the tent and load our bicycles, they keep their eyes fixed on us. What do they want? They don't seem bent on taking our cycles. Nor do they look like rapists. If only Andrik were here now!

Escorted by the four of them we get going. Straight through the woods, in exactly the opposite direction from our original destination.

At last we stop at a railroad embankment. We are told to stand still. We stand for a long time. We stand longer and longer. Our guards have made themselves comfortable. Lying flat on their bellies they play a game of throwing knives. Like children they are delighted at each lucky hit. They scarcely pay us any mind. But as soon as we make the slightest move, they glance at us suspiciously and draw nearer.

The time passes at a snail's pace. Finally, with the sun well past the zenith, a patrol officer appears. The soldiers jump up and report.

"Identification documents," an interpreter barks at us. We show our papers. "Open your bags, your purse, your backpack."

Obediently we follow his order. Within five minutes it all is jumbled up.

"Why are you camping in the woods?"

"Because . . . because we . . ." Frank and I look at each other help-lessly.

"Well?" the interpreter urges, sharply casting a meaningful look at his gun.

Frank pulls himself together. "We love the woods," he says simply. With an engaging smile, he turns to the officer: *"Lyu-blyu lyess."*

The officer smiles back. He has understood and displays some understanding. *"Vratch?"* he asks quickly but amiably. "Doctor?"

Frank nods and points at the small tubes of Pyrimal. Within a moment they are distributed. Our supply is much too small.

Within a few minutes the scene changes. Bent over a prescription pad, surrounded by his patients solemnly watching, Dr. Frank Matthis writes sulfa prescriptions.

"Your name?"

"Ivanov."

"Pyrimal one O.P. . . . Your name?"

"Stepanov."

"Pyrimal one O.P. . . . Your name?"

"Ivanov."

Frank hesitates. "Ivanov?"

"Ivanov," the person in question confirms with a sly smile. The others all keep a straight face.

Stepanov and Ivanov—there can't be any two names that are more common in Russia. Müller or Schulze. Schulze or Müller. What do we care about their names? What do they care about their own names? They change them like shirts to be laundered and hide behind them like goblins under a magic hood. A disturbing difference between East and West. What seems most important to us, the unchangeable and individual name, means nothing to them. Today Ivanov, tomorrow Stepanov. And in reality who knows what the name is. The Soviet Union is one indivisible entity and not the sum of countless individual beings. It is not the first time we encounter this tendency toward anonymity in our liberators. But certainly it is not the last time that this will alienate us. It teaches us more about their collective spirit than any Communist Party platform.

Four Ivanovs and five Stepanovs are taken care of. They write down our address and promise to pay us a visit. "With schnapps," the officer smilingly assures us.

They release us. Seven hours after our arrest, we mount our bicycles again. "A nice little stopover," Frank says. "A few more delays of the sort and it'll be two weeks before we get to the Oder."

For about an hour we pedal in earnest.

"What time could it be?" Frank pulls his spare watch out of a secret pocket. "Three-thirty—about time we had some breakfast." Ahead of us is a village. We ride along its main street.

It looks desolate. It seems completely deserted. Not a soul to be seen. A cat runs across the road and quickly disappears beneath the nearest hedge.

"Have they all gone to bed already?" Frank wonders. "Or have they died?"

"The Lion's Inn," reads a sign on one of the houses. Smoke rises invitingly from the chimney. Frank presses the door handle. It's locked. He knocks. With his fists he pounds on the door. "Open up! We're customers!"

No answer. Complete silence. It's beginning to feel eerie.

"Let's go on," I urge. "Who knows what's . . ." I want to say "happened," but Frank interrupts me.

"If they're cooking there must be someone there. Stop and wait a second!" Somewhere the sound of a window latch.

"Through the yard gate," a woman's voice whispers. Obediently we go around the corner. There is a gate into the yard. A key is being turned. We gaze into this frightened face. Her face drawn deep into the scarf, muffled up like an old woman, a still young peasant woman stands before us.

"What do you want?" she asks nervously. And then, as if rattling off something memorized, "We have nothing. Neither food nor drink. Neither cups nor plates." With a hopeless gesture, she points across the yard. "All empty . . . all gone . . . all taken."

We look around. Empty sheds, a deserted barn, broken-down doors dangling from twisted hinges. Here and there a bit of dirty straw. Scattered in the corners an indefinable jumble.

"Russians or Germans?" Frank asks. The woman shrugs her shoulders.

"Robbers," she says dully. What does she care about nationality? Fear is all she feels. Fear of a knock on her door, of being grabbed and raped, of shouts and shooting, of plunder and pillage.

We pull two boxes next to the well and sit down to breakfast. Greedily she looks at our sandwiches.

"You can already buy bread!" She knows nothing about Berlin. For eight weeks she has been sitting there in her desolate house. Helpless and hopeless as a mouse in a trap. There are no men left in the village. Those who weren't rounded up by the storm troopers have either fled or been taken away. Hitler's order to keep fighting to the last has had the effect of depopulating entire areas and robbing millions of their belongings.

Fear prevails wherever we go. It lurks behind boarded-up doors. It stares at us from deserted houses, overgrown gardens and fallow fields. Two girls are walking ahead of us.

"Which way to Frankfurt?" we call out. Startled, they let out a scream. Fear created the ugly disguise behind which the women of the Eastern occupation zone have been hiding their youth for weeks.

A black-and-yellow sign shows us the way to the Autobahn. We climb over an embankment and then stop short as if petrified. Good Lord! Is this an exodus?

In front of us an endless stream of wretched-looking people is moving slowly East to West. Women and men, old and young, randomly mixed, driven together by fate. From Posen or from East Prussia. From Silesia and from Pomerania. They carry their belongings on their backs. To someplace or other, as far as their legs will carry them. A child staggers by. A miserable little boy.

"It hurts," he is sobbing. Turning up his bleeding feet, pitifully he tries to balance himself on his bare heels.

"While baking bread . . . directly from the oven . . . ," a woman behind him is babbling. On her long way from home she must have repeated it a thousand times. She says it again and again. In the same inalterably desperate tone of voice. "While baking bread . . . directly from the oven . . ." Across her back two pots dangle, ringing out a rhythm to her steps.

Old and young, men and women. Wandering along the highway, sleeping on the highway, dying on the highway. Someone is dying there, I suppose, as I look dismayed at a man pulling a flimsy wagon. It's a child's wagon—short, narrow and low. Two pillows have been stuffed into it, some straw and a quilt. On the quilt lies an old woman. White-haired, in her rural Sunday best. Her hands folded over her chest, solemnly she stares at the sky. Blue shadows around her nose. The wagon jolts. Weakly her head sways back and forth. After another breath or two the man will be pulling a dead body. He does not turn around. He trudges ponderously on, seemingly unaware that behind him a human being is dying. Only the children who follow, led by a nun, notice. But the children do not show it. Perhaps they are too weary. Too weary to be shocked.

"You must have come a long way?" Frank inquires sympathetically.

The nun looks at him as if she wanted to cry. "We were thirty when we left Kreuzberg. Now we're twelve. The others . . ." With a vague gesture she falls silent.

We dare not ask what's become of the others. If one can't help, one shouldn't pry.

"We all shall die," a girl sighs. "And why not? Dying isn't the worst." Emaciated from hunger and exhausted, millions of people are dragging the curse of their fate across the ruined remains of Germany.

"It would be sheer madness to transplant ten million people from their homeland," Churchill had said during the war.

But they have done just that. And they keep doing it. Ten million have been driven from house and home, just mercilessly driven away.

"Have a heart, Frank," I say. "What's going to become of them? Where are they going to send ten million people?"

"Where? Who knows where? Maybe to heaven. Unless they find a way of adding another story to Germany." He looks at the passing crowd. "The harm being done here . . . who's going to want to assume responsibility for that?"

Nobody will want to assume any responsibility. Human suffering concerns only those who suffer it. And maybe those who see it. Of course there is sympathy. But sympathy is limited. What concern is it to world politics that German refugees are walking without shoes, without socks, on bleeding feet? Other issues are at stake. More important . . . more crucial.

And how much did we care when Hitler depopulated the Ukraine? When thousands of forced laborers from the East died of exhaustion in their squalid barracks? When thousands upon thousands perished in gas chambers?

"Let's not fool ourselves," says Frank. "Having pity and shedding tears mean nothing. Would we be jubilant if we had to put up a Pomeranian refugee family in our cramped and wrecked home? It's damned easy to preach about charity as long as one doesn't have to practice it. But try to practice it. With eight square meters of living space per person. With the walls full of holes and the doors not closing tight. With everyone sitting on top of everyone else and everyone getting on everyone else's nerves. Just try to imagine this sort of idyllic life in the pickle barrel. You want to go to the bathroom—its occupied! You go into the kitchen and there are diapers hung up to dry. You escape to your room—your neighbor turns up his radio. Finally you end up hating one another because you can't endure one another. You get as mean as the devil and as quarrelsome as Xanthippe. Wait and see. No one's keen on putting up with these millions. Neither you, nor I, nor anyone else in Germany. Not because we're hard-hearted, but because it just isn't possible. Because a tub already full to the brim won't hold another drop, let alone a torrent."

We've gotten off the highway. The sun is setting. Gray and shadowy, the stream of refugees disappears into the distance behind us. If we want to get to our destination before dark we had better hurry.

"Stop!" someone suddenly shouts. In front of us appear three pedestrians gesticulating vehemently. "Bicycle trap in the next village! Don't go on!"

That's all we need an hour before curfew. We turn off. It's a detour of six kilometers. Dripping with sweat, we work our way through broom and heather. If only they don't catch us! Like lynxes we prick up our ears, like owls our eyes pierce the darkness.

"Damn it!" With full force a branch as thick as an arm hits my forehead. Groaning, I rub my hurting head. "It'll be all right," comforts Frank. "It's still better than walking back to Berlin."

• • •

SATURDAY, JUNE 16, 1945

We arrive at our destination at one in the morning. It seems odd to see so much activity in the village. Men patrol the streets, suspiciously keeping watch in all directions.

"What are you guarding?" we ask one of them.

"Our women," he replies, his eyes full of hatred.

We stop at the manor house. "Burgomistr," we read, shining our flashlight at a piece of paper on the door. Beneath is the name we are looking for. They are alive then. That takes a load off our mind. We knock, we pound at the door, we shout, we rattle the door.

"Well for heaven's sake, it's you!" our friend Fritz von Hallberg calls out in stunned surprise, shining a candle into our faces. Booted and spurred, he steps outside. A red armband shines on his arm. Fritz von Hallberg is an old schoolmate of Frank's. His schoolmate and our comrade-in-arms. A slightly built man, whose high, domed forehead always reminds me of fine porcelain.

Around the middle of April he left Berlin in order to rejoin his family. "One ought to go down together," he had said at the time.

"So you haven't died," Frank says jokingly. "You're even the . . ." He looks at the red armband. "Bur-go-mistr," he spells it out with mock deference.

Hallberg nods. "One should take an office if it falls to him, even if it . . . ," he looks troubled, "is as difficult as mine is these days."

We have, in the meantime, entered the building. At a table in one corner a young man sits reading a book. "You may go to bed now," Hallberg tells him. The boy disappears.

"You seem on the alert," Frank says smilingly. "Do you really need to be?"

Hallberg frowns. "Necessary? When night after night three hundred villagers must fear that at least two hundred of them will be in danger of rape, pillage, plunder or robbery, you needn't wonder whether it's necessary or not."

"Hmm! And what's the reaction of the occupation forces?"

"Because we surrendered without a fight they're doing their best. They help as much as they can, but even they can't do much. They can't overnight turn an army of soldiers drunk with victory and a legion of released laborers into paragons of virtue." He puts the candle on the table and pulls up two chairs for us.

"I wonder if Stalin knows what's at stake here," Frank says pensively. "Though even if he knew, it wouldn't change much. By the time we have peace, the war will have destroyed so much that all propaganda will fail. Our conquerors will lose the game not through war, but through their behavior in peace. You can tell the women whatever you please—that Russia is paradise and Bolshevism is heaven on earth. They'll think of those who raped them and will answer: No! And no power on earth will be able to change their minds."

Until morning we sit and exchange experiences. Four times during the night Hallberg is summoned. Once to treat someone suffering a gall bladder ailment, twice to lead his "militia" in putting down a dozen rowdy ex-laborers, and the fourth time to catch the Russian commander's runaway dog.

"You seem a jack-of-all-trades," I say sympathetically as he sinks into his chair, exhausted after his last expedition.

"Right you are! Detective, registrar, veterinarian, general practitioner, pastor, Soviet spokesman, farmer, mayor and junkman. All in one. They ought to tack another twenty-four hours onto the day," he adds, looking at his watch. "Twenty to six. In twenty minutes it'll be time to get up." He yawns and rises to his feet. In the light of dawn his translucent face looks even more translucent.

"He never changes," Frank praises him as we go to our room. "You think he does nothing and suddenly he's doing everything. The good, the appropriate, and all that's necesssary."

• • •

SUNDAY, JUNE 17, 1945

On the way back we ride through devastated countryside scorched by blazing summer heat. Mangled forests, strewn with war material, deserted vehicles, wrecked tanks, steel helmets on soldier graves, dead horses and the stench of putrefaction. This is the battlefield of Halbe. German combat units were trapped like rabbits here.

It isn't pleasant to bicycle across battlefields. And even more terrible to do so under a radiant sun. Isn't there a leg sticking out of the ground over there? Silently it reaches toward the light-green tops of the beech trees. We look neither left nor right. We would prefer to keep our eyes closed. But the road is too rugged to permit us this luxury. Potholes and nails, pieces of broken glass and sharp metal ruin our tires. Three times we have to stop to patch them, and twice more to elude an imminent bicycle hunt.

"I guess they want to equip their entire army with bicycles," Frank complains when we're forced, for the fourth time, to take a roundabout way.

By evening the battlefield of Halbe is behind us. Before us lie fields and meadows undisturbed and peaceful. This miracle surprises us again and again: that war's destruction is so sporadic, and contrasts so starkly with that which has been preserved. In its wake it leaves chaos alongside the idyllic, the idyllic bordering chaos. Where will the preservation leave off and the destruction begin? No one knows and none can foresee it.

"Silesia is safe," it was said two years ago. "Take your belongings to Silesia . . ." Thousands followed this advice. They jammed the trains, overloaded the freight cars with evacuees' baggage. They went to Silesia and disappeared.

How does one know when things will disappear? How can one anticipate what will be reduced to rubble? The region ahead of us has been spared by the war. "Here is a good place. Let's stay here," says Frank and hops off his bike. Half an hour later we crawl into our tent next to some bushes along the bank of a stream.

• • •

MONDAY, JUNE 18, 1945

The morning is cool. The mist that rises above the meadow soon melts away in the rising sun. The grass is wet with dew and smells fresh as in spring. We laugh out of sheer joy at being alive.

"Let's go swimming," Frank suggests. He takes off his clothes and dives into the water. "Come on," he calls out, "it's wonderful."

Together we swim down the river. The sun casts wide beams of light over it. Dancing upon the waves they look like sparkling rings of gold. Water lilies among the reeds. Cowslips and gently swaying cattails. Now something is rustling between the reeds. A duck whirs up and, quacking, flies toward the riverbank. How warm the water is. How clear and transparent. I think of the pool in Linkstrasse. The grass-green bathing suits. If one didn't know of the ruins, one might think the world perfect. And it is perfect. Right now, at this moment. Just as it seemed perfect to the girls as, amid the ruins, they took their morning bath. The light is in us and not in things.

In the distance we hear the hoofbeats of horses and the barking of dogs. We clamber up the riverbank and carefully peer through the thick willow shrubbery.

"Look," I call out delightedly, "so many horses." Before us in the bright morning light there stretches a meadow surrounded by woods. Hundreds of horses are grazing there. Large and small. White, black and brown. Shoving against each other, they gallop through the grass. A mare slowly trots toward us. She must have just given birth. On thin stiff legs her reddish-brown foal trots unsteadily at her side, fearfully pressing its body against its mother's thigh. Somewhere a stallion is neighing. His love cry pierces the air.

"God, how beautiful," whispers Frank.

So must look the Russian steppes or the Khirgiz pastures. It's Asia. Asia in all its splendor.

At the edge of the pasture five peasant carts are standing. Plump and covered with tarpaulins, their poles pulled up, they mark off a campsite with a fire burning at its center. Three Russians are sitting around it. Their arms propped on the ground, they lie there at their leisure. An accordion sits next to one of them. In a moment he will pick it up and play a melancholy song: "Make no red caftan for me, babushka . . ." How good man is if one lets him be good.

Tomorrow they will drive the horses toward the East. German horses with their Russian herdsmen. Over another meadow will sound the song of the caftan and the smoke of campfires will rise.

Are we still in Germany? Are we already in Asia? All is flowing. The breath of Genghis Khan blows through the forests of Brandenburg. *"Niechevo!"* the Russians say. "What do we care? What do we care whether we're here or there."

In a pensive mood we swim back to our campsite at the riverbank. Everything is exactly as we left it. Nobody has, in the meantime, stolen our bikes or taken away our clothes. We are grateful for so much luck.

It is eight-thirty. Time to think about heading home. We still have forty more kilometers to cover. But the god of all travelers seems kindly disposed toward us. No bicycle traps, no detours, no dismaying delays. We make it into Berlin without a hitch.

There red flags greet us. They wave from all the buildings. Some are at half-mast, others carry black crepe. "What's happened?" we ask some passersby.

"They say Zhukov is dead," says one. "Maybe Stalin too," someone else says.

At Potsdamer Platz we spot a news vendor. People crowd around him and tear the papers out of his hand. "Hero of the Soviet Union: General Bersarin," states the black-rimmed front page. "Untimely death of the military commander of Berlin in a motorcyc[i]e accident," we read farther down.

"How unfortunate for the man," I say. "He certainly wasn't the worst."

"Unfortunate for Berlin," Frank corrects me. "He was certainly one of the best."

"What a misfortune," Andrik greets us. "He supported the arts like no one else."

At home they gaze at us in amazement, as if we have come directly out of a den of thieves. "A wonder they didn't catch you! That they didn't take your bikes!"

"It cost us exertion enough," laughs Frank. "One seven-hour stop-over, a thirty-two-kilometer detour, nine prescriptions and sixty Pyrimal tablets."

Fabian looks at me attentively. "But otherwise you're feeling well?" he asks in an allusive tone of voice. "No nausea, no morning sickness, no craving for pickles?" I know what he is hinting at.

"How come you always right away think of rape?"

"Not me, the Russians."

Jo gives a little cough. "Perhaps the Germans too?"

"Come on," Heike says indignantly.

Jo pulls a face. "They talk a bit too much about it, as it seems to me."

"Are you out of your mind?" Dagmar bursts out. "When night after night we . . ."

"Not everybody, of course," Jo Thäler admits. "But certainly some. Talking about rape can also be a kind of compensation."

I wonder whether there isn't some truth to his words. No doubt, the predicament of our women sometimes does have some suspicious side effects. The conversations among certain people circle around the tragic subject like bees around the honey. "Raped twelve times . . . raped twenty-seven times . . . raped fifty-nine times." It is described with glistening eyes. They dwell on the awful details with frightening minuteness . . . Good heavens, who would there be to keep accounts of the various stages of horror and who wouldn't make a mistake in counting the revolting details? Never before have civilized people talked as bluntly about sex. Are they really concerned with the victims?

Or isn't it rather out of sensationalism? In this city, so short of men, there is a lot of craving for love. And a number of compensatory ways to satisfy it unconsciously.

. . .

FRIDAY, JUNE 22, 1945

Ten days ago the victorious military leaders met in Frankfurt am Main. "In the spirit of cordial friendship," comment the papers. Zhukov presents Montgomery with the highest Russian order, Montgomery bestows on Zhukov the highest English order. They exchange photographs, drink to the peaceful cooperation between all nations and stress the "important role Truman has played in maintaining Russian-American friendship." With each gesture the need for mutual understanding is emphasized. Mutual understanding means teamwork. Teamwork means reconstruction. Reconstruction means work, means the way out of chaos. When the kings are building, the carters have work.

"It smells of hope," says Fabian, cheerfully sniffing the air.

It smells of hope, they say with a sigh of relief all over the city. What is beginning now will shape our future. Each step becomes a new beginning. Every movement is carried out with the importance and weight of a founding ceremony.

"Let's get to work" is the motto of the carters.

District X urgently needs a mayor. "Let's get to work," decides actor Y of the State Theater and jumps into the unfamiliar position with courage.

At the former National Opera the first opera collective gathers. The stage, a pile of rubble; the roof, a sieve; the square in front, an arsenal of rusty battle equipment. "Let's get to work," says the director. Two dozen opera singers roll up their sleeves and begin cleaning out the Augean Stables.

Let's get to work! Musicans work as carpenters; factory managers run coupon-issue offices. Lawyers become construction workers; pilots become bakery assistants and dancers turn into clerk-typists.

Let's get to work! The tasks are countless. Of the twelve hundred

61

kilometers of the streetcar system's overhead wires, a thousand are torn apart and dangle onto the streets. In the center of the city there is still neither water nor gas. The power supply is so irregular it can scarce be counted on.

Let's get to work! Workshops spring up like mushrooms. Classrooms turn into theaters; former movie theaters become concert halls. Hospitals are opened up in storage sheds. The labor service barracks are turned into refugee camps. There is an urgent demand for axes, shovels, nails and wrenches. A great many offers of Russian language instruction, Russian interpreter courses, Russian phrase books and Russian translation services. Whether raw materials or finished products, expertise or workers, whether it is space for living, offices, production or entertainment, all are in demand. Everything must be improvised, bartered, bargained for and salvaged from the ruins.

Banks and savings institutions are closed. Whatever may have been left in their vaults fell into the hands of the victors. But there is no need for money. Never before have the contents of our purses seemed less important. When something is needed one barters, steals or scrounges it from the ruins.

In the beginning was chaos! We feel like God on the first day of creation. We try hard, we work hard, we run like clockworks that have been wound up to the last possible turn. Those who do not know their creative goal are made restless by the general frenzy of activity. They go and visit friends. Walking for hours with restless perseverance. Seldom have Berliners visited each other as much. If one doesn't have anything to exchange, one can at least exchange one's experiences. Everyone's heart is overflowing with memories of the fighting. There is a need to pour out one's heart and talk, to comfort one another and to let off steam. Plundered—arrested—killed in action—missing in action—raped. There isn't much positive to talk about. The best one can say about the past is that one survived it. Survived it to do the cleanup work which in the last ten days has begun to have "the smell of hope."

• • •

One o'clock in the afternoon. Very upset, Andrik returns from a rehearsal. "They've arrested the director of the Titania Palace," he reports unhappily. I look at him with disbelief.

"How come? Such a nice man. Didn't he get along really well with the Russians?"

"He got along with everyone," Andrik replies, "He just forgot to mention that he had been head of an SS training camp for five years. And that, as a civilian again, he killed a Russian just two days before the fighting ended."

"SS training camp? . . . Killed a Russian?" I repeat feeling confused. "But how could we . . . ?"

"Could . . . could," Andrik interrupts me. "That's the problem. We seem to have no eyes to see with. No instinct for separating the wheat from the chaff." He shudders. "Why are people so miserable? So eager to always skim the cream off the milk."

"Because they want to live," replies Frank. "Nobody likes to cut the ground out from under his own feet. Or did you imagine that sometime between April 28 and May 10, all the Nazis had turned into penitents? That because Hitler was dead, morals had changed?" Having stepped to the window, he angrily drums on the wire mesh of what used to be shatterproof glass. "They'll all try to conceal their pasts," he continues. "The major scoundrels and the small fry, the instigators and the hangers-on. Because they haven't been trained to stand by their acts. 'The Führer takes the ultimate responsibility' had been preached to them. The Führer is dead. If you want to live you must eat. If you want to eat, and eat well, then you'd better not be a Nazi. So they aren't Nazis. Therefore they weren't Nazis and they swear by all that's holy that they've never been."

"A promising reconstruction," remarks Fabian, "with seven million party members in disguise as our democratic starting capital. How can we find them out and separate the sheep from the goats?"

Andrik sighs. "Perhaps one should allow them to make amends.

63

—Put on your party badge, comrade! Put it on as the Jews put on the Star of David, and get to work. Clean up what you've destroyed. Clean up for a year, clean up for two years. With the swastika in your buttonhole and remorse in your heart. The objective of punishment, if it is to be effective, should be to punish the guilty. Work is no disgrace. And certainly no reason to feel degraded. Seven million rubble removers, bridge builders and roofers. Imagine what that would do. Not only for reconstruction but also for national education."

"And who should be the educators?"

"Those who claim to be better than the Nazis. Just condemning them serves no purpose. Denouncing and condemning don't help in the perfection of men. Help them get up when they've fallen. Give them a chance to atone for their sins. And then no more reprisals. Once and for all."

"You think the Allies will be capable of that?"

Andrik shakes his head. "They'd better be. Otherwise we'll have to contend with the Nazi problem for another ten years. And by then nobody will know anymore what's right and wrong."

• • •

THURSDAY, JUNE 28, 1945

Another success for the kings and new hope for the carters. Two days ago at the international conference in San Francisco, the delegates of fifty-one nations signed the United Nations Charter.

"A great instrument of peace, security and human progress," Truman calls it, telling the fifty-one conferees: "Between the victory in Europe and the final victory in Japan you have won a victory against war itself."

Fifty-one nations! A World Security Council, a World Economic Council, a World Social Council and an International Court of Justice.

"Not a weak League of Nations," says *Izvestia*, "torn apart by contradictions and undermined by windy discussions; but a strong international organization, strong enough to prevent any future aggression."

Let's hope so! The world certainly needs a little while to recover from aggressions.

Germany, Austria, Italy and Japan are not members. How could they be? Yesterday's aggressors can't be today's pacifists. For the time being we are grateful if they let us live. Ourselves and the rest of our collapsed country. If there is no more plundering and dismantling, but reorganization and reconstruction. No more injustice for injustice, perversion of justice for perversion of justice, but justice for guilt and order against chaos. And once the arbitrariness is ended . . .

World Security Council! World Economic Council! United Nations! Brotherhood of Nations! Indeed, these words are music to our ears.

• • •

TUESDAY, JULY 3, 1945

The Americans are here! Frank has seen them with his own eyes. At least one of them. Near Schlosstrasse. It's highly unlikely there would be only one. So they have come at last. The victors from the West for whom we have waited since the beginning of April. More and more eagerly with each day, more and more urgently each night.

It had been rumored for quite a while. For the last seven days, garlands and welcome signs have hung withering upon the lampposts of the main western arteries. We had stopped believing it and had resolved once and for all not to fall for that tale again.

But now the fiction has become reality. Bent over a city map, we mark off the occupation zones, district by district. Russian, French, English, American. Four victorious nations—four occupied zones. How strange, I think, that international reconciliation should begin with the division of Berlin into four sectors.

"Steglitz remains Russian," Dagmar claims to know from reliable sources.

Frank shakes his head. "Steglitz will be American. They are taking the entire south. The west becomes English. Russia keeps the east and the French get the north." His blue pencil zigzags over the streets of Berlin.

"What about Unter den Linden? Who gets Unter den Linden?" Dagmar asks. We look at each other. Before our minds' eyes appear the remains of what used to be a splendid boulevard. Rubbish heap after rubbish heap. An image of desolation. It definitely has seen its day.

Frank reaches for an eraser. "All right then, let it be Russian," he decides benevolently. Two blue pencil marks from the castle to the Reichstag—with a simple movement of his hand, Unter den Linden is Russified.

"Let's hope that they stay in agreement with each other," says Heike, sounding like Cassandra. "If these four start fighting . . ."

". . . then we have had it!" Frank finishes the sentence.

But why fear the worst? For the time being there is the United Nations Organization. There is friendship in Frankfurt and cordial goodwill all along the line.

Will we need a visa to ride our bikes from Steglitz to Grunewald? Or an identification card? Or a permit to travel from one occupied zone to another? Will they erect barriers? Will one have to pay duty? We have a hundred questions and, once again, are sure of only one thing—that we don't know anything.

"At least communication will be easier," Fabian consoles us. And while rolling a cigarette out of some butts, he smiles at Heike. "Hallo old girl," he says in English, "how do you think about a Chesterfield?"

We laugh. Tomorrow, or the next day at the latest, we will be American.

In the afternoon we ride our bikes to the broadcasting center. In a convoy, as bicycles are still in short supply. If one travels alone, one still risks losing one's bicycle.

"*Machina . . . machina . . .*" Just yesterday Jo Thäler managed with great difficulty to escape an involuntary change of ownership.

At the broadcasting center they are inaugurating the "Cultural Society for the Democratic Renewal of Germany." Andrik and the Philharmonic Orchestra provide the musical setting for the festivities.

The auditorium is packed. People want democratic renewal. They are sincere in their willingness to work hard for reconstruction. If only there weren't always so much talking. Frank, who is sitting next to me, despairingly glances at his watch, already for the third time. For two and a half hours one speech has followed another. "We, men of the arts," it rings in my ears, "we, men of science . . . we, men of the new Germany."

Indignant, I pull at Frank's sleeve: "Have they forgotten that there are women among us too?"

Apparently they had forgotten. Just like the fact that democratic renewal can't start with Nazi superlatives. Hardly anyone of the eight notables, who are talking here about coming to terms with the past and renewing our cultural life, seems to notice how little they've so far managed to renovate their own way of talking. It is all still about the greatest, the ultimate, the largest, and most magnificent. Without the least self-consciousness, they talk about reeducation, fighting morale, fulfillment of objectives and targets, and marching.

"With firm steps we're marching into the battle for pacifism," a politician proclaimed the other day, probably not realizing how paradoxical his well-meant zeal sounded being phrased that way. Learning to cut out the exaggeration might not be so easy.

After the last speaker has finished Andrik stands up, mounts the platform and conducts Tchaikovsky's Fourth. In a calm, confident and natural manner. "At least one act after all those speeches," whispers Frank, relieved. "A wonder how the Germans can never seem to get to the point."

I have to agree. Also I still feel annoyed about the forgotten women. Somewhat disappointed, we meet in the green room to go home together. Somehow we had all imagined the inception of democratic renewal differently. More practical, so to speak, more active and more enterprising.

"We cannot expect everything to happen overnight," Andrik tries to appease us. "In any case, they meant well."

"At least for you guys," I cannot help but remark somewhat sarcastically.

As we turn from Kaiserallee into Schlosstrasse, an idyllic sight meets our eyes. Leaning back in a cane chair, a vase filled with flowers at her feet, a chubby Russian girl sits in the middle of the intersection. Highbosomed, with military blouse and cap. As we approach she gets up slowly, assumes a soldierly pose, and vigorously waving a little red flag, she starts directing traffic. Clear to pass, the little flag signals.

Then the girl sits down again and gently plucks at her bouquet of marigolds.

"There you have your women," Andrik laughs amused. "Culture in the middle of an intersection. In medias res, even without the blessing of the cultural society."

With a grateful feeling of solidarity I look at the policewoman and her way of displaying culture. For the time being the "honor of the women" is saved.

• • •

SATURDAY, JULY 7, 1945

The whole city is in a frenzy of expectation. One feels about to burst with eagerness to work; one would like to have a thousand hands and a thousand brains.

The Americans are here. The English, the Russians. Supposedly, the French as well. Perhaps they have already occupied their zone. We don't know for sure.

Rumors abound, are defended and disproved. But they are not important. What's important is that we are at the center of activity. That four world powers have met in our ruins and we may prove to them how earnest our zeal, how deadly in earnest our efforts toward reparation and reconstruction. Berlin is running at full throttle. If they would understand and forgive us now, they might obtain anything from us. Anything!

That we shall renounce Nazism, that we shall prefer the new, that we shall work and demonstrate our goodwill. Never before have we been so eager for salvation. So tired of terror, fear and injustice. If only the victors keep their promises . . .

How little trained politicians know about the simple trick of winning people over by offering them something better than what they've previously known. The liberator is cheered by the masses, considered the deliverer from evil. Did we deliver the Ukraine from evil? The Dutch or the Norwegians?

"People of Alsace-Lorraine, come back home to the Reich," Hitler said in 1940. "For twenty-five years you have suffered under the yoke of the foreigner. Now come back to Mother Germany." And what did they get from Mother Germany? Plundering of their resources, devaluation of their currency, loss of their savings accounts and arrests upon arrests. Because we only made things worse, they could only come to hate us.

The people of the Russian-occupied zone hate the Russians because they've only contributed to their misery. Is it their regime that is to blame? Is this the way fate takes care that dictatorships don't last forever, that their own mistakes ultimately cause their downfall? The Americans will do it differently. So will the English and also the French. They will correct the first occupying power's psychological mistakes and restore justice and confidence.

• • •

MONDAY, JULY 9, 1945

The doorbell rings. It startles me out of my sleep. Alarmed, I glance at the clock. Ten to six. God be with me. When the doorbell rings before six, it can't mean anything good. Arrest. Like the neighbor next door. Like the hundreds and thousands who, during the war and since, have been taken from their beds straight to prison without being given any reason.

Should I play dead? Choked with fear I sneak to the door and peek through the peephole. No one in sight. But wait a second, what's that? Something dark cowers on the stairs. Now it moves. I hear a suppressed cough.

"Who's there?" I call out under my breath.

"Mail from the West," answers a voice.

"Mail?" I quickly pull the door open. Can there be mailmen again? For more than two months we haven't seen any.

But I still don't see one. Before me on the steps sits a bundle of rags with the hollow-cheeked face of a man sticking out of it.

"What do you want?" I inquire, feeling ill at ease.

The stranger rises to his feet. "A glass of water and . . . ," he hesitates, ". . . if possible a piece of bread." As if embarrassed by his request he hastily searches his pocket and pulls out something crumpled. Without saying a word he hands it to me. Indeed, it is a letter. I read my name on the dirty envelope. The sender's name: Conrad Bauer, Bad Homburg.

"You came from over there?"

He nods.

"On foot?"

Again he nods and points at his dusty shoes. "It took three weeks. Across the border illegally."

The first messenger from the "other world." The first mail since the end of the war. Hastily I tear open the envelope.

"My dear friends," our friend Conrad writes. "My very dear friends. We are alive and hope that you are too. In spite of all the horror stories we hear about Berlin. Let us know. Take care. Love, Conrad."

Conrad! I think, feeling moved. You made it! Then, carefully, I smooth the crumpled envelope and turn to its deliverer.

"Would you like to come in for a moment?" He follows me. He is so exhausted that he trips over his own feet as if he were drunk. "You must be very tired," I say and pull up a chair for him at the kitchen table.

The power company is merciful. Fifteen minutes later, breakfast is ready. "Tell me about it," I ask my guest. "We know so little and hear such a lot of rumors."

Slowly be begins his tale. Originally from Cottbus, he had felt unbearable longing to rejoin his family. It had been more than five months since he had heard from them. The Soviets caught him at the border, but released him after four days. He'd been deprived of his watch, his money and lighter, but otherwise unharmed. He had heard rumors of plague in Berlin. And he asks if it is really true that everyone who attends a Communist meeting here receives two cigars and half a pound of butter.

I clap my hands at so much nonsense. But when I tell him my suppositions about the West, his reaction isn't much different. It's all wrong; none of it is true. If one of us was speaking Malay, it couldn't be more difficult to make ourselves understood, one to the other. Separate fates create separate worlds. How long will it take before fate reunites our worlds, and our lives will no longer be lived behind closed doors within the four walls of an occupied zone?

Battleground Berlin

. . .

The Chamber of Cultural Affairs has become the focal point of cultural life in Berlin. Music department, theater department, film department, literature department—over them all presides the actor Paul Wegener as if he were God Himself. Andrik is a member of the steering committee. It stands as a model of democratic artistic aspiration. He likes being an example. The other members probably like being one too. It's too bad that in their sessions they so rarely attend to their tasks and so frequently give in to the temptation to bicker. As if none wished to allow any of the others to be an example. And these days we need examples more than ever before. The right individuals in the right positions.

Perhaps part of our misfortune is that among us there are so few real individuals. To each nation, nature has allotted around the same percentage. Ten percent leaders, versus ninety percent followers. That means that among sixty million Germans there are six million from all walks of life who think independently, act independently and judge independently, versus fifty-four million who are indifferent, immature or "hangers-on" in principle! How many remain of these precious ten percent after the past twenty-five years? The First World War, the Second, emigration, gas chambers, the Gestapo cellars and the concentration camps, they all claimed their share, and claimed it in particular from among the leaders. Not ten percent anymore but at most five percent of the best have been left to us. A dangerous disadvantage vis-à-vis other nations. Even more dangerous if some day it should become evident that those who remained were not enough to clean up the German mess. That we are dependent on the second, third and fourth generations, because the first is dead, was hanged, suffocated in gas chambers or emigrated.

The right individual in the right position. Of course, they are trying. At the Chamber of Cultural Affairs a "Committee for the Rehabilitation of National Socialists" has been formed. A real tribunal including a presiding judge and associate judges to separate the sheep from the

71

goats, it is supposed to bar former Nazis from responsible cultural positions. But who will bar whom here? Who in the world is objective enough to pass Solomonic judgment upon seven million party members?

●　●　●

THURSDAY, JULY 12, 1945

The Americans confiscated the Titania Palace. As a clubhouse for their troops. Andrik desperately runs around. The sole concert hall within the American sector! What will become of the Philharmonic Orchestra? The Ahornschlösschen also has been confiscated. Heike and Fabian submit one petition after another.

A questionnaire: "Report your yearly income since 1933. Which party did you vote for in 1932? List all your bank and savings accounts as well as those of your parents, siblings, uncles and cousins." It is hair-raising. How is one supposed to remember all that. Must one commit perjury just because one has a bad memory?

●　●　●

SUNDAY, JULY 15, 1945

The confiscations continue. Apartments in Dahlem, apartments in Wannsee. Entire residential areas in Zehlendorf and Charlottenburg. Of course, they need quarters for the troops. They cannot live in ruins. Our soldiers also confiscated quarters in Russia and in France. Except that it seems one feels more bitter about it when one is affected oneself. Order to vacate within a few hours. Just the barest necessities are allowed to be taken along. When the door slams shut behind the evacuees they may consider themselves totally bombed out. And just as with the bombed-out people, the lot of misfortune is cast indiscriminately. Whether Nazi opponent or Nazi follower, whether rich or poor, whoever is ordered to get out must get out. And then it's up to him to find new accommodations.

Andrik laments: My concerts! Fabian moans: My cabaret! It is painful to have to leave behind, from one moment to the next, what one has created out of nothing in two and a half months of hard work.

But over the radio it was announced tonight that Stalin, Truman and Churchill have arrived in Berlin to hold a conference. The confiscations are unaffected, but at least it cheers one up. All that has happened so far must be considered the aftereffects of the war. Including the rapes, the plundering and the confiscations. The Big Three conference will establish order and prepare the ground so that the good may grow.

. . .

WEDNESDAY, JULY 18, 1945

Andrik has succeeded. After bicycling for days on end from one administrative department to the next, after numerous applications and endless negotiations, the Titania Palace has been derequisitioned. At least part of the time, for concerts and rehearsals. The fact that the officer in charge deems it necessary to keep the main gate closed and to require the host of concertgoers and performers to use the narrow back door humiliates him more than us. Using the "delivery and personnel entrance" detracts not at all from the joy of listening to Beethoven and Mozart.

In Charlottenburg the English are in charge of culture and art. A Philharmonic Orchestra concert for English troops, held in the former Popular Opera. The Philharmonic Orchestra concert, held at the same place, with the same program for the German residents of the English occupation sector.

As we are bicycling the long way from Steglitz to Charlottenburg, we see a newly posted sign on one of the main roads leading into the city: "Attention, refugees! Newcomers banned from settling in Berlin. Use detours. Avoid entering the city limits. Continue westward."

"A hospitable order," remarks Andrik. "The West won't want them either."

Just the thought of it is horrible. Like pendulums the refugees from the East go back and forth between the towns. No settling, no admission, no accommodations, no ration cards.

"Three times already we have walked back and forth between Fürstenberg and Genthin," reports a refugee family of six. "Fifty-one times we've been rejected, seven times we've been told to wait until later, and twelve times we've been promised accommodations for three nights at most. What are we supposed to do with accommodations good for three nights at most? Or with a questionable promise that something might be available four weeks from now?"

Their number is legion, their suffering boundless. Hitler's program of German settlement in the East has turned out to be the "most gigantic depopulation of all times." And I think along with Frank: All that is destroyed here . . . who is going to take responsibility for that . . .

• • •

THURSDAY, JULY 19, 1945

Our neighbor, whose husband was arrested in May and who was left alone with five children, lies in her bed and does not get up anymore. "Because of hunger," she whispers faintly as Heike looks after her. Housewives, unemployed people and Nazis get food ration cards grade five. What does a mother do who gets only three hundred grams of bread per day? She divides it among her children and has to satisfy her own hunger by watching them. Nobody ever gained weight from watching. Not even if one's husband was a Party member. Our neighbor now weighs barely eighty pounds. And lies in bed "because of hunger." Moving less, one saves calories. She is not the only one to discover that. The mobility of grade five ration card owners has waned considerably over the last few weeks. To save shoe leather, to save energy, to save calories.

More and more frequently one hears the same reasoning. "While the grass grows the cow dies," the saying goes. In Potsdam the Big Three are holding a conference. The entire area is sealed off. No German is allowed to set foot on the sacred grounds where the negotiations are taking place. May they succeed in letting the grass grow. May it grow before the cows have died.

Battleground Berlin

. . .

The day of Witzleben and Stauffenberg.* A year ago today we thought that the terror would be over within a few hours. It wasn't over. That it didn't end that day cost the world millions of lives, hundreds and thousands of apartments and houses, and billions in national wealth. Why didn't the world powers help us then? Why did they let slip this last of many chances to end Hitler's life?

The occupation of the Rhineland, Austria, the Sudetenland, Czechoslovakia, Danzig, Poland. Hitler's aversion for war on two fronts—a host of possibilities, of neglected chances for intervention, of lost opportunities. Will Potsdam make up for it? A terrible rumor has been spreading in the city since this morning. That things have not been going well in Potsdam. That they have been of very different opinions at this conference. Definitely not as amiable as in Frankfurt and San Francisco.

"Perhaps there will be war," people whisper, looking scared. "They say it is possible" . . . War! We just had a war. Only eleven weeks ago. It's out of the question . . .

In Potsdam they are conferring very discreetly. No sound penetrates the cordon that is several kilometers wide. Nothing except the exciting news that the foreign heads of state "visited the center of the city and the Tiergarten district and looked at the ruins and the air raid shelter of Hitler's Chancellery . . . Salutes were fired in their honor, and the creation of a new Europe formed the background for the present events." That's what the papers say.

People put their heads together and whisper: "Concentrations of troops . . . shoot-outs between Americans and Russians every night. They don't even greet each other on the street, the Allied soldiers. They don't seem to like each other, our Allied occupation powers."

But we are not allowed to say it aloud. When we cautiously mention to the Americans and English that there have been some problems

---

* Two of the high officials involved in the assassination attempt against Hitler a year earlier.

75

under the Russian occupation, their faces turn to ice. Our Allies, their cold look says, and it makes us fall respectfully silent.

In the evening an American musician visits Andrik. A black man. He is beautiful like a panther and more passionately interested in Bach and Beethoven than most Germans are. He has traveled all over the world, given concerts in countless countries.

"They come in droves to my concerts," he says and looks at us with the eyes of Ahasuerus. "Though not for my music, but because they want to see what it's like when a Negro plays their music. We are the most disdained people in the world. Even more than the Jews or . . . ," and again he looks at us with the eyes of Ahasuerus, ". . . the Germans."

Is it a victor who is standing in front of us? In his elegantly styled American uniform, beautiful like a panther and passionately interested in Bach and Beethoven? Suddenly we all feel ashamed. Until Andrik embarrassedly reaches down to the shelf where he keeps his scores, pulls out a Bach cantata and hands it to our beautiful guest, saying in English, "If you would like to have it . . ."

• • •

WEDNESDAY, JULY 25, 1945

The Committee for the Rehabilitation of National Socialists has been temporarily suspended by the city council and the presiding committee for "clarification of jurisdiction." In the course of its existence it has decided three cases. Three or five. Perhaps even seven. If it goes on at this pace, the last Party members will have their rehabilitation documents put on their graves by our grandchildren and great-grandchildren. For the time being they are in a jurisdictional dispute. And when it comes to the crunch, they get quite unfriendly with each other. The emigrants who have returned from Moscow—people call them Muscovites—believe they've been the best anti-Nazis and they, more than anyone else, are therefore entitled to shape our future. Those who stayed believe the contrary. Anti-Nazis versus anti-Nazis. How naive we were to believe just a few weeks ago that we might all join forces.

In apartments barely cleared of rubble, it's a struggle for every minute of electricity. It comes and it goes, capricious as the weather in April.

"Broken cables," some say.

"Not at all," others object. "When the Russians left the Western sectors, they took the coal reserves with them to their occupied zone."

Who is right? Probably either of them. Perhaps neither of them. Only one thing is for sure: whether we like it or not, we have to go back to our brick stove.

• • •

FRIDAY, JULY 27, 1945

This time we've set it up on the balcony. Because of heat and smoke. After all, we are not smoked ham, and in the course of the last two months, despite ruins and improvisation, we have again become accustomed to a more civilized way of life. While I am busy with pots, poker and cooking spoon, Heike comes running.

"They've turned out Churchill," she says. "And Eden. Attlee has supposedly become prime minister."

I drop the cooking spoon. And all this in the midst of the conference? "An outrageous ingratitude!"

"It's not ingratitude," Andrik joins in from inside. "It only proves how objectively the English deal with politics. For war Churchill had been their best man. For peace, particularly if it is to be an allied peace, Churchill as a Conservative might not do so well. Attlee is a Labourite. Between Social Democrats and Communists there shouldn't be insurmountable differences. In any case, not at a joint conference."

I understand. And despite my sympathy for Churchill, I am glad about the decreasing risk of war.

• • •

MONDAY, JULY 30, 1945

Oh great God! How miserable can it get? Sometimes, when walking through the streets, one can barely stand to look at all the misery.

Among the smart American uniforms, the well-fed figures in the occupying forces, the first German soldiers appear ragged and haggard, sheepishly looking around like caught offenders. Prisoners of war from who knows where. They drag themselves through the streets. Seeing them one wants to look away because one feels so ashamed of their shame, of their wretched, pitiful looks. Are these the glorious victors whom Adolf Hitler years ago had sent into the war so well equipped? They shamble around like walking ruins. Limbless, invalid, ill, deserted and lost. A gray-bearded man in a tattered uniform leans against a wall. With his arms around his head he is quietly weeping. People pass by, stop and shyly form a circle around him. He does not see them. Looking helpless, his arms around his head, he sobs like a little child. "Mother . . . mother . . ."

"Are you hungry?" a woman asks, and embarrassedly searches her shopping bag. "Maybe you're ill . . . ?"

He does not hear her. He weeps. It is terrible to see gray-bearded men cry, unable to stop crying . . .

Sometimes all that's left is the trunk. Amputated up to their hips, they sit in an old box supported by wheels. With their arms they push themselves forward like raftsmen, maneuvering their pitiful vehicles through the stream of cars and trucks.

"Heil Hitler!" one feels like cursing out of angry compassion when one sees them.

• • •

TUESDAY, JULY 31, 1945

The war against Japan has entered a new stage. All the forces no longer needed in Europe are assembling in the Far East, in preparation for the invasion of Japan. Daily the bombing of Japanese cities intensifies. America, England and China have delivered an ultimatum to Japan. From Potsdam of all places! Since the heads of the respective states are gathered there. They demand unconditional surrender. "The alternative for Japan," the ultimatum states, "would be total destruction." Without a doubt. So now the war against Japan is coming to an end. No head of state can be so suicidal as to ignore such threats.

Battleground Berlin

Following the electoral victory of the Labour Party in England, Attlee has replaced Churchill at the Potsdam Conference. Supposedly the negotiations will be concluded within the next few days. Our attention is divided between Potsdam and Tokyo, between power outages and continued apartment confiscations.

• • •

SATURDAY, AUGUST 4, 1945

Big headlines in all papers. "The Potsdam Agreement. Joint policy for all occupied zones." That's a load off our minds. It means no new war. "Joint efforts for reconstruction and order. The tripartite conference has strengthened the relations between the three governments and further improved their collaboration and mutual understanding," emphasizes the closing communiqué. "The statesmen leave the conference with new confidence that the governments and people of their countries, in conjunction with other nations, will guarantee the creation of a just and lasting peace."

It sounds almost too good to be true. They do not want to install a central German government yet, but for a start they plan to appoint several undersecretaries who will be responsible for the transportation and communication systems, finance, foreign trade and industry, uniformly for all of Germany. For the duration of the occupation, Germany will be treated as an economic unit, particularly in regard to mining, agriculture and industry, food distribution, the banking system, the transportation system, reparations and currency.

If that happens, sooner or later all borders between the zones will become superfluous. I already see the dove of peace.

"Don't see it too soon," warns Frank. "Not all these resolutions are going to be realized as easily as it sounds on paper. As for the article on reparations, the cession of territory and the western border of Russia, not to mention the repatriation of the German minorities, the refugees from the ceded territories, I shudder to think of the consequences. My politically untrained mind doesn't quite grasp it."

"Why?" I ask.

79

Frank counts on his fingers: "Königsberg and the adjacent territories, Russian. East Prussia, West Prussia, Posen, Silesia and Pomerania all the way to the Oder, Polish. For the satisfaction of Russian reparation claims, dismantling of industrial plants in the Russian-occupied zone to an as yet undetermined extent. Reparation claims by the Western Allies covered by assets and resources in the Western-occupied zones and German foreign deposits."

Having gone through all his fingers, he clenches his fists.

"What do you think?" he asks gloomily. "Which resources are the Germans to fall back on, under this program, in order to, as it is stated in the resolutions, maintain their existence without any outside help? What if this madness is carried through! Repatriation of German minorities from Poland! If they regard Pomerania, Posen, Silesia and half of Prussia as Polish, that means the expatriation of millions of Germans. No thank you! These are nothing but elastic clauses! To be interrupted according to their whim."

Feeling depressed, I fall silent. That's not how I had imagined it. The Potsdam Agreement begins to make me feel uncomfortable.

• • •

SUNDAY, AUGUST 5, 1945

Mail service has been restored in Berlin. As of yesterday, mail is being delivered again. Real mail, delivered by a real, official-looking mailman carrying a mailbag. Also here and there, a mailwoman. The return of civilization continues.

• • •

MONDAY, AUGUST 6, 1945

Something oppressive is in the air. As if a storm were gathering. After Japan rejected the Allies' demand for unconditional surrender, something ominous seems about to occur. Japan expects the invasion at any time and wonders which island will be attacked first. It would serve better to wonder about how peace might be achieved as soon as possible. Self-sacrifice to the verge of a people's extermination is no heroism, but rather a crime.

• • •

WEDNESDAY, AUGUST 8, 1945

It has happened. He who chooses war will be destroyed by war. Not invasion, but the atomic bomb. Yesterday the terrible weapon, about which there had been rumors for weeks, was employed against Japan. On Hiroshima. With an explosive force two thousand times greater than the English ten thousand kilo bombs. It must have pulverized that city and its people.

What if Hitler had succeeded in creating such a powerful weapon of destruction. Retaliation weapon X. Unimaginable! However, the grotesque thing about it is that three of the scientists who invented it are German emigrants. So he might have played the murderous trump if his racial hatred—oh what a vengeful nemesis—hadn't blocked his way. Another proof that dictators at the decisive moment destroy themselves by their own measures. Hiroshima lies in ruins. Tomorrow perhaps it will be all of Japan.

• • •

THURSDAY, AUGUST 9, 1945

The world holds its breath. Will they surrender? More bombs are to follow. While the smoke of death still is billowing over Hiroshima, the radio announces that Russia has entered into the war against Japan. At the eleventh hour. They say it was decided in Potsdam.

• • •

WEDNESDAY, AUGUST 15, 1945

In front of the Hebbel Theater on Stresemannstrasse—formerly known as Saarlandstrasse—then Stresemannstrasse—then König-

81

grätzerstrasse—people are crowding. In a continuous succession, cars carrying prominent members of the occupying forces pull up. The theater is opening with a new production of the *Threepenny Opera*. The beggar's opera, what coincidental symbolism.

It is four in the afternoon. If one thinks about it, it is a strange time to be in a festive mood for theater. But curfew begins at eleven. Those who are still out on the streets after eleven risk being arrested or even shot. And by the time one has walked from the Hebbel Theater to the various suburbs . . . This is why the performance begins at an hour that, afterward, permits one to get home without risking one's life.

The ensemble has been working for a month and a half. Struggling with great effort through one bottleneck after the other. A cable breaks. Five thousand volts. The premiere has to be postponed for at least three days. The costumes have been stolen, the props demolished. Replacing them means overcoming a mountain of obstacles for each little thing. Then rain leaks through the roof and runs into the auditorium. A summer storm nearly washes away the set.

The ensemble continues rehearsing indefatigably. Sometimes beneath umbrellas, other times in total darkness. It takes tremendous idealism to keep rehearsing the *Threepenny Opera* day after day with undiminished enthusiasm, especially after hours of walking and scarcely more than a dry piece of bread in one's stomach.

Every morning Heike struggles to maintain her enthusiasm, and dead tired every evening she is convinced she will not be able to bring it off.

Today is the premiere. Once again we ride our bikes in closed convoy through Berlin's streets of rubble. Thank heavens, no new cable break. No cloudbursts or other nuisances.

"You masters who tell us to lead an honest life, to avoid crime and sins," we hear them sing.

I feel choked with emotion. It was the song of our illegal days. Providing solace and comfort during many desperate hours.

". . . First give us something to eat, then talk: that's how it begins."

A storm of applause breaks out, rousing me out of my self-absorption. Whom do they mean? How embarrassing, I think. Must we begin our first attempt at free expression by criticizing others?

Battleground Berlin

• • •

The war in Japan is over. On August 10 the Japanese declared their willingness to accept certain conditions for surrender. On August 11 the Allies responded. On the fourteenth the Japanese surrendered unconditionally. At two o'clock yesterday morning the war's end was announced in London, Moscow, Washington and Chungking.

The Japanese news agency reports that War Minister Korshika Anami has committed hara-kiri, "accepting his responsibility for having failed in his duties as His Majesty's minister." When will people finally begin to see heroism not in the destruction of life but in its preservation?

• • •

SATURDAY, AUGUST 18, 1945

Destruction of life or preservation of life. Public health officials in Berlin discuss this question for five hours.

At issue is Article 218 of the Criminal Code: "A pregnant woman who willfully aborts her fetus or kills her unborn child will be punished with up to five years' imprisonment. In case of extenuating circumstances, with imprisonment of at least six months. The same penal stipulations apply to any individual who assists with or performs an abortion with the consent of the pregnant woman."

Also at issue are Articles 177 and 178 of the Code: "The use of violence or threat of endangerment to life and limb in order to force a woman to suffer extramarital intercourse is punishable with imprisonment . . . . In case the act of violence results in the death of the victim, it is punishable by imprisonment for no less than ten years and for as much as life."

The seeds sown by the victors during the last week of April and the first weeks of May are bearing fruit. Another six months and thousands of children will have been born who will never know their father, who

83

were begotten in violence, conceived in fear and born in horror. Must they be born?

Public health officials meet at the Charité hospital under the chairmanship of Dr. Sauerbruch. Behind closed doors and without the presence of occupation authorities. Their reports confirm that half of all the women in Berlin have been raped. Ten percent of them have paid for their involuntary sexual encounters with venereal diseases. Of course, venereal diseases can be cured. Provided that they are known and the necessary drugs are available. Pyrimal or Salvarsan.

On the black market a Salvarsan treatment costs two pounds of coffee. Two pounds of coffee or one hundred marks per injection. Sulfonamides are hard to find. But supposedly those who suffered the misfortune of having caught "Mongolian" syphilis cannot be helped at all. Perhaps penicillin would help. But penicillin is not available to us. The privilege of using it is limited to the Allies.

The girls and women sit in the doctors' waiting rooms, looking utterly bewildered. Their faces bloated, dark shadows under their eyes. Terribly weighed down by the burden of their fate.

"Am I going to die? Am I going to stay sick?" some of them ask.

"Must I have this child? Must I give birth to it?" others worry. Article 218 is still in force. Never before has it seemed so obviously questionable.

"Of course we approve of abortion under these circumstances," Frank says emphatically. "Being forced to give birth to unwanted children violates human dignity. A woman has a right to self-determination too. It's about time we stopped thinking of a woman as a mere breeding vessel. As a means to an end. As a milk cow for population purposes."

"But what about respect for the unborn child?" I object. "Are the fetuses to blame that they were unwanted? Perhaps a Goethe is among them, or a Leonardo or . . ."

". . . a Hitler," Frank says coldly. "Of course, the disruption of nascent life is not desirable. But as long as women are not allowed to decide for themselves whether and when they want a child, abortion remains an unavoidable emergency solution. At least in cases where a woman's health is at stake, or on social grounds, or in cases of rape. Tell me," he continues, "what becomes of a woman's dignity and equality when she is forced to assume responsibilities she is unable to bear, to fulfill duties for fifteen or even twenty years of her life which she didn't choose out of her own free will? Of course you might say that it is up to her to remain continent, forego love and lovemaking entirely. But then you aren't a human being and are made of wood. A frigid creature who hasn't discovered the wonders of eros. Because eros is an end in itself as well. Through thousands of years of human spiritualization, it's freed itself from the basic instinct of procreation and emerged as an end in itself. Ultimate fusion between two lovers means fulfillment in itself too."

"Maybe," I answer, "but not the kind intended by nature."

Frank shakes his head. "Are we still living in the stone age? Do you think nature's original intention for the milk cow was to just endlessly produce milk, or for the hen to keep laying eggs? Does nature mean the asceticism of saints, or the heavenly love of nuns? On one side you say yes, on the other side you say no. May I ask how you justify that? Let people have the freedom and enlightenment, the responsibility and availability of choice, without risking their health, without interference with their feelings and without a guilty conscience, whether or not they want children. If they love each other and are ready for it they will gladly choose to have children. Mankind won't die out if Article 218 is repealed. But keeping it on the books certainly won't make people more responsible. Nor any freer or more dignified."

"But will it be kept on the books?" I ask. "I mean now, under the present circumstances?"

Frank looks at me. "How do you expect to repeal it without governmental power, without legislative power? Of course it stays on the books. But under tacit agreement . . ." He falls silent.

". . . its enforcement will cease temporarily," I interpret his silence. And I feel relieved that given the present population surplus, the hunger, misery and lack of housing, tens of thousands of Russian children will not be born in the course of the next nine months.

• • •

THURSDAY, AUGUST 23, 1945

Andrik performs more and more frequently. At the Titania Palace and the Popular Opera. The program keeps changing, as does the audience. American troops, English troops, German civilians from one sector, German civilians from another sector. So far there is little inclination to allow the various groups to mingle. Fraternization is not permitted. Only on the park benches at night, to the extent that they have been spared by the wood thieves, it is practiced in secret.

In Andrik's green room also, one forgets about victors and vanquished while talking about Tschaikovsky, Beethoven and Richard Strauss. Tonight we've been invited by an Englishman. Yesterday two Americans invited us to be their guests. We are pleased at every occasion that furthers understanding, for each opportunity to convince the victors that German people aren't necessarily different from them. Only if we understand each other will we be able to treat each other fairly.

Do we understand the other peoples? Would we treat the Indians fairly, were we in charge of them as an occupying power? Misjudging a foreign people is not a fault. But if it fell to one to govern a foreign people, it would be a critical mistake to fail to utilize all opportunities to get to know that people. We are dying to be understood. To be understood the way we really are. We would like to get this message to all ears, all minds and hearts. We want to . . . for Heaven's sake what wouldn't we do in our passionate desire to clear up the mess.

At seven o'clock a car sent by the English colonel is supposed to pick us up. He loves music. He loves Bach, Handel and Brahms. And he won't hate us and we won't hate him.

• • •

FRIDAY, AUGUST 24, 1945

At seven o'clock the colonel's car takes us to his villa in Grunewald. We sit in comfortable chairs, drink whiskey and eat unbelievably white sandwiches with unbelievably real meat. We talk about Bach and Germany. We are being listened to and are pleased to feel that we are among friends. The time passes quickly. A quarter to eleven. Curfew in fifteen minutes. Alarmed, we remind ourselves that there are occupation laws.

"I'll take you home," the colonel says.

Battleground Berlin

Swift as an arrow we seem to fly through the streets. Hardly any Germans are still out. Only once in a while a foreign soldier stands by the roadside demonstratively holding up his thumb. Hitchhiking, we interpret the gesture and are proud to have learned a new word.

Hildegardstrasse . . . Kaiserallee . . . Kaiserplatz. Three shadowy figures stand under the railway overpass. Are those flashlights they are holding in their hands? Hitchhiking! . . . Hitch-hiking!

Andrik sits in front of me. I see his beautiful profile facing our English friend. They are talking about the Third Brandenburg Concerto.

"Next time I'll bring you Bach's . . . ," says Andrik.

A strange noise. As if someone were throwing a handful of pebbles against the car. Pebbles or . . . oh dear God! I hear noise. Hostile noise it seems. I slip deeper into my seat. Deeper and deeper. Now a loud bang. Something is being spattered around my face, hits my arms and shoulders with biting force. The smell of gunpowder. Pungent and sulfurous. And then a different kind of smell. What is it that smells so strange . . . Tack-tack-tack . . . tack-tack-tack . . . The car stops. About ten meters beyond the overpass. Did someone shoot? Am I hit? Feeling dazed I sit up.

"Andrik!" I call. "What happened? Andrik!"

His shoulders bent forward he quietly sits in front of me. His hair blowing in the wind looks like a crown of fire around his head.

"Andrik!" I call out once more.

Silence. Andrik sits in his seat, his shoulders bent forward as if he were lost in thought. Why doesn't he answer? I jump out of the car and pull his door open. My God, what is this? Dripping it flows toward me. Dripping it runs down Andrik's shoulders. Darkly, viscously. Like a stream . . . like a stream. Blood, I think in horror, it is blood. I hear it dripping like a gutter, I see it flow. It is sticky. It sticks to my hands and my feet. Everywhere . . . everywhere.

"Help," I scream. "He's bleeding to death . . ."

Our English friend is coming toward me from the overpass. His face looks ashen. Why is he coming from over there? Hadn't I even noticed that he'd jumped out of the car? With an expression of infinite gentleness he steps up to me.

"I am afraid . . . ," he says haltingly. "I am afraid it is too late . . ."

Ruth Andreas-Friedrich

Everything around me ceases to exist. It all seems unreal and shadowy. Andrik is sitting there. His shoulders bent forward. Quietly . . . more and more quietly. As if from a gutter it drips across his hands onto the car's floorboard and into the street.

I walk up and down in front of the car. Someone says an ambulance has been called. That it will pick up Andrik. Our English friend puts his arm around me. Through the green of the trees shimmers the yellow light of the streetlamps.

Andrik . . . Andrik. Has one hour passed? Or several hours? Mechanically we walk up and down the street. Arm in arm. Suddenly my companion staggers. He staggers, then falls to the pavement. Everything seems unreal. Everything seems foggy. Is he dead? Someone picks him up.

"He fainted," I hear someone say.

Then the ambulance arrives. And then it is night. Endless night. Until I see myself climb up the stairs at home. Back at the housing complex at the water tower. I wake up Frank, Jo, Heike and Fabian.

"Andrik is dead," I say. "Get up and get dressed. We can't wear pajamas when Andrik has died."

Day is breaking. We've waited a long time for it. At eight o'clock our English friend appears. There is so much to be done. It cannot all be done on a bicycle. One cannot get anything done at all if one is German. They still take the dead bodies in handcarts to the cemetery and lay them, wrapped in a horse blanket, to eternal rest in a mass grave. Andrik must not lie in a mass grave. He deserves better than being carted to the cemetery, than lying on the cold tiles of a mortuary while we are sitting right now at his table, in his chair, in front of his books. Body next to body. Stranger next to stranger.

"Help us to do it right," I ask our English friend.

He has pulled a few sandwiches from his pockets. Unbelievably white bread with unbelievably real meat.

"You must eat," he says and puts them on the table.

All day long we drive all over Berlin. Frank, he and I. From one administrative department to the next. We always ask for the same things. A coffin for Andrik. A grave for Andrik. A decent way of transporting his body. A decent funeral. We ask in vain.

88

"American soldiers are buried in tarpaulins too," they tell us. "We see no reason for treating a German any better."

"Not even after you shot him?" I want to ask. But I don't say it. It wouldn't bring Andrik back to life again. So it makes no sense.

We keep driving. Stamps, certificates, impounding of the body, release of the body. During brief moments when I've recovered my senses, I hear it rushing as if from a gutter. Andrik is dead . . . Andrik is dead, it keeps echoing inside my head.

We should contact Makar Ivanov, it suddenly occurs to me. Makar Ivanov is Andrik's friend. A childhood friend from Moscow. When the Russians occupied Berlin they took him as an interpreter. In some administrative department. That is where he has been working since. He also sleeps there. But where is his office? Two blocks from the Friedrichstrasse station.

"Let's drive to Friedrichstrasse Station," I ask our English friend. "We've got to reach Makar Ivanov."

He nods. Half an hour later we stop in front of a freshly painted apartment building. Suspiciously, the Russian sentry inspects the English military car, the British colonel's uniform.

"We'd like to see Makar Ivanov," we ask him through an interpreter. He shakes his head and looks at his machine gun.

"It's about an accident," says our English friend. "The conductor of the Philharmonic Orchestra . . . In my car . . . I am an English colonel . . . We'd like to inform his friend, Makar Ivanov . . ."

The sentry shakes his head and tells us to move to the other side of the street, away from the building's entrance. Is he afraid we might throw a bomb?

"Can't you at least summon him?" I try for a third time through the interpreter.

Lengthy arguments go back and forth. Ten minutes later Makar Ivanov appears.

"Andrik has met with an accident," I tell him. "Maybe they'll let you take a few days off for the funeral."

Makar Ivanov disappears. We wait on the other side of the street. Ten minutes later he comes back. He has been granted a leave of absence. As we get into the car, feeling relieved, a Russian officer comes running across the street, pulls the car door open and shouts

89

something. It does not sound friendly. But we do not understand it. And I don't think to ask Makar Ivanov to translate it for us.

· · ·

SATURDAY, AUGUST 25, 1945

Now we know how it happened. An unfortunate chain of fateful circumstances. During the night before the twenty-third there was a shoot-out between Russians and Americans. In the center of the city, like almost every night. Perhaps it was somewhat worse than normal, more widespread and hostile. Perhaps that had prompted the American authorities to order their sentries to stop any car that passed the checkpoints after eleven o'clock at night. And to shoot immediately if it did not stop. To fire at the car, because the Russians would not respond to shots fired into the air. Our friend's car has very bright headlights. Apparently they did not see the car's English license plates. They thought it was a Russian car. And when it failed to stop, they opened fire. They fired at it because the Russians do not respond to shots fired into the air. Perhaps they only meant to hit the tires. Or just the roof. The street slopes there. They fired. Six shots one after another. With the fastest machine gun the American Army has. They did not mean to shoot Andrik. It was because of the order to shoot and because of their anger at what had happened the night before. But their shots hit Andrik. And no matter who is to blame, it will not bring him back to life.

In the early evening we drive to the Popular Opera. The Philharmonic Orchestra is performing. Andrik's program, rehearsed with Andrik, with a new conductor. Tchaikovsky, Beethoven and Richard Strauss. They've changed only the Beethoven piece. Instead of the First Symphony we hear the mournful and heavy "Funeral March." I think of Andrik and wonder why I cannot cry.

Later our English friend takes us far away to the outskirts of the city. In a room at the English hospital lies Andrik. On a white bed. Quiet, thin and solemn. They put a bandage around his head and a bouquet of roses in his folded hands. At his feet stands a white-covered table and on it lies the open score of the Third Brandenburg Concerto and a baton.

90

"Thank you," I say to our English friend. "We all thank you."

"He will get a coffin too," the colonel says gently. "And a hearse will take him to his own grave in the cemetery."

"Thank you," I say once more. And suddenly I feel that now I could cry. Dear, gentle English friend!

• • •

MONDAY, AUGUST 27, 1945

The funeral must be postponed because the coffin is not ready yet. It is difficult to find a coffin in Berlin, even for an English colonel. However, the weather is hot and at the hospital they begin to worry. Perhaps Tuesday, but under no circumstances later than Wednesday. They say they have no ice and are not usually prepared for anything of the sort. On Tuesday they want to take Andrik to the cemetery. Makar Ivanov's leave of absence lasts till the weekend.

• • •

WEDNESDAY, AUGUST 29, 1945

The cemetery chapel has been destroyed by bombs. Everything has to be improvised. But there are flowers, many flowers, and there is a coffin, and the sun is shining. They have dug out a grave under an oak tree.

"May the Lord let His countenance shine upon you and be merciful unto you," the minister prays.

The sun is shining. It shines upon the grave, the coffin, the flowers, and upon all of us. It shines so gently, but Andrik is dead.

• • •

FRIDAY, AUGUST 31, 1945

"To the German People. The Allied Control Authority. The Allied Control Council. Proclamation No. 1 . . . Pursuant to the public notice of June 5, 1945, the supreme governmental authority over Germany

91

has been taken over by the governments of the United States of America, the Union of Soviet Socialist Republics, the United Kingdom of Great Britain and Northern Ireland, and the provisional government of the French Republic. . . . By virtue of the supreme governmental authority which has been assumed by the four governments, the Allied Control Council is hereby established as the supreme governmental authority, and all matters concerning Germany are delegated unto it."

So it is the Allied Control Council! Now we know at least who governs us. Why is there so much talk in the papers about democracy? Democracy means the people rule. We are ruled by the Control Council. We should beware of abusing the beautiful word.

"And that's supposed to be democracy," people grumble while waiting in line or while angrily trying to get on overcrowded trains, or when confronted in any other unpleasant way with the consequences of the Nazi regime. "That's what they call democracy! No thank you."

Nobody in his right mind would call the present situation in Germany democracy. It is not democracy. It cannot be a democracy as long as we are governed by a Control Council. Only a first attempt perhaps, a slow way of "getting used" to it.

Sometimes it makes one almost feel odd to be unable to fall back upon traditional national customs. Not that we are nationalists. It is only that one becomes aware of the difference. In front of an American administrative office sentries take down the flag. Standing to attention, they raise their hands to salute. How odd it actually is for a people to be without a flag. At the beginning of each concert performed for English troops their national anthem, "God Save the King," is played and the audience solemnly rises to its feet. It is not our anthem. We have no anthem. We have no king and hardly any occasion to rise to our feet in honor of any head of state. Often it is a strange coincidence that suddenly reminds one that we have lost something. Something one has never really been aware of, something one was born into, so to speak. They should not give too many Germans the opportunity to be suddenly reminded of this. They might draw wrong conclusions from it.

• • •

MONDAY, SEPTEMBER 3, 1945

Makar Ivanov wants to ask for a few more days off. This morning he went to his office. He wanted to be back at two o'clock. It is almost ten o'clock. In an hour the curfew begins. Where can he be?

• • •

THURSDAY, SEPTEMBER 6, 1945

We ask for him, we look for him, we wait for him. There is no trace of Makar Ivanov. Our English friend doubtfully shakes his head. "We must be careful. Too much interest could arouse suspicions."

We dare not ask at his office. At some of the administrative agencies they act very secretive. Perhaps it was wrong to have driven there the other day. Perhaps . . . If only Andrik were here now. It is so difficult when one does not even understand the language.

• • •

SUNDAY, SEPTEMBER 16, 1945

At the Hebbel Theater the writers of the time of the Weimar Republic are honored. What has been burned on pyres in front of the University of Berlin in 1933 is now solemnly resurrected there. Toller, Tucholsky, Brecht, Heinrich Mann, Erich Mühsam, Frank, Rubiner, Feuchtwanger and many others. The audience sits there, deeply moved. It seems incomprehensible that they were banned.

"I already turned in my Rosenberg," I hear someone say amid the applause. "Burning of Nazi literature. It was announced today in all the Sunday papers."

Astounded I turn around. The lady who just spoke smiles unpleasantly.

"On a pyre," she says sarcastically.

93

Her smile annoys me. I feel like answering her sharply. Why must it be today of all days that another pyre is ordered, no matter how justified it might be? A dubious counterstroke.

At home I take a look at the paper. "Eradication of all Nazi literature. . . . Expurgation of all libraries by October 1. . . . Public burning," I read. And I feel very unhappy and lonely . . .

• • •

SUNDAY, SEPTEMBER 23, 1945

. . . so unhappy and so lonely! One month ago Andrik died. Today the first sign of life of Makar Ivanov reaches us in a surreptitious way. "Help him," the anonymous messenger implores us. "Help him, for Christ's sake . . . They are breaking their clubs over him. They say he is a spy."

What terrible certainty! Poor Makar Ivanov. Why have we done this to you? The English car, the English colonel. And of all places in front of a Soviet agency. An agency whose name and address you should never have disclosed!

They are breaking their clubs over him. Perhaps on your back. Or your hands. There wasn't anything said about that. Only that you need help. But how can we help you? Against their clubs and their crazy suspicion. Perhaps one day they will call us spies too. Frank Matthis and me, or Heike and Fabian. Who knows? As of today we know only that they are breaking clubs over you. How can one live knowing that?

Two days ago the Russians published a report on all the destruction caused by Germans in the Soviet Union. They say 1,670 orthodox and 237 catholic churches have been burned, 69 chapels and 532 synagogues. About four million apartment houses have been destroyed, one and a half million horses, nine million cattle, twelve million pigs, thirteen million sheep and goats. As well as an immeasurable amount of household goods, machines, engines, motors, cars and books carried away, requisitioned or rendered unusable. One understands why they hate us, why they vent their anger at us. But what does Makar Ivanov have to do with that? Or the English car in front of the Soviet agency?

Battleground Berlin

• • •

MONDAY, OCTOBER 1, 1945

No help for Makar Ivanov. In two months they want to put him on trial. On account of espionage for England. However, the source of our information is dubious. One bottle of brandy and two hundred cigarettes for each piece of information. "As a bribe," our dubious source of information says. I wonder whether he does not use the bribes himself? Whether it isn't he who drinks the vodka and smokes the cigarettes and then tells us shameless lies? Needing connections to GPU prisons, one is at the mercy of very nasty characters.

• • •

WEDNESDAY, OCTOBER 3, 1945

I talk to the head of a Russian agency. He is intelligent and obliging. He is frighteningly intelligent, like most officers in key positions of the Soviet military government. "The Americans sent their second-raters to Germany, the English their third-, and the Russians their elite," the Berliners sum up five months of occupation.

The major receives me kindly.

"Makar Ivanov," I begin to plead with him. "It must be a mistake. A series of misunderstandings. The agency on X Street . . ."

The Red Army major puckers up his face into a smile in which his eyes are like boarded-up windows.

"Which agency?" he asks obligingly. "I don't know of any agency on X Street."

Oh God, I think horrified. He is lying! Every child knows that the GPU is there. As usual, when someone is lying, I become embarrassed and insecure.

"I could try and find out," says the major, "and ask the commander . . ."

I nod mechanically. His eyes look right through me. As if I were made of glass. In which corner of my soul shall I hide Makar Ivanov?

95

Ruth Andreas-Friedrich

Hide him from the power behind those eyes? There is no Makar Ivanov, I feel like shouting. Forget it, for Heaven's sake forget about Makar Ivanov.

Politely I get up and offer my hand. "Thank you," I hear myself say.

The major bows. His eyes look right through me as if I were made of glass. Makar Ivanov is lost. Now, at this moment, I know for sure that nothing on earth can save him.

At home, cold and darkness await me. Military headquarters ordered the city administration to reduce the power supply drastically. Which means power outages for indefinite periods of time, gathering firewood in the ruins, buying candles on the black market, returning to the brick stove, and an unpleasant winter. The coal shortage is turning into the worst postwar difficulty. And that in a country which once supplied half of Europe with coal.

Slowly even the optimists begin to realize that we have not yet reached the bottom of the abyss. "So, we have to carry on," the positive types say. "It means ultimate destruction," sigh the exhausted, the disappointed and the despondent. Should the bottom of the abyss still lie far ahead of us, only a few will remain to cross it uncowed. According to official reports, the infant mortality rate in Brandenburg is about eighty to ninety percent. The city of Ruppin reports that of forty-five newborn infants, forty-one die within their first year of life. Five months after the war ten thousand orphaned children roam about Germany subsisting exclusively on begging and stealing. Misery and hardship wherever one looks. As soon as one difficulty has been taken care of another one opens up.

"Redistribution of land to workers and refugees," they proclaim in the Soviet occupation zone. A perfect solution! "Expropriation without compensation of all landowners holding more than one hundred hectares," the administrative authorities in Brandenburg declare their solution to the problem. Seven thousand landowners become homeless overnight. Not even a small plot of their own land is alloted to them. In the Western zones there is no land reform. No expropriation, and, as rumor has it, not even any freezing of bank accounts. Why aren't we living in the West, think the seven thousand dispossessed. Should the solution to the German problem be that each zone is slowly turned

96

into a colony of the respective occupying power? In that case, adieu to German unity. Farewell to all postwar hopes of a joint Allied reconstruction policy.

"For the duration of the occupation Germany is to be seen as an integral economic unit," the Potsdam Agreement states. How can an integral unit be formed if each of its components develops in opposite directions? Or could it be that we are condemned to bear evidence to the fact that the wartime alliance of the victors will never turn into a peacetime alliance.

· · ·

TUESDAY, OCTOBER 16, 1945

Frank comes home with a whole bunch of papers. "Now we've got them," he says, throwing them onto the table.

"Whom do you mean?" I inquire.

"The parties. The political mouthpiece of popular will, if you prefer it more poetically." He points to the names of the papers. *"Neue Zeit,* Daily of the Christian Democratic Union of Germany. *Deutsche Volkszeitung,* Official Party Organ of the Communist Party of Germany. *Der Morgen,* Daily of the Liberal Democratic Party of Germany. *Das Volk,* Daily of the Social Democratic Party of Germany."

"Strange," says Heike. "They all call themselves 'Party of Germany' and three out of four call themselves 'Democratic.' While in fact, since the end of the war, to us Germany consists only of Berlin, and democracy only of orders issued in agreement—or rather in disagreement—by the occupying powers. Why all this pomp?"

"Because this 'pomp' expresses our willingness to assume political responsibility," Frank explains to her. "Because freedom begins by assuming responsibility. It's the first step from underling to citizen."

"But they don't allow us to assume any responsibility," Heike murmurs, somewhat confused.

Frank frowns. "Perhaps. But that doesn't relieve you of the duty to care about the future. 'Never again Hitler,' we vowed in April. Put into action that means no more and no less than learning how to think, act and judge for oneself. Do you think a people can learn that in three

97

weeks? It took England a couple of hundred years. No less in America. Should we be able to achieve it sooner? But in order to see to it that in addition to the two or three hundred years of citizenship, we don't waste another couple of weeks or months trying to figure out how to begin—this is our responsibility. Yours and mine and that of all our contemporaries. And that's why today . . ."

"Well, what?" I interrupt him.

". . . I joined the Social Democratic Party."

Perplexed, we look at him. "But why the Social Democrats?"

He shrugs his shoulders. "What other choice is there? I am too much of a scientist to join the Christian Democrats. I'm not Soviet enough for the Communists of today. And the Liberal Democrats? After thirteen years of Nazism, with seventeen million refugees and twenty million in surplus population, we can't afford any individualistic points of view. Mass misery requires social solutions. Social democratic ones."

"And what if one day this party membership is on trial, too?"

"So be it. At least no one will be able to claim he was forced to join."

In the evening Frank, Jo and I go to a Social Democratic meeting. It is not easy to join a party if, during all one's life, one has been against any kind of association, insignia or membership. But Frank is right. Daydreaming will not make the world any better, nor will it transform an underling into a citizen. In spite of that it makes us wince the first time we are called "comrade."

• • •

In Nuremberg an international tribunal has gathered to sit in judgment on the "main war criminals of the Axis." That is, the main war criminals who have not escaped international condemnation. Hitler, Himmler, Goebbels and Bormann, the actual ringleaders, are not seated in the docket.

Hitler shot himself. Goebbels shot himself as well. Himmler poisoned himself. Bormann has repaired to parts unknown. Fritzsche has the dubious honor of playing Goebbels's stand-in. Twenty-four defendants. The trial is supposed to begin in thirty days. The text of the indictments fills seven densely printed pages in the newspaper. Extermination of the Jews; crimes against humanity; crimes against peace; murder of hostages; maltreatment of prisoners of war; euthanasia; gas chambers; concentration camps; slave labor; gallows.

A conglomeration of human atrocities. How come it doesn't anger and shame us? Watching people indifferently skimming the shameful seven-page document, it almost seems as if it doesn't concern them at all. Neither the crime nor the criminals, neither the guilt nor the punishment. "Incomprehensible!" the Allies say. "Utterly baffling! Where is the hatred that supposedly consumed millions of Germans?"

It is . . . where actually is it? Seven months of hunger, desperation, of struggle to survive, of insecurity, have taken the wind out of its sails. Yes, back then in February, in March or in April, during the weeks of the final battle, when denunciations were rife, and even the biggest fool understood how villainously he had been deceived by Nazism . . . back then people were ripe for retribution. If there had been a three-day period between the collapse and the conquest, thousands and thousands of Germans, disappointed, humiliated and abused by the Nazis, would have wreaked revenge upon their enemies. To each his personal tyrant. "An eye for an eye," people swore back then. "The first hour after the collapse belongs to the long knives!" Destiny had it differently.

The first hour, the first day, the first weeks after the collapse belonged to the terror of rape. There wasn't a moment between one atrocity and the next. Before the night of the long knives could take place, yesterday's bloodsucker had become today's fellow sufferer—a comrade-in-arms against common misfortune. How can one settle old accounts when constantly beset with new ones? So we missed our chance and have wasted the force of our anger.

Keitel, Rosenberg, Ribbentrop, Frick—who are they to most people? Out of a hundred thousand scarcely one knew them; scarcely a one had suffered personally at their hands. Revenge is an instinctive reaction to personal humiliation. In the spring "the long knives" were sharpened, not against the Nazi idea, but against those who used it against us—the block warden who had harassed us, the concentration camp guard who had maltreated us, the informer who had denounced us to the Gestapo. Fate has cheated us of our private retribution. Now the big shots are being brought to trial. Not by us, but by a foreign tribunal. And for the missed personal retribution, we have had to settle for a nebulous collective guilt. Too nebulous to seriously discomfit the average German. Too collective to be comprehended as individual responsibility.

• • •

MONDAY, OCTOBER 29, 1945

A rumor is spreading in Berlin. A nervous whispering. One passes it on to another—whispers it into the next one's ear—anxiously, triumphantly, gleefully or desperately—depending on what his conscience allows him. "The Americans have found the lists. The entire membership list of the NSDAP. Seven million party members. No, ten—no, eleven, or even twelve million. That would mean . . . ," people exchange frightened looks, ". . . twenty percent of the German people!"

"Nothing but a bluff," say the lighthearted. "They only want to find out who was involved."

"But what if it were true?"

Three weeks ago the first measures were taken against Party members. Elimination of all Nazis from prominent positions in industry and commerce. Exclusion of Party members from cultural occupations. Former NSDAP members may only be employed as workers. Anyone who violates this law will be prosecuted. Anyone who conceals his membership will be strictly accountable. Additionally, as of November 1, ration cards will be issued only upon presentation of an employment record. Ill tidings, especially for those who, after the war, were not very particular about telling the truth. Now their conscience, troubled by questionnaires, is entrenched behind an air of personal affront.

"Unbelievable, this terror! Outrageous, this latest injustice. They can't put twenty percent of the population under special law."

But they can! Have they forgotten how easily it can be done? Has it escaped them that these special laws are almost identical to those of eight years ago against the Jews? Along with having lost their memory of Party membership, the majority of Party members seem to have also lost their memory of Nazi legislation.

"Elimination of the Jews from German economic and cultural life. As of January 1, 1939, there shall be no Jewish shops, skilled laborers, or managers. Reparation payments from all German Jews to the German Reich of one billion Reichsmarks. Signed in November 1938 by Hermann Goering, Frick, Goebbels, Gürtner, Schwerin-Krosigk, Funk."

Who complained back then about terror and injustice? Who groused about special laws when that ordinance was published in the papers? They ought to refresh their memories for the benefit of their lost sense of justice. They ought not to forget the causal connection between the swastika and the Star of David worn by the Jews.

．． ．

THURSDAY, NOVEMBER 1, 1945

As of today there is mail service throughout Germany. Another step out of isolation, a wonderful chance to get in touch legally with friends on the other side of the Elbe. The day is spent writing letters. "Are you still alive? Have you survived? Is your house still standing? Do you have enough food?" So many questions, so many uncertainties. One would have to fill up a hundred pages to sketchily convey what has happened in the meantime. "Andrik is dead," I write fifteen times that afternoon. And even when writing it for the fifteenth time, I know that I myself don't believe it.

．． ．

SUNDAY, NOVEMBER 11, 1945

Winter has set in appallingly early. Much too early for our paltry wood supply, the windows without glass, the wind which, from day to day, blows more icily through the cracks in the walls. Nobody mentions the coal allotment. The newspapers do not mention it either. I suppose we have to survive without coal . . .

• • •

. . . Not only survive, but even perform in the theater. To get enthusiastic about a four-hour performance of Macbeth at several degrees below zero. Oh, lovable Berlin! Who on earth would emulate you? Shivering with cold, the lady stands onstage. The actors' breath steams from their mouths like a cloud. The trees, upon which the witches sway, are covered with ice. And the audience? Figures covered with blankets. Feet in muffs, collars raised, hats pulled down over the ears. Bravely the people in the audience freeze. Bravely the lady in her thin silk gown freezes. Bravely Heike, the youngest witch, freezes on her ice-covered tree. The heat that the outside does not provide we must generate from within. That we manage this, despite hunger and cold, despite ruins and collapse, is and remains a miracle. A miracle that one must have experienced to appreciate in all its consolatory effect. The intensity of suffering awakens an intensity of living. What makes the weak give up seems to strengthen the strong. As if fate had rewarded them for their years of training in misery and death with an increased awareness of existence. Never before in Berlin has as much passionate will to live and desire for culture been displayed as now, when every step upward must be struggled for so strenuously. This is how we are compensated in comparison to those who are blessed with a better-fed existence. We are no longer humiliated if we have to do without nail polish in the latest fashionable color. We don't mind if the hat we have to wear is outmoded. We never again want to get ourselves into a situation where we bother about such things. Life is more important than nail polish. Shakespeare is more important. And more important is the incomparable delight in discovering him at several degrees below zero in a totally new and passionate way. Similarly, we discovered yesterday, while collecting wood, that a tree is a tree and it can be a miracle to experience a leafless tree against a wintry sky. For years we have balanced on the borderline between

102

being and nonbeing. Perhaps it is a blessing rather than a curse to be
allowed to balance on this final borderline.

• • •

MONDAY, NOVEMBER 26, 1945

"Strange," says Frank while looking at the blond, curly-haired girl
in the supplement of the *Tagespiegel* newspaper, "how badly the victors
succeed in assessing the effects of their actions."

I read over his shoulder: "Two photos of Eva Braun in summer-
time, that have been found by American military specialists on an
estate in Bavaria."

So that is Adolf Hitler's mysterious lover. The woman who died
with him twenty-four hours after the wedding. "A pretty girl," I must
admit.

Frank looks at me. "That's the problem. Do you think it's our task,
seven months after the war, to find Frau Eva Hitler, née Braun, a
pretty girl? After they've spent half a year trying to drive Nazism out
of the minds of the German people, they now, in all innocence,
are rekindling it." He points at the paper. "With photographs like
that. With sentimental reports about Adolf Hitler's last hours, last
words and last farewells. As if they don't know how dangerous it is
to confront average people with sentimentality. The worst killer
would get their sympathy if, under the blade of the guillotine, he
were crying for his mother. The wedding in the bunker of death.
Poison capsules at the wedding banquet, a funeral under artillery
fire. Gasoline-drenched bodies, arms outstretched in a last salute toward the smoke-blackened sky. An exemplary collection of sensation-
alist titles for dime novels. The most successful way to bring about
a Hitler renaissance."

"But how come they're doing that?"

"Because they're badly advised and much too suspicious to take any
advice from us. It is an old law. Anyone wishing to colonize cannot
live in 'splendid isolation.' Almost all victors go about it the wrong
way. Through their haughtiness and lack of understanding of the
vanquished, they ruin their chances for success."

103

I had noticed that too. As if upon an isle of the blest, most of the occupation forces live in separate areas of the city. Almost none of them know the language of the conquered. How can one judge the culture of a country if one doesn't know its language? How can one do justice to its inhabitants if one passes them only in a car? "Let us help you!" we have often implored. "Let us convey, from our experience, an understanding that you as foreigners cannot have. Take our word for it when we tell you we are honest. Allow us to help you avoid mistakes. Mistakes that could become dangerous. For you—for us— for our common cause." Rarely, too rarely, they allow us this. It seems to be difficult to transform oneself from victors and vanquished into fellow human beings.

• • •

SATURDAY, DECEMBER 1, 1945

The first mail from the Western zone. It took four weeks to finally reach us. A letter from Germany to South America used to take no longer than that. The news from Stuttgart, Cologne, Hamburg and Frankfurt sounds strange to us, as if from another continent. Nevertheless—it is news. And at least one can hope for an answer within two months to a letter sent today.

• • •

MONDAY, DECEMBER 3, 1945

The Chamber of Cultural Affairs has been dissolved upon orders of the commander. Rumor has it that the "arguments between East and West" have led up to this. That the Muscovite emigrants insist on their claim to leadership and do not acknowledge the emigrants who returned from the West.

To be "anti-Hitler" means less and less to be standing on the same side. An alarming rift becomes apparent. The Social Democrats are debating a merger of all left-wing parties. Will that prevent the rift? For the time being one has the impression that it is not entirely voluntary. As if there were a purpose behind it that does not have much to do anymore with German interests but with maneuvering world politics. But what are the German interests? As long as mail from Frankfurt to Berlin takes four weeks, as long as they keep dissolving today what was founded yesterday, as long as there is little regard for individual life and nobody knows who is in charge, it all just seems like a turbid river with the individual swimming in its whirling waters like a castaway. Content if he manages not to drown in his struggle against the waves, grateful for any little straw he can get hold of.

• • •

TUESDAY, DECEMBER 11, 1945

In the Tiergarten area—in the English sector—lives Makar Ivanov's friend, the Baltic Count X. When he was adjutant to Canaris, the Nazis put him into a concentration camp.

"I love Russia," he said after the war. "And even if I am not a Soviet, I still—because of that love—want to communicate with its government."

So he came to Berlin. From the West. And moved into his former quarters in the Tiergarten area.

Several days ago two men came to see him. Politely they ask him to come along to the English commander's office in order to supply some information.

"Of course," he readily agrees, gets into the car that is waiting outside, and drives away together with the two men. Three hours pass. His wife begins to worry. At last she goes to the commander's office.

"Your husband?" they ask, surprised. "We don't know anything about him."

"For Heaven's sake! . . . The GPU." The wife laments.

The English commander calls the Russian commander.

"Impossible," he protests. "Nothing like that happens in our sector." Of course, he would inquire about it and get back to him within the next twenty-four hours.

105

Twenty-four anxious hours. Then the answer comes. "Count X. cannot be found in any of our agencies."

No one will ever find him. Unless one should walk through all the concentration camps of the Eastern zone and through all of Russia. Perhaps then one would also find Makar Ivanov who, as our dubious source of information whispers, is being tortured at every interrogation. And threatened with twelve years in prison.

Countess X. sits at home and weeps. "If at least he had some poison on him," she cries. How can they take a man away from his home just like that?

Indeed, we are swimming in turbid waters. Night after night civilians are brought to Jo Thäler's hospital. During an argument with some unidentified soldiers, they are wounded, beaten or killed. Usually these "incidents" are caused by alcohol in combination with the soldiers' habit of immediately reaching for their guns. What about the law? What about security?

A week ago a jeep was stolen from in front of our house, practically from under its owner's nose. The night before last the gasoline was taken out of Frank's car. Yesterday the car itself was stolen. The moment one turns one's back a tire is taken off, the battery removed, or the entire car disappears. Sometimes one finds the sorry remnants in a junkyard. And has the chance to sell it as junk or scrap iron. But what good are a few hundred marks if a pound of butter costs twice that on the black market.

In the shadows of the ruins of the Reichstag is the black market— so far the only commerce that has flourished since the war. Anything unobtainable through ration cards is traded there, sold illicitly and for a high price. Sometimes, during a raid, a commando unit drives the buyers and sellers apart, loads those who did not get away quickly enough onto a truck and takes them to the police station for the night in order to check their identification papers and frisk them. But five minutes later the area in front of the Reichstag's ruins is bustling again with people. Men, women, youngsters and, in between, the uniforms of occupation forces. "Bacon . . . would you like bacon? Cigarettes? Chocolate?" A night in the jail at Alexanderplatz? There is worse than that. Prison is no disgrace anymore since it has been abused millions of times for infamous purposes.

Battleground Berlin

. . .

Rumor has it that the mark will be devalued as of January 1.

"Pay your debts." "Pay your rent in advance." "Use your money buying goods or take it to the bank." Different advice is coming from every quarter. Nobody really knows what to do. Open a savings account? Just to have the money confiscated for a second time, as happened to all bank accounts after the conquest. Resorting to goods whose 100- to 500-fold inflated price might exceed the rate of the devaluation? To save or not to save, to invest or spend. Between ruins, hunger and the black market, slowly the respect for money and the value of money have been equally devalued.

. . .

"If you want me to I can get you in touch with the outside world," our English friend said a month ago.

I wanted to very much, because it might take forever before a German is allowed to communicate beyond the border. I gave him three addresses: that of my foster mother Salomon, in California, and those of Karla Simson and Erich Tuch in Nanking. It's nearly five years since I last saw Karla and Erich. On April 7, 1941 we said goodbye at the station. It is hard to think for five years about someone you are close to without the possibility of a reply. Will they still care about us?

Today the answer came to our English friend's army post office number. I pore over five densely written pages and cry like a baby. My beloved friend Karla! My dear foster mother, far away!

107

Ruth Andreas-Friedrich

. . .

SATURDAY, JANUARY 5, 1946

TUESDAY, DECEMBER 25, 1945

The first Christmas since the war. How differently we had imagined
it. No tree. No presents. No Andrik. Just that the day before yesterday
the curfew was lifted, and if one dares, one may go out after eleven
P.M.

. . .

SATURDAY, JANUARY 5, 1946

The money has not been devalued. Once more the rumors have
been false. One continues bartering on the black market, trading
things one can do without for bacon, sugar, brandy, coffee or cigarettes. And slowly one gets used to the fact that for a portion of the
population small change is a thousand-mark bill, while for another it's
a five-pfennig piece. The differences between economic extremes become more and more grotesque. The maximum rate of public assis-
tance to men and women unfit for work is between thirty and forty
marks a month. About twenty-one marks is what a Berliner needs to
buy his food ration cards. The number of men and women in Berlin
who are unfit for work is large. After buying their ration cards, nineteen marks a month remain to buy everything else they need. Which
means they have to watch every pfennig. And to walk rather than spend
twenty pfennigs for the streetcar.

Twenty pfennigs! How much is twenty pfennigs? It is the price of
the seventy grams of butter the average person is entitled to every ten
days. On the black market it buys one and a third milligrams of butter.
Ten grams, enough for a sandwich of bread and butter, costs fifteen
marks. Seven legal butter sandwiches for every ten days will not help
much and certainly will not fill the average person's stomach.

The problem of obtaining additional butter sandwiches imperceptibly restructures the entire social order and forms new social classes,
a new economic hierarchy. One cannot fall back on savings in the

bank. Yesterday's capital has ceased to exist. There is a new capitalism and a new proletariat. Those depending solely on food ration cards belong to the unpropertied class. To be a new capitalist means to possess sufficient scarce goods to be able to live as in peacetime. Expressed in monetary terms, that means black market goods worth about twenty to thirty thousand marks a month.

The new capitalists are the dealers in scarce goods, the producers of scarce goods, the providers of scarce services, the black marketeers, the factory owners, the farmers, the craftsmen—in food-supply terms they represent the upper classes of today's Germany. Those to whom the monthly rations are providing a basic existence, but are not the sole means of subsistence, form the new middle class. Petit bourgeois in terms of life-style. Their modest sources of capital are—in case of need—their connections to farmers, chance bargains, Sunday hoarding excursions, and the exchange of remaining tangibles for additional calories. I wonder if Karl Marx ever envisioned the restructuring of bourgeois society in such a way?

• • •

MONDAY, JANUARY 14, 1946

Independence or fusion? This question is debated with increasing urgency at all district and division meetings of the Social Democratic Party. Fusion of course, our feelings tell us. What more could the Socialists wish for than a fraternal unification with one another. Together they are unbeatable. United they will stand for the world's good. For Moscow's good? worries the party's chairman. Or for the good of the world proletariat? For the good of Marx or the good of Stalin? For the good of the International or the good of the Soviet Union? A disturbing conflict to a Socialist conscience.

For twenty-nine years socialism was embodied by the Union of the Soviet Socialist Republics, which meant separation from the world community, meant state capitalism, GPU, fear, unfreedom and manipulation of opinion. Are these the ideals of the program established in Erfurt?

For nine months the embodiment of the German Communist Party meant taking orders from Moscow. If we walk into that trap not only will we be lost, but also Berlin and all of East Germany.

• • •

TUESDAY, JANUARY 29, 1946

"And thus we vow to you, the German people, that our work and our knowledge shall only serve your welfare and that of mankind," the student representative solemnly vows.

Reopening of the University of Berlin. A ceremonial act at the Admiralspalast. Together with Frank I sit in the overcrowded parquet. The sweet and melodious sounds of the *Rigoletto* quartet fill the air. Furtively I glance at the faces of people around me. Ascetic heads, fine profiles. Never before have I seen so many intelligent faces in one place. Berlin's elite have gathered here. Legal and medical professionals, theologians and scientists, scholars and leading men of the city government. Oh century, oh sciences, what a pleasure to be alive, I think, and my heart is throbbing with joy. If we carry on from there to build new bridges . . .

". . . shall only serve your welfare and that of mankind . . ." This resolution and promise seems written all over everyone's face. Nothing is lost. Nothing can be lost if this promise comes true.

• • •

WEDNESDAY, FEBRUARY 6, 1946

Frank was offered a chair at the university. For the time being, however, his "service to the welfare of the people and of mankind" consists mainly of trying to get a new roof for his hospital, of clearing out rubble in the laboratories, of procuring beds for patients and the struggle to find glass for the windows. The hospital has been hit by shellfire seventy-five times. And before one may think about devoting one's life to research, at least one room must be established where dust, rain or snow no longer fall on every test tube. The Russian authorities help as much as they can. From sunrise to sunset, the site of the Charité Hospital is bustling with activity like an anthill. Construction workers, craftsmen, architects, trucks. Ardently trying for a new beginning of cultural life.

"Culture!" our victors from the East say. "We respect culture! Nothing is more important to us than to generously support it."

Two hundred meters farther down is the building that houses the GPU, where Makar Ivanov disappeared five months ago. Where they "broke their clubs over him," where they tormented and tortured him.

Where lies the truth? From which perspective can these opposites be united?

• • •

FRIDAY, FEBRUARY 22, 1946

There is a certain perspective. And when one finds it many contradictions may be understood.

"New fundamentals of Soviet population policy," the news reports. "Two billion rubles for Russian mothers. Sanctity of matrimony. Special taxes for single people. Drastic ways to make divorce more difficult to obtain. The law prohibiting abortion is in effect again."

We read and read and cannot believe it. "Women with ten children or more receive a medal and the title of 'Heroic Mother of the Soviet Union.' The medal 'Glory of Motherhood' will be bestowed on those who give birth to five or six children."

All that in a nation that introduced marriage before a civil magistrate, that supported free love and repealed the abortion law. Are the Russians changing their ideals like shirts to be laundered? No. It is only that every ideal, no matter what it is about, is subordinate to a main ideal. The ideal of ideals, so to speak, which says: Good is what serves the interests of the state. If today it serves its interests to keep the population figure low, the abortion law is repealed. If tomorrow it serves its interests to increase it, it goes into effect again tomorrow. It is almost as with Chinese pictures. It is not the viewer the perspective relates to but the principal point of the picture. The principal point of the Soviet picture is the state. All is viewed from its perspective. If only we knew how the question of unification will be dealt with from this perspective.

• • •

It looks bad, frighteningly bad, if one is to believe the rumors that circulate in Berlin. A united front, say the Communists. . . . Dictatorship all the way to the Elbe. If the Social Democrats do not unite voluntarily they will just be forced to do so.

"We shall see about that," the comrades say, outraged. "The times when we let ourselves be forced into decisions without any protest are past and gone."

Mr. Grotewohl, the chairman of the Social Democratic Party, seems to be of a different opinion than his party colleagues. Rumor has it that he has already agreed to the merger. On behalf of the executive committee of the Social Democratic Party of Berlin. Without asking anyone, without authorization, without any vote. The day after tomorrow, at nine in the morning, in a speech at the Admiralspalast he supposedly intends to inform his functionaries about it.

• • •

What is actually going on? Caught up in the whirlpool of events, it is difficult to see things in their context.

"Never again internecine strife," the Social Democrats proclaimed after the war and proposed to the Communists the formation of a common party. The Communists wavered and demanded that ideological differences should be clarified first. Did they fear their influence was not great enough? So instead of one party, two are formed, of which one, since the day it was founded, enjoys the special support of one of the occupying powers. It is not the most popular occupying power that favors it. We have not always fared well with their methods.

In December all of a sudden it is on their initiative that the unification of the left-wing parties in the Eastern-occupied zone is promulgated. One party, one will, one government authority. Now, to the Communists, who just a few months ago were so concerned about "ideological clarification," the unification cannot take place soon enough.

"Before we join forces, the partiality of the occupying power toward your party must end and both parties must have agreed to the unification by resolution at a national party conference," declares Otto Grotewohl, chairman of the Social Democratic Party in Berlin.

"That's not necessary," the Communists urge. "We can unify locally also, in districts, provinces or states."

"One can force it, perhaps. But we don't want to be forced into it," Grotewohl retorts. "We're not against collaboration, but we're against overly hasty and undemocratic methods of achieving it. How can there be a united German working class if this union is created separately in one zone?"

The headquarters of the Social Democratic Party is situated in the Russian sector. On December 21 its functionaries in Berlin gather to discuss the unification, to carefully consider all the reasons for and against it. They wait for Grotewohl. They wait for many hours. At last it turns out that he has been called to a meeting in Karlshorst. His meeting there lasts until the early morning hours. As Paul he went there, as Saul he returns. As a fanatic apostle of an immediate merger. The functionaries are stunned. Members of the party throw up their hands. The entire Social Democratic Party is like a nest of hornets. The way its chairman, Otto Grotewohl, has been talking, writing and acting since December 22 has nothing to do anymore with Social Democratic principles. Nor with justice or freedom.

"Should we for a second time subordinate to dictatorship just because we abhor strife among Socialist brothers?" the comrades ask themselves gloomily.

• • •

THURSDAY, FEBRUARY 28, 1946

"No matter how one looks at it, it remains a problem," says everyone with whom we discuss the matter. "If you say no, the Russians will turn against you. And it isn't good to have them as your enemies."

We know that. Ever since the collapse of the Nazis we have striven for communication. For a balance of interests between East and West. Can we afford to be at daggers drawn with one of the occupying powers? Aren't we rather compelled to strive for a peace that is agreeable to our neighbors? Those in the East as well as those in the West, the south and the north. To please them all becomes more and more difficult.

• • •

FRIDAY, MARCH 1, 1946

The party conference at the Admiralspalast begins at nine o'clock. Long before that time all seats are already taken. The auditorium is packed with people. With grim tension fifteen hundred functionaries wait for what their party chairman has to tell them.

On February 11, after meetings with party representatives of the Russian occupied zone. Mr. Grotewohl, while attending a conference of the Free Labor Union in the Soviet zone, endorsed, on behalf of the executive committee of the Social Democratic Party in Berlin, the unification of the workers' parties in the Russian-occupied zone. At the same conference their decision was announced.

"You didn't ask us," the Berlin functionaries protest. "You only asked those who aren't allowed to say no. Those who by order of their occupying power expel anyone from the party who doesn't agree. But we want to say no. We came here to defend this right for all of Germany."

The atmosphere in the auditorium is explosive. From minute to minute the general mood turns more and more irritated. Even before the principal speaker appears, dozens of topics are registered for discussion at the table of the executive committee. At last Otto Grotewohl takes the floor.

"Lackey!" the audience begins to jeer. "Go back to Karlshorst, Otto!"

Mr. Grotewohl stands firm. "Damaging separatism. . . . Reactionaries waiting to seize the moment. . . . Activity of the Vatican. . . . The return of Nazism is imminent." He invokes the consequences brought about by a refusal to unite.

"We don't want a forced unification," the audience retorts with hostility. Angry heckling and stamping of feet. "We won't let ourselves be raped!" The protests intensify. They turn more and more angry, more and more passionate. The speaker's words drown in them as if in a spring tide. "Traitor . . . fraud . . . resign . . . stop . . ." A few isolated voices of consent go unheard in the general uproar. "A strike vote! We demand a strike vote!" can be heard more and more distinctly above the tumult.

Hands are raised. By an overwhelming majority a resolution calling for a strike vote is accepted. Someone begins to sing: "Onward, brothers, to light and freedom . . ." His lips form the words automatically. And automatically the comrades join in. Everybody's face is glowing with pride and excitement. "This time we didn't eat crow. For the first time in thirteen years we have defended our freedom."

• • •

SUNDAY, MARCH 3, 1946

In *Das Volk*, the party newspaper of the Social Democrats, one searches in vain to find anything about this defense. Not a word mentions the resolution for a strike vote at the conference of the functionaries. The behavior of the executive committee of the party in the Russian sector seems increasingly odd. Instead Wilhelm Pieck, chairman of the Communist Party of Germany, has summoned a countermeeting and has told his audience that the unification would be ordered. By whom, if one may ask?

• • •

MONDAY, MARCH 4, 1946

The battle has begun. No one knows how it will end.

115

• • •

TUESDAY, MARCH 5, 1946

Frank was summoned by the administrative director of the hospital and sharply rebuked for having supposedly made anticommunist remarks. The hospital is located in the Russian sector. One almost feels tempted to join the fools who ask: "Is this what they mean by democracy?"

• • •

THURSDAY, MARCH 7, 1946

It is said that the occupying powers would not give their consent to a strike vote. In the city council, too, they are opposed to it. Mr. Pieck and Mr. Grotewohl pose together for a photograph.

• • •

SATURDAY, MARCH 9, 1946

"Help us," we implore our English and American friends. "Do all you can so we can vote."

They shrug their shoulders. "This is a German domestic matter," they say evasively. "Our Russian allies . . ."

• • •

MONDAY, MARCH 11, 1946

The *Tägliche Rundschau,* the mouthpiece of the Russian allies, seems less convinced that it is to be regarded strictly as a "German domestic matter." From day to day its tone against the "opponents of unity" becomes sharper.

Battleground Berlin

• • •

"Help us . . . help us," we beg our Western friends. Why don't you understand that this matter is your concern as much as it is ours? If the Social Democratic Party in Berlin is swallowed up by the Communist Party, it will be the end of democracy in Berlin, the end of democracy in Germany and—sooner or later—the end of democracy in Europe.

• • •

Our party chairman tries everything to render a strike vote unnecessary. He plans to meet with the merger's opponents individually in order to more effectively change their minds. At a hundred and seventy-five planned rallies, skilled speakers are supposed to refute any objections to the merger. A meeting of works council delegates is scheduled for tomorrow, in which a spontaneous call for the merger will be underscored by demonstrators entering the meeting room. Specially prepared identification cards are being sent only to those functionaries known to be reliable supporters of the merger.

The split between the rival factions becomes more and more passionate, and the rivalry more and more personal. People who just a year ago helped each other against the terror of the Gestapo and risked their lives for each other now vilify one another like mortal enemies. For or against the merger. Scoundrel or man of honor. Our old friend Dr. Flamm is of a different opinion too. He has become editor-in-chief at an Eastern newspaper. Yesterday's allies are turning into today's political adversaries.

117

• • •

MONDAY, MARCH 18, 1946

Mr. Grotewohl floods the city with propaganda material. Pamphlets, handbills, extra editions of newspapers and magazines. Indeed, he spares no expense. With our money, in our name and without any regard for our interests. Help us . . . help us, we implore all the Allied agencies to which we have access.

• • •

TUESDAY, MARCH 19, 1946

The city council threatens all opponents to the merger with loss of their jobs and worse. No doubt, those who support an independent Social Democratic Party will not fare well in the future, neither in the Eastern-occupied zone nor in a Communist-ruled Berlin.

"Should we once again form an opposition?" the workers ask themselves. "Once again risk our jobs, our freedom, perhaps even our lives for an unforeseeable length of time?"

It is a hard decision. Doubly hard for those who, for thirteen years in concentration camps or in hiding, had impatiently awaited the hour of liberation.

"Help us . . . help us," we beg our Western friends. "Don't let it happen that the best of us are destroyed by this conflict."

• • •

WEDNESDAY, MARCH 20, 1946

The district delegates meet. Unanimously they decide against the merger. All we need now is the Allies' permission to vote.

• • •

SATURDAY, MARCH 23, 1946

The district leader of Tempelhof, the district leader of Kreuzberg and the head of the youth organization in Charlottenburg have been expelled from the party by the executive committee. "For having acted detrimentally toward the party by forming factions and for handing out pamphlets aimed at destroying the party," the party headquarters at Behrensstrasse explains the decision. Members are attacked more and more fiercely. Five other district leaders are expecting their expulsion. Fifteen employees opposing the merger have been dismissed without notice.

• • •

SUNDAY, MARCH 24, 1946

The permission for a strike vote has not yet been granted. If the Allies refuse to grant it, it will be their own fault if Berlin cannot be held . . . In any case, the Social Democratic and the Communist Party leaders already have let it be known that they would not submit to a strike vote decision. In the Eastern sector they are already setting up offices for the Socialist Unity Party.

• • •

WEDNESDAY, MARCH 27, 1946

Yesterday, at a conference of the Berlin functionaries of the Communist Party and Social Democratic Party who are in favor of unity, it was decided to request the district leaders of both parties to immediately prepare all necessary measures for a merger. A strike vote was declared unnecessary.

Yesterday, at a conference of the district leaders of the Social Democratic Party in Berlin, it was definitely decided to proceed with the

119

strike vote on March 31, provided the permission of the Western Allies has been obtained. Because the party newspaper does not let opponents of the merger voice their opinion, the *Tagesspiegel* and the recently founded *Telegraph* offered their help.

• • •

SATURDAY, MARCH, 30, 1946

Tomorrow the strike vote will take place. Our party chairman blocks preparations wherever he can. Total confusion prevails in all districts of Berlin. One is missing its membership lists, another its ballot papers. Here, the list of candidates is missing and there, eligible voters have not been notified. We lack ballot boxes, posters and pamphlets. We lack voting booths, pencils and envelopes. Far into the night we fumble with building a ballot box, searching our meager supply of cloth for a voting booth curtain. The party newspaper did not deem it necessary to publish the addresses of the polling stations. Thousands of eligible voters still do not know where they are supposed to go to vote. If they do not come across one of the papers "hosting" the event, they will not get to vote.

The anti-unity comrades work like coolies. Writing out voting lists and notices, preparing announcements and designing pamphlets. They do it all of their own accord and with their own means. For the majority of them these means are quite meager. That they are being found and offered in such a matter-of-course way is truly admirable.

The Allies have promised their support for a properly conducted election. The Soviet authorities alone make their permission for a strike vote in their districts contingent upon the clarification of issues that are so complicated that no one will be able to answer them satisfactorily by tomorrow. Eight of the twenty districts in Berlin are under Soviet control. We worry about the voting results in these districts. If the Western Allies were as skilled and intelligent as we wish them to be, they would negotiate the same kind of control over voting procedures in their districts as the Soviets have in theirs. If they had the same experience of dictatorship as we, they would certainly do so. But unfortunately . . . It is bad enough that circumstances force us to consider their fortunate inexperience "unfortunate" . . .

Battleground Berlin

. . .

MONDAY, APRIL 1, 1946

The die is cast. With 82.5 percent the Social Democratic voters of Berlin decided against the merger. The Communists call the result of the strike vote "an overwhelming victory for the united front." What manner of mental gymnastics allowed them to reach that conclusion would remain puzzling even to a mathematical genius.

Our party chairman resisted to the last. But it was to no avail. Despite violence, threats and propaganda the will toward self-determination triumphed, even if only in twelve of the twenty districts. The permission to vote was not granted in the Russian sector. "Due to technical difficulties," they explained. To these same "technical difficulties" must be attributed the fact that at some of the polling stations in our occupied zone Russian sentries arrived in the early afternoon, that many stations were already closed at nine in the morning and the rest later in the morning, and that all voting materials were confiscated or destroyed.

Upon finding their polling station closed and guarded, 539 voters of the Prenzlauer Berg district decided to vote in another sector. They turned around, walked to Wedding and voted under French protection. There is great rejoicing among the comrades. Almost as great is the displeasure of their party chairman. Next Sunday the representatives of the twelve Western electoral districts will decide on a definite secession from him.

. . .

WEDNESDAY, APRIL 3, 1946

The day before yesterday, mail service to foreign countries was restored. We have little time for writing letters. We are very busy trying to keep our victory from turning into defeat. The entire left-wing press angrily condemns us. The majority of the city council angrily boycotts us. The party treasury is at headquarters in the Eastern sector. Propaganda costs money. How, with nothing but our bare hands, are we to

121

stop a wave of tanks, rolling from East to West, flattening everything in its way? What is the use of being reconnected to the world by mail if the world forsakes us? "Our allies . . . ," our English friends justify themselves. And for the first time a tone of resignation can be detected in their voices.

• • •

MONDAY, APRIL 8, 1946

A party conference of the Western city districts. Yesterday afternoon at the Zinnowald School in Zehlendorf, the Social Democratic Party was reconstituted, and disassociated itself from its former party chairman.

"The Zehlendorf secessionists," their adversaries jeer. They behave as if the election results had not been 82.5 percent.

"It will be to no avail," our Communist acquaintances say. "On the first of May unity will be established. Then an antifascist united front will swallow up the Christian Democrats. The few votes of the Liberal Democrats will be cast aside, and within six months we will call for a merger."

So that is what they are aiming at. For the first time they have let the cat out of the bag, and the features of that cat look alarmingly Soviet. Are we really fighting a losing battle?

• • •

SATURDAY, APRIL 20, 1946

For the time being it looks as if we have to help ourselves. Adam and Eve upon their expulsion from the Garden of Eden could not have been more naked than we. The entire inventory of the Social Democratic Party: cash, offices, stationery, papers, every chair, every table remained with its former executive committee. With a donated table, a borrowed typewriter and several dozen sheets of typing paper scrounged together, the "Zehlendorf secessionists" set out anew in their struggle for democracy. "It will be to no avail" rings in their ears.

Battleground Berlin

It is not easy to start a counterpropaganda campaign when the allotment of paper needed to print it on is dependent on the victors, when
the issuance of a licence for a party organ is subject to filling out
countless questionnaires, and when we are continually reminded that
we have not even yet been registered as a separate party. Should the
struggle for democracy fail due to the bureaucracy of the democrats?
The threat of "May First" hangs over us like the sword of Damocles.
Eight tons of paper for posters and flyers have been made available to
the unity committee by the Soviet occupation authorities. Eight tons
means three million flyers. Three million flyers versus a handful of
have-nots who have to beg for every scrap of paper. The bourgeois
parties watch us without lifting a finger.

"It doesn't concern us," the Christian Democrats say. Only the
Liberal Democrats come to our aid with a flyer. "Never again dictatorship! Democrats, there is still time to act!" say their posters
on the street corners, and thus they at least help us to call a spade a
spade.

• • •

WEDNESDAY, MAY 1, 1946

It is an unequal battle! Nevertheless the battle goes on, and will be
won. The May Day celebration of the Socialist Unity Party that was
founded in the Russian sector of the city and the Russian-occupied
zone occurred on Easter Sunday. A big parade. The Social Democrats
do not take part.

There is no "swallowing up" of the Christian Democrats, no "casting aside" of the Liberal Democrats, no call for union with the East.
It was a triumph of spirit over power. The Social Democratic Party
remains a party in Berlin. Whether it will be allowed to do so in the
Eastern sector and the Eastern zone too, remains to be seen.

So far, the Soviet occupation authorities do not appear to be accom-
modating. Neither toward the "secessionists" nor toward the people of
Berlin. For the past few days the city's railways have been in a chaotic
state. The miserably shrunken postwar fleet of railway cars has been
further reduced by thirty trains, as part of reparation payments to

Russia. If one thinks justly, one can't really blame the Soviets for taking back what we took away from them. Except that they couldn't have chosen a worse moment to do so. The endless-seeming span of time between trains, the overcrowded platforms and the miserable sight of the battered replacement cars lacking windows and seats make the loss so noticeable. "They make us ride like cattle, they pack us like freight," people in Berlin complain and show no disposition to the idea of unity.

• • •

TUESDAY, MAY 14, 1946

Dagmar has lost all desire to live in Berlin. She is not the first to set out on foot toward the West. Wearing a beret, ski boots and a track suit, she stands before me to say goodbye. "Here I'll never get anywhere," she says and resignedly lifts up her sixty-pound knapsack.

Dagmar Meyerowitz. Only now do I become aware of how we've almost totally forgotten about her during the past months. Little Dagmar, I think, feeling ashamed, and suddenly I want to make up for it all. For the forgetting and the leaving, the lack of friendship and her disappointment with Berlin. But I cannot make up for it. The more I try, the more I become aware that a change has taken place not only in our relationship, but in others as well. Did we ever really mean it? Or wasn't it rather about our shared hatred of the Nazis, the exchange of news broadcasts by the English station, our fear of bombs and the daily if not hourly danger of losing our lives. Friendships that serve a certain purpose can be good friendships too. Except that once the purpose is achieved they do not necessarily last for the rest of one's life. The magnet that kept anti-Nazis together has lost its force. Forgive me, Dagmar, I think, but I do not say it. It makes no sense to voice such sentiments now. "Farewell," I say instead. "Write us if you ever need anything."

She nods. "You too." And then suddenly, as if overcome by memory, we embrace and kiss each other's cheeks three times. The way Andrik used to do it. "Don't get lost," we whisper, our old farewell from Nazi times.

• • •

SATURDAY, MAY 25, 1946

Fabian does not roll his cigarettes at our place anymore either. He writes books and plays, and one day he swears by the West and the next day he toasts the East. He always was a nomad. It was only the "anti-Nazi magnet" that temporarily forced him to settle in one place. Occasionally we run into each other, and then we smile at each other and ask, "Do you remember?" or, "Do you still think about it?"

We often think about it. The white ox, the times spent in the cellar, and the raspberry jelly at the cemetery. It seems like a fairy tale. It all seems so long ago, so unimaginably long ago.

• • •

WEDNESDAY, MAY 29, 1946

We have succeeded. In yesterday's session the Allied Control Council recognized the Social Democratic Party and the Socialist Unity Party as independent parties in all four sectors. So our struggle has not been in vain. In fact, it is gaining more and more support from the Western victors. Not officially, but certainly noticeably. As if, after all, they have come to appreciate the fact that there are people among us who do not unconditionally say yes to any given situation. Even if the "Yes" were to comply with the wishes of one of the Allies.

The Socialist Unity Party announces its platform with triumphant proclamations. "Our slogan is: Not a one-party system, but the consolidation of a united antifascist democratic front. The future belongs to the Socialist Unity Party. Next to this party, which represents millions, there will be, in the long run, no room for any splinter groups," the official paper of the Socialist Unity Party, *Das Neue Deutschland*, writes. How is this to be understood? "Not a one-party system," but on the other hand, no room for any other parties. Isn't that a contradiction?

Nevertheless, we did achieve our goal, and what we have to do now is discontinue the fraternal strife and show our willingness to cooperate as brothers. With all parties, including the Socialist Unity Party.

• • •

THURSDAY, JUNE 13, 1946

Trouble is brewing. The willingness to cooperate as brothers leaves much to be desired. Not least, among our occupying powers. The tone of communications among the members of the Control Council has become alarmingly irritable during the past weeks. And this irritability is echoed among the people. We do not know what they have in mind in Moscow, London and Washington. And the less we know about it, the more prolific become the rumors, and the more one feels inclined to reduce them to a common denominator.

The Russians did not recognize the Social Democratic Party in their sector. They do not want it is their sector. What if things continue to develop in this direction . . . "Surrender of Berlin . . . separation of the Eastern zone . . . a third world war." Our imagination escalates the terrible possibilities.

• • •

MONDAY, JUNE 17, 1946

"Do you believe there will be war? Do you believe the zones will be separated?" I ask Andrik's English friend as I sit with him, drinking cocktails on the terrace of the villa that serves as his official residence.

He smiles. "I believe none of it. What makes you think that way?"

"Because everybody thinks that way."

"Everybody?" he asks doubtingly.

"Almost everybody," I correct myself.

He looks at me pensively. "Not now. Maybe in ten years. But whether it will come to war or not ten years from now, we will know in two."

To then anticipate the catastrophe for eight years. What a terrible prospect. "But can't we do something about it," I implore him.

"We can stop talking about it and other than that . . . light candles. Each little light will help to make the world brighter."

"That's all?"

"That's all," he nods. "Except that most of us haven't done it yet."

Light candles, I think on my way home. Perhaps that also means holding out in Berlin, fighting against despotism and renewing the toilsome struggle against terror and collectivism. If one looks at it that way . . . My heart beats faster. I resolve that we must ask everybody to stay here, whatever the price. Never before in Berlin has the attitude of each individual mattered as much as it does now. Never before has each individual had to mediate as much, and prove as much, and assume so enormous a responsibility.

• • •

SATURDAY, JUNE 29, 1946

"If you feel like it," says Frank, "we could take a trip to Werder tomorrow. The train leaves at ten to seven."

"The train?" I totally forgot there were trains in Germany too. "All right," I say. "But how does one get tickets?"

Frank fumbles for something in his pockets. "By waiting in line, the way you do for everything else. Luckily it didn't take longer than the trip will take." He pulls out two third-class tickets. "Why they still issue third-class tickets when there is neither a second nor a first class is beyond me," he says, handing me the tickets.

I look at them as if they were a miracle. Real tickets. Exactly the way they used to be. I can hardly believe that there still are things that are exactly the way they used to be.

• • •

SUNDAY, JUNE 30, 1946

The sky is as blue as one could wish it. Equipped with provisions we set out around five o'clock in the morning. Beyond a drink of water, we cannot expect to be offered anything. The streetcars are not running yet. So we have to walk from Steglitz to the Anhalter Station.

127

We feel as if we were about to travel around the world. The place that was once a popular spot for Berliners taking Sunday excursions seems so far away to us, at such an adventurous distance.

The area in front of the station is crowded with people. Clusters of travelers hang on to the waiting train. Using the straps of his knapsack, Frank ties me to the train with my feet resting on two buffers.

"Are you standing comfortably?" he worries as he himself climbs on top of the caboose.

"It's all right," I tell him. I never have been a great climber.

The train leaves twenty minutes late. We arrive in Werder one and a half hours late. All along the way rusty railroad tracks are piled up next to the embankment. Why have they dismantled them, I wonder. And if they had to do it, what is the purpose of leaving them there? *Nietchevo*, I give myself the answer.

On arrival in Werder, I climb off my buffers, stiff as a stork. "Bicycling is easier," I say to Frank and, seeing his face smeared with soot, I add, "and obviously cleaner too."

He laughs. "In return for it you're now in a foreign country."

I look around. Indeed. The signs that catch my eye might as well be standing in Russia. Cyrillic letters, Russian roadblocks, Soviet uniforms and a foreign atmosphere that bespeaks another world. Berlin's cherry tree paradise seems like a provincial town in the Ukraine.

We shoulder our knapsacks and start walking. The flat open country is shimmering in the splendor of the summer day. Fields and meadows are in full bloom. Did the dog roses ever smell as sweet as this year? Has this normally rather barren countryside ever had so many cornflowers, such blazing red poppies, and displayed such an exuberant will to live? Nature appears to have tried its best to make up for what man has destroyed. Flaming yellow mulleins adorn the roadside. The cherry trees bend under the weight of their fruit. Frank squeezes my arm. We are alive and can feel it with each step. And all around us, below us and above us everything is vibrantly alive. We enter a small wooded area. Just a few pine trees. But to our eyes even those pine trees are remarkable. Their branches seem like delicate feathers. We keep walking as if intoxicated.

"Do you hear that?" Frank asks, listening attentively. From the

128

opposite banks of the Havel, the wind is carrying sounds in our direction. "Volga, Volga . . . ," sounds from a loudspeaker. "Volga, Volga . . . ," the waves of the Havel seem to murmur.

A Russian soldier passes us on his bicycle. His round face looks shiny in the heat as if covered with oil. *"Otchen sharko . . . very hot,"* he calls out to us with a friendly smile. A few meters down the road he gets off his bike, takes off his shirt, pants and shoes, and jumps headfirst into the water. *"Otchen sharko"*—this image too is part of the scenery.

A Soviet cemetery stretches along the roadside. Red is the fence that surrounds it. Red shimmer the five-pointed stars on the wooden pyramids marking the graves.

"Volga, Volga . . . ," I keep humming. The sun is in the west now. Slowly we are approaching the place from which we will return home. It is as like the one from which we started out as two peas in a pod. Banners with Russian inscriptions. Red barricades. Red posters that, in large letters, clearly visible even from a distance, inform people that racism is unknown in the Soviet Union. Larger than life-size portraits of meritorious Soviet heroes are displayed in a semicircle on the market square. Frank takes a closer look at one of them. "The artist seems fond of bright colors," he remarks. "But unfortunately he wasn't as fond of perspective."

Beneath General Zhukov's medal-adorned portrait, three children are playing marbles. "Volga, Volga . . . ," comes to my mind again. How different from last year everything here seems. In the wake of conquest came possession. In the wake of rape came—fusion. I glance at a freshly painted sign above the entrance to a building. "Local branch of the Socialist Unity Party," I read.

After waiting for two hours at the crowded station, we once again climb onto the slow train that runs between Werder and Berlin. This time we travel standing on the outside steps. At a snail's pace the train jogs across the countryside. Starts with a jerk, stops, starts again, to slowly puff along for a short stretch. By the time we reach Anhalter Station, the last subway has long since left. A delay of three and a half hours. Three times longer than scheduled. "Volga, Volga . . . ," we sigh while walking home on tired feet. Not always do Russian standards adjust to German conditions.

Ruth Andreas-Friedrich

• • •

TUESDAY, JULY 16, 1946

Still that irritable tone at the Control Council. Still the Socialists make life a perfect hell for one another. Following the motto "First you stop your aggressiveness, then I will stop mine," everyone ends up being aggressive with everyone else. People wonder warily where all this will lead.

Friends have brought us the first news of Kurt Eckhardt, the Putschist and Nazi-saboteur. He too survived and now is supposed to be working in the West. Strange how our clique is going such separate ways.

• • •

SATURDAY, AUGUST 3, 1946

"In case Berlin is surrendered . . . in case the Eastern zone is separated . . . in case of a third world war." We are fed up with being continually in the opposition. We would like to be a "bridge," but everything seems to indicate that fate intends us as a bridgehead.

In two months there will be elections in Berlin. In six weeks there will be elections in the occupied zones. Every vote counts. Every word weighs double when uttered, here or there, in favor of understanding. Behind the Socialist Unity Party stands its big and powerful patron from the East. Who is behind the Social Democratic Party? . . . "Help us," we continue begging with increasing urgency.

• • •

THURSDAY, AUGUST 29, 1946

Sometimes we feel like children trying to prevent their sand castle from being swept away by the waves. Who are we to stand up against the pressure of a world power? In the Eastern zone the merging process advances with steadfast relentlessness. It encloses Berlin on all sides. Only a narrow corridor, a single-track railway line, connects it with the West. Our vegetables, our fruit, our potatoes—nearly all our food is obtained from the neighboring provinces. In a twinkling the occupying power there could sever our lifeline. All they need do is prevent a few trains from passing through—block a bridge, or let the single-track railway line deteriorate . . . The possibilities are numerous. Especially for an occupying power that dislikes saying yes. If necessary, will the Western Allies supply three million Berliners with potatoes? With fruit, vegetables, coal and electricity? Or will they tell us that this problem, too, is a "German domestic matter"? "Help us!" We keep repeating the refrain—like Cato, always the same.

• • •

FRIDAY, SEPTEMBER 6, 1946

"Did you hear Byrnes speak? . . . The American secretary of state delivered a speech in Stuttgart. They want to return the East to us . . . There won't be a war . . . There won't be a separation of the zones . . ." With lightning speed the news spreads across Berlin. "The Eastern provinces will be returned to us."

Ten million refugees cherish new hopes. Of all that has been said in Stuttgart they've heard and remembered only one thing: The Oder-Neisse line is not definite. The Eastern provinces will be returned to us. "Home," they rejoice. "A day will come when we will be permitted to return home."

Rarely has a foreign minister's speech raised so many hopes as has Byrnes's speech before the ministers of the Western zones.

I wonder whether they understood it correctly. Already, wishful thinking on the part of the refugees has turned this promise into a fait accompli.

"The Oder-Neisse line," a spokesman for the Russian occupying power smiles obligingly, "is a fait accompli. Surely! What do you want from us? Germany took the Eastern provinces by conquest. Burgundy once was German too. Is Burgundy worse than Silesia? We moved our border three hundred kilometers to the west. Why don't you do that as well? We'll help you. It's very simple."

Luckily this conversation didn't spread with lightning speed among the general public the way Byrnes's speech did. The public is cheerful and optimistic. "Finally," people say, "the Western powers are showing some understanding. At last they begin to treat us Germans as human beings too."

• • •

WEDNESDAY, SEPTEMBER 11, 1946

It is difficult to claim humane treatment when misery, greed and chaos have dispensed with all scruple. Nearly all of us do things we would not have imagined a few years ago. Unimaginable back then to be chewing on a crust of bread in the lobby of a theater. Unimaginable to scrounge for other people's cigarette butts, to greedily snatch them away from one another, to pick them barehanded out of the ashtrays in buses and trains. Unimaginable to rummage through trash cans in search of calories, or to search the garbage from Allied kitchens for something to eat.

Unimaginable? When one suffers from gnawing hunger nothing is unimaginable anymore. When a smoker has nothing to smoke, his dignity falters. "Catch," an American soldier says, tossing his half-finished cigarette at a German. Like a chicken, he rushes for the butt, bends down and picks it up. The soldier laughs. If he would think about it, it would make him cry instead of laugh.

The areas around the Allied officers' mess halls abound with trophy hunters. Catch, they think, and take home the cans that have been thrown away, to scrape them out, lick them clean or wash the remains with water into their soup. Catch! If you are hungry enough it doesn't disgust you. In the years since the war, thousands who "once knew better days" have ceased feeling disgusted.

• • •

TUESDAY, SEPTEMBER 17, 1946

On Sunday the first local elections were held in Brandenburg, Mecklenburg and the Western zones. In the Eastern zone an absolute majority for the Socialist Unity Party. The remaining third of the vote went to the Christian Democratic Party and the Liberal Democratic Party. The Social Democratic Party does not exist in the Russian-occupied zone. One cannot vote for something that does not exist. Not all Christian Democratic and Liberal Democratic voters in Pomerania, Mecklenburg and Brandenburg supported the platform of the party they voted for. And certainly no one had imagined this first democratic expression of their will since the collapse of the Nazis as an act of compensation.

The results in the French and British zones are different. The methods of the Socialist Unity Party in the Eastern zone are ill-becoming to the Communists in the West. Among the four largest parties they rank last nearly everywhere. Let's wait and see what comes next. On October 20 elections will be held in Berlin.

· · ·

SUNDAY, SEPTEMBER 29, 1946

A verdict on the Nazi big shots is supposed to be reached within a few days. For nearly a year the foreign press was full of articles on the Nuremberg trial. "It's typical of the Germans that they, of all people, show the least interest in the fate of their war criminals," the Allies still scold, forgetting to allow for the fact that the rest of the world is certain to be much more interested in the Nuremberg trial than the Germans.

"Why did we enter the war? For what was my son, brother or father shot and crippled in a foreign country?" an American citizen, a Canadian or Australian farmer must be asking.

"To send these criminals to the gallows," answers the Allied press with daily reports from the courtroom in Nuremberg, with spotlights and impressionistic descriptions, with documentation material and detailed descriptions of the procedures. The Nuremberg courtroom reports have to justify the deaths of millions of people. That's why they are good, and that's why they are necessary. Not so much for us but for the farmer in Oklahoma who has to make some sense out of the fact that his son has lost a leg.

Ruth Andreas-Friedrich

• • •

TUESDAY, OCTOBER 1, 1946

They have been sentenced. Twelve of the twenty accused condemned to death by hanging. Three were sentenced to life imprisonment. Four received prison sentences of between ten and twenty years. Schacht, Papen and Fritsche were acquitted. Radio broadcasts, telephone and telegraph cables transmit the news all over the world. Special editions, announcements, photographic coverage. Flash pictures of the judges passing judgment. Flash pictures of the defendants receiving their sentences. An interview with Fritsche. An interview with Papen. The defendants in their prison cells. Petitions for pardons. The date of execution. Encoded texts whiz through the ether. Even the world's most remote villages are interested in the fate of the German war criminals.

"Not speaking of them is the best form of execution," says Frank and turns off the radio, which has, for the seventh time, just informed us of every detail of each defendant's emotional reaction to his sentence. They never fussed as much over Witzleben's feelings. And I wonder if it's such a good idea to depict all these details to the farmer in Oklahoma, or whether it's advisable to let the Germans know about them?

• • •

SUNDAY, OCTOBER 6, 1946

More and more details are being described. How they sigh, what they say, how they pray, how they are turning desperate. The sentimentality of the "last hour" is a smokescreen to the minds of many. This cannot be the way to learn about democracy. Perhaps a way of practicing it in countries which no longer need to learn it. We find it hard to react to this sensation mongering, whether it be in malicious redress or unembarrassed thrill seeking. Not speaking of them is the best execution. And isn't it maybe also the most dignified?

134

Battleground Berlin

In Berlin, seventy-five thousand workers go on a brief strike to protest the acquittal of Papen, Schacht and Fritsche. What do the former Nazi Party members have to say to that? Millions of them still sit and wait for their denazification. They fill out questionnaires, procure certificates of good character, write autobiographical statements, explanations and justifications. They starve on grade five ration cards, break rocks, clear rubble, run errands, and once they have been finally denazified, they have to wait months for official approval of their denazification by the Control Council. Until then no employment contract. Until then no employment in any higher positions. "What did we do that Papen didn't?" they ask, embittered. "Did we interpret Goebbel's speeches on the radio, or did Mr. Fritsche? Mr. Fritsche has been acquitted. Mrs. Goering lives in her country house in Bavaria and every day poses for a photograph with yet another Ally while we're breaking rocks. What kind of justice is it that forces us to break rocks while Mr. Papen goes for walks?"

• • •

WEDNESDAY, OCTOBER 16, 1946

Goering too escaped punishment. Three hours before he was supposed to be hanged, he committed suicide in his cell. Hitler, Himmler, Goebbels, Goering. None of them suffered the kind of death he made millions of people suffer. None of them would—if things had gone differently—have let his adversary escape. Why do democracies allow their adversaries to slip away? The public is not impressed by the executioner waiting in vain at the gallows, but rather by the criminal who has given him the slip. So many mistakes might be avoided if the Allies allowed us to advise them once in a while. Do not arouse German sentimentality, we would advise them now. Most definitely do not arouse it in connection with the Nazis. The will to assume responsibility is more important than sensationalism. Once the evil spirits have been conjured up it will be hard to get rid of them.

• • •

THURSDAY, OCTOBER 17, 1946

Hermann Goering is dead. Ribbentrop, Keitel, Rosenberg, Frank and Frick are dead. So are Julius Streicher, Kaltenbrunner, Sauckel, Jodl and Seyss-Inquart.

"Ribbentrop was prounounced dead after fourteen minutes and forty-five seconds. Jodl's death took a little longer," writes the Berlin paper *Der Abend*. Dangerous how the last words of the condemned build themselves a nest in the hearts of the susceptible. Don't play with fire, we feel like imploring the Nuremberg reporters. To no avail. They don't spare us any sentimentality, no matter how poor in taste.

• • •

SATURDAY, OCTOBER 19, 1946

All night long Heike, Frank and I put up posters. As soon as we finished our route, our adversaries showed up and pasted their posters on top of ours. Vote for the Social Democratic Party—vote for the Socialist Unity Party. In the course of this one night the political posters on Berlin's southern artery changed at least three times. "Let's not get too upset about it," says Heike, looking at the demoralizing result of her last hour's work. The posters of the Christian Democratic Party have disappeared too. "Nothing beats a proper supply of paper."

• • •

SUNDAY, OCTOBER 20, 1946

Election fever, election heat, election frenzy. Nearly ninety percent of the eligible voters in Berlin voted. Eight hundred and fifty-one thousand men, one and a half million women.

"The women of Berlin have decided against the Russian lovers," a Socialist Unity Party member says sarcastically as the election results

136

become known in the late evening: 48.9 percent for the Social Democratic Party, 21.5 percent for the Christian Democratic Party, 20.4 percent for the Socialist Unity Party. Our "sand castle" held up. Those prepared to do likewise, under the same circumstances, may cast the first stone at postwar Berlin.

• • •

TUESDAY, OCTOBER 22, 1946

The Social Democrats had not imagined such a triumpant electoral victory. Probably, here as well, a majority were voting for a front against the East rather than for the party's platform.

"Now we must avoid two pitfalls," say the more insightful ones among the Social Democrats. "We must stop the fraternal strife, and we must stop antagonizing the Russians."

• • •

WEDNESDAY, OCTOBER 23, 1946

We have already managed to antagonize them. We have done exactly what should have been avoided "for the sake of the bridge."

As their first official act, after their election victory, the Social Democrats call a conference of functionaries at the *Neue Welt.* Franz Neumann and Schumacher speak. The situation is not very encouraging. Deportation of German workers to the Soviet Union. It began during the night of the twenty-first and has not stopped since. In the Soviet zone and the Russian sector of Berlin, skilled workers, scientists and specialists in various key industries are being taken away unexpectedly and deported to an unknown destination in the East. Democrats call this murder. Dictators call it "fulfillment of previous obligations." Who is obliged to whom in this case cannot be made out from the commentaries. Panic prevails in the families of the deported. Franz Neumann, the chairman of the Social Democratic Party, protests. He shakes his fist against the Socialist Unity Party and fervently appeals to the conscience of the responsible occupying power. No one is more

137

courageous than he. But, considering the fact that the Social Democrats came into power with a minimum of support, so much courage can make one feel uneasy.

. . .

WEDNESDAY, OCTOBER 30, 1946

The deportation of the workers is discussed in the Control Council. "We'll investigate the matter," declares the Soviet representative. "We'll set everything in motion . . ."

Merciful heavens! It is already set in motion. The trains carrying the specialists are already rolling eastward.

"Why are these crooks at the *Telegraph* and their comrades so excited?" wonders the *Tägliche Rundschau.* "It's common knowledge that, based on agreements, German specialists have previously traveled to the Soviet Union in order to work there." Certainly. But it does seem strange that their departure takes place under cover of darkness, after entire residential areas have been cordoned off. The trains are rolling. And no questions in the Control Council can stop them.

. . .

SATURDAY, NOVEMBER 2, 1946

Power outages . . . power outages. The Social Democrats take over while beset with tremendous difficulties. They already have more than enough problems finding suitable persons for all the positions unexpectedly accruing from their electoral victory. As strange as it may sound, neither the Social Democrats nor the Christian Democrats have as many prominent personalities available as their new city council contingent requires. The functionaries are debating makeshift solutions. Did they say no on March 21 in order to be completely at a loss on November 1 as to how to put that "No" into action?

Councilmen needed, administration officials needed, mayor, departmental heads and district leaders needed. Members of the Socialist Unity Party smile ironically. We had claimed to know what to do. We should not need to rack our brains about finding the right appointees. Nor about the occupying power's approval of these appointees, think the Social Democrats, who are waiting with increasing urgency for their coming to power to be recognized in the Russian-occupied city districts, too.

• • •

WEDNESDAY, NOVEMBER 20, 1946

People in Berlin pull up their collars against the cold, blow into their hands and put their last piece of wood into their stoves.

In Berlin's Western press, they are arguing about whether or not there was a resistance movement in Germany. Gabriele Strecker, who was the first German woman to travel to America in October, denied it there. The *Tagesspiegel*, too, says no. And the world draws the corresponding conclusion from this "No."

In Germany the fighters against Nazism still have not organized themselves as have members of the resistance in Poland, France, Holland, Belgium and Norway. All that has so far been realized here is a union of the victims of Fascism. A union of those who suffered, an association of sacrificial lambs. It is right to commemorate those who suffered. And only fair to compensate those who were abused. But why limit it to the passive ones?

• • •

FRIDAY, DECEMBER 6, 1946

Along with the drop in temperature, the quicksilver prop to our optimism has dropped as well. Will we survive this winter? "Those still alive today have only themselves to blame. Enough bombs have already fallen," say melancholy Berliners, shivering with cold, as they retire into their snailshells.

Ruth Andreas-Friedrich

• • •

MONDAY, DECEMBER 16, 1946

Last night it was twenty degrees Centigrade below zero. In the morning the water was off in our district. We haul our buckets, and are sadly reminded of the days following the conquest.

• • •

SATURDAY, DECEMBER 21, 1946

"Would you like a Christmas tree?" Frank asks me this morning.

"Very much," I say, "except that there aren't any. Unless you're registered as having many children or as a victim of Fascism."

Frank laughs. "Or if you own a saw," he adds slyly.

We are sitting around the breakfast table. Bread, margarine and lukewarm coffee. The clock has just struck six-thirty. At six o'clock the power was cut off. Twenty minutes after the alarm clock rang, and ten minutes after we knocked the ice out of the water bucket and put it in the coffeepot to boil it. Once more we feel defeated by the power company. How annoying! We are cold enough already. It's twenty degrees below zero outside, one degree below zero in the kitchen and four degrees below zero in the bathroom. Twice it has happened that during the night the water in Heike's hot-water bottle froze in her bed. The water supply in our housing complex has been shut off since last Monday. More than seventy pipes have burst, claims the superintendent. And no solder available. It would be at least three months before they could be repaired. Fine prospects, indeed! One feels like cursing. In the cellar there are twenty-two briquettes remaining, power outages of eight to ten hours daily—in the British sector these days the lights are on only for twenty minutes a day—no water, no way to cook, and no possibility to use the bathroom or take a bath. In little packages people in Berlin carry their bodily waste out of the house and discreetly bury it in the nearest pile of rubble. A degrading state of affairs.

Frank puts his nose against the top of the kerosene lamp—bought

140

on the black market and made out of a gas mask. "Are you as cold as I am?"

Instead of an answer my teeth are chattering with cold. "If one could at least obtain kerosene or a good candle."

"Six marks a piece," says Frank. "As many as you like, under the table." He pulls up the collar of his coat and wraps several woolen scarves around his neck. "So, what about the Christmas tree?" I nod. "At three o'clock if you can. It's dark by six."

After he has left I crawl back into my bed. What else can one do when the average temperature inside the apartment is one degree below zero, when one's feet are numb and one's hands blue with cold? The brain, too, begins to give up, when stuck into the refrigerator.

At ten o'clock Heike arrives. Red-nosed, wearing a fur coat and galoshes. "If I don't drink a brandy right away I'll never thaw out!" she says miserably.

I pour the last drops from the cognac bottle. "Take it with due respect, my dear," I tell her. "You're drinking pure gold." Seven hundred marks a bottle is no chickenfeed.

Together we light a fire in our newly acquired iron stove. It smokes as it does nearly every morning, and the little heat it provides gets lost as we, coughing, open the windows. Carrying water, splitting wood, waiting for the electricity to be turned on, dragging waste water into the ruins. Until three o'clock, time passes in drudgery. Then Frank, hiding a saw under his coat, and I set out on the Christmas tree mission we had agreed on.

The snow along the banks of the Teltow Canal is up to our ankles. The canal's icy surface sparkles in the sun. "Strange," I say, "that one feels colder inside one's rooms than outside."

Frank laughs. "You're free to set up your bed in the Grunewald."

After an hour we meet up with scarcely anyone. Like cotton wool the snow covers the deserted gardens. The ruins seem as if wrapped in cotton wool, as do the burst iron girders of the blown-up bridges across the canal. Shaking his head Frank looks at the silent country-side. "And that calls itself a city!"

"Not anymore," I correct him, "five minutes ago you entered the Russian sector."

For many Berliners the world ends at the sector boundaries. What lies beyond seems desert and wilderness to them. Many people from the Western sectors haven't set foot in the Russian sector, let alone the Russian zone, since May 1945.

In the distance the Teltow lock looms up. A Russian checkpoint. Checking identification papers. "For heaven's sake, I've forgotten my papers." Paralyzed with fear I go through all my pockets.

"Oh my!" Frank says, aghast. Quickly he pulls me behind the picket fence of the inn near the lock. Murmuring excuses, we work our way through kitchen and back rooms to the restaurant. Its exit is about three yards beyond the checkpoint.

Standing at the bar we try to appear as innocent and carefree as possible. One is liable to prosecution if caught on the street without papers. Liable to be arrested. By the Russians? Unpleasant, most unpleasant! A good many people thus arrested have not returned for several weeks, if at all.

Sipping a rye whiskey, we discuss our predicament. The rye costs five marks fifty pfennigs. But at least it is available. That is the advantage of the Russian zone. "A fine advantage, indeed!" complain those living there. "It uses up half of our potato harvest."

That, however, is not our problem right now. Frank suggests he go and get the lay of the land. Five minutes later he returns. "In fifteen minutes the bus to Stahnsdorf will arrive. As soon as the sentries are busy inspecting it, we take off around the nearest corner."

Everything happens just as he predicted. Our luck holds. Unsuspecting, the sentries at the checkpoint turn their backs on us and we run across the road in suspect haste.

Behind the Teltow lock, the forest begins. We look around in all directions. There are not many spruces around Berlin. "A pine tree will do just as well," Frank decides after we have struggled through knee-deep snow for twenty minutes without seeing a single specimen of the type of tree we are looking for. Quickly he gets out the saw. Forest theft—the thought pricks my conscience. Nonsense, I assure myself, the forests of Brandenburg will not begrudge us a little tree. A quick glance to the right and to the left—Andrik used to call it the illegal glance—and a beautiful pine tree, neatly sawed off, lies next to us in the snow. Satisfied, we pack up our tools.

At the Dreilinden Station we head for the compartment reserved for travelers with oversize luggage and inside the dark compartment we discover an entire collection of Christmas pines. Abashed, their illegal owners stand next to them. So we aren't the only ones out this afternoon equipped with a saw. Rarely has a Christmas tree seemed so precious to us.

. . .

SUNDAY, DECEMBER 22, 1946

"If we only knew what to put on it," Heike muses, looking at our trophy of yesterday. What to put on it and what to put under it. A difficult problem. Of course, there are stores. Except, one does not feel like buying what they sell. And what one feels like buying cannot be bought in them. After all, we cannot present each other with an ugly decorated tile on every occasion, or a new ashtray, a boutonniere or some other useless handicraft. The need for pokers, potato mashers, ladles and skimmers is limited too, even when made of precious high-grade steel.

In their longing for construction and production, eager entrepreneurs produced millions of pokers and ashtrays during the first year of peace. Partly out of the army's supplies of high-grade steel. But why pokers? Why ashtrays, of all things, when one gets only six cigarettes a month? They say the machines needed for more complicated products are not available. That they have been dismantled or destroyed by bombs. Ten pokers for every Berliner, a statistician calculated. What can one person do with ten pokers? How many pokers then go to a family of five? It's inconceivable!

On the other hand, the rationing office allots a pot, pan or coffeepot only to households having at least three members. Are smaller households supposed to make their coffee in ashtrays or to steam their vegetables on pokers?

In the meantime a greater variety of products is being offered. Nothing useful, however. What is displayed in the shop window is either luxury articles or junk. The things one really needs lie under the counter, are bartered on the black market or, at best, may be obtained by bringing in the trimmings oneself. Dolls are made upon delivery of sixty-five centimeters of material and fifty meters of thread. A new gramophone record upon delivery of an old one. New gloves upon delivery of . . . new slippers upon delivery of . . . blouses, hats, ties, sweaters. Goods, made to measure or not, from your own stock, out of existing materials, hold complete sway over commercial activity. Sometimes you even have to supply a few briquettes and some wood to help with heating the store.

On the black market, it's only racketeers who have adequate purchasing power. A bar of soap—40 marks. A Christmas goose—1,400 marks. A pair of shoes—1,000 marks. A pound of chocolate—500 marks. Fabric for a suit—3,000 marks. Nobody can legally earn as much as he needs to pay for the bare essentials. Due to the high black market prices on the one hand, and the tax laws on the other. Because no matter how hard you try, it is impossible to earn more than a thousand marks a month. Whatever you earn above that, no matter how much it is, is devoured by taxes. Why should I work so hard, the citizen asks himself. For the revenue office? For the public purse? So he adapts to the circumstances. He slows down and works for only so much as he can earn without paying taxes.

Beyond that he lives on bartering. A different kind of bartering, however, than in May 1945. Tax-evading black marketeering versus black marketeering. Silverware from one's dowry for cigarettes, coffee, a winter coat or suiting. Great-grandma's Dresden china for ten pounds of sugar, five bottles of schnapps, three packs of tobacco, twelve hundred pounds of coal and a pair of galoshes. The price depends on the demand. Among the victors, there is great demand for valuables and art objects. And great—almost shamefully great—is our eagerness to part with them. Eighty-five percent of all Berliners live on additional products beyond their ration card allotments, a recent American opinion poll revealed. That means more than three quarters of the population is now involved in the black market. What does that say about moral recovery?

"So what shall we put on the tree, and what shall we put under it?" Heike interrupts my thoughts on the economic situation.

After discussing this for an hour and counting up our cash, we agree on a dozen candles for seventy-two marks, two packs of tinsel at eight and a half marks each, a dozen candle holders which, because they are legally obtainable, cost twenty pfennigs apiece, and the necessary ingredients to bake four platefuls of Christmas cookies. The rest will have to be made up by handiwork, by "rummaging through our things," and charitable contributions out of American relief packages.

"My handiwork will be to volunteer ten times to fetch water," Heike offers.

"Splitting wood ten times would make a good gift too." Together we draw vouchers for the respective services offered. Then our things are "rummaged through." For Frank there is an almost new wallet, for Jo a silk necktie. Our Christmas party is assured. All we need now is the power company to present us with electricity.

• • •

TUESDAY, DECEMBER 24, 1946

They have given us that. With an even more generous gesture they have suspended the power cuts for the duration of the holidays. We are delighted by the unimpeded cooking and lighting possibilities. Only water is still a problem. Day after day we carry buckets from three blocks away. Night after night their contents freeze. Nevertheless, it is Christmas. And suddenly there are even Christmas trees. Nobody knows from where they have come. Obtainable without a coupon, and not at black market prices, at every freight depot. We stick to our Christmas pine. One shouldn't be ungrateful.

As darkness falls Heike and I go to church. What is Christmas Eve without Christmas carols? Ice-cold darkness greets us. Six forlorn paraffin candles are lit on the high spruces to the left and right of the altar. Like gray shadows, two dozen woebegone people are crouched about the pews.

"Peace on earth," says the minister. As he raises his arms for the blessing, a gray woolen vest becomes visible under his robe. He looks miserably cold. We are freezing too. Everything is frozen. Around us, inside us, next to us. Our breath forms thick clouds. The Christ figure on the cross, too, seems to be freezing. And as if from frosty breath congealing, the word of his teaching makes its way to our ears. In vain I seek an echo in myself. Is this the message that feeds the hungry,

145

that comforts the forsaken, that consoles the wretched? Gray and depressed, the listeners crouch in the pews. That's how they might have sat in the churches after the Thirty Years War. So pitifully tired, so wretched and miserable.

"Do you believe the church can still work?" Heike asks me on the way home.

I shake my head. "Perhaps the words can, but not their intermediaries. They aren't luminous enough. At least not the one tonight. It's no coincidence that the theological faculty has the fewest students. During the Middle Ages it was the reverse. Simply because people believed differently, more deeply and in a more childlike way."

Heike nods. "More childlike," she agrees. "Among us, children seem like bitter old men already."

Frank and Jo are waiting at the door for us. "Merry Christmas!"

In honor of the day we have set the table in front of the fireplace. "Silent night, holy night," peals from the radio.

"The day before yesterday the second refugee train arrived from Poland carrying frozen bodies," Jo reports. "Fifty-three people frozen to death, one hundred eighty-two badly frostbitten, twenty-five amputations. Supposedly there were children among them too. About thirty, I think."

Frank jumps up and turns off the radio. "Shame on them, allowing such a thing to happen," he says angrily.

Jo pulls a face. "Allowing it—there already are twenty million people too many here."

Heike shutters. "Don't talk like a brute."

Wordlessly Frank turns the radio on again. "Oh happy, oh blessed Christmastime," sings a clear-voiced children's choir. The candles are burning. Andrik, I think. Dearest Andrik!

• • •

MONDAY, DECEMBER 30, 1946

No electricity, no water, no coal. And still between fifteen and twenty degrees below zero every night. People are freezing to death in their beds. It's impossible to do any work. Countless businesses have been closed due to lack of fuel. Not much can be done with a fuel allotment of one hundred pounds of briquettes!

On the black market the price of coal has risen to ninety-five marks for a hundred pounds. But it is rarely available. At least not to ordinary people. Coal dealers, too, want to be bribed. With cigarettes, butter or other luxuries. It is quite sad how corrupt we have become. No repairman comes without the requisite enticement. No shoemaker repairs shoes, no tailor fixes a coat if you haven't slipped him something. That's only for his work, as nails and soles, thread, needles and sewing kit, solder, gasoline for the soldering iron and whatever else might be needed, you have to supply yourself anyway. We carry our bodily waste in little packages into the ruins; we use forks, spoons or dishes sparingly so as not to waste a drop of water.

At night, around the kerosene lamp we sit, wearing coats and fur hats, and when we go to bed we coil up like earthworms. To divert us, Frank reads poems by Goethe to us.

"They're still beautiful, even at twenty degrees below zero," he claims.

They are. And when you come to think about it, they seem even more beautiful at twenty degrees below zero, and without electricity, water or coal.

• • •

TUESDAY, DECEMBER 31, 1946

New Year's Eve. We are sitting around the fireplace. We feel like crawling right into it. We roast in the front, while our backs are cold as ice. None of us is in a particularly festive mood.

Will this next year be any better, I wonder. Jo Thäler makes a hopeless gesture. "Not next year nor the one after that. The game is lost for us. For us and the Western world."

He expresses what is haunting all of us like a nightmare. We have no hope left. Our high spirits from 1945, our intoxication with the feeling that on the strength of our faith we would achieve recovery, have given way to despondency and disappointment. We have come to realize that it has nothing to do with us anymore—that it concerns a power struggle between two ideologies. And it is being waged on our backs. Whether it will be decided today or tomorrow we, no doubt, will be the last to know. Neither Frank nor Heike nor Jo nor I will have a say in the matter.

Everyone has gotten tired during the past two years. The Party members still waiting for denazification have long since given up trying to understand the connection between their position as today's helots and their political attitude of yesterday. They just feel offended and find no good word to say for any of the occupying powers.

"The mass—the people—that part of a nation that doesn't know what it wants," as Hegel said, is angry that things do not get better. Their stomachs dictate their opinions, and their opinion is "Why aren't there any potatoes? In West Prussia and Posen, in Pomerania and Silesia, the fields lie fallow. Why do the fields lie fallow? Why can't we get any potatoes? Under Hitler the fields didn't lie fallow. Under Hitler there were plenty of potatoes. The English and the Americans, the French and the Russians, they would like to see us starve to death. Otherwise they would give us potatoes. That must be why there aren't any potatoes."

And what about the opponents of the Nazis? Often I am forced to think of Andrik's words: "It's much easier to be in solidarity *against* something than *for* something." Today we show solidarity only when it comes to complaining about someone else, about the mistakes of the occupying powers or about the poor living conditions. Here the Social Democratic Party—there the Socialist Unity Party. Here Bavaria—there Prussia. Here the women's magazine *Sie*—there the women's magazine *Für Dich*. Here the *Tagesspiegel*—there the *Neues Deutschland*.

They all talk about a common cause, but they mean only themselves. And does it make any sense at all to think in terms of a "common cause"? From one month to the next, each zone more and more takes after its respective occupation power. From one day to the next, the gulf that separates the zones grows deeper. Who knows whether it won't be final in the end?

On the radio the clock strikes midnight. "Happy New Year," someone shouts outside. But that shout does not sound especially happy either.

"To the rebirth of the West," says Frank raising his glass of black market cognac.

"To the rebirth of the West," we repeat, clinking our glasses. Then we take the candle ends off the Christmas tree, put them in our pockets, and head for the cemetery. On Andrik's grave there are six small pine trees. After we have lit the candles on them, we suddenly feel a solidarity again "for something."

• • •

THURSDAY, JANUARY 2, 1947

The whole city talks about the frozen refugees. "They let them perish," people say angrily. "They gave them nothing to eat and nothing to keep warm, neither water nor bread, neither blankets nor straw. They knew that they would die. They wanted them to die."

When you try to remind them that Hitler also knew that millions of Jews were dying in the gas chambers, they look at you angrily and fall silent. Stool pigeon! says their hostile look. Allied lackey! Miserable traitor!

Sometimes we wonder whether we really are such bad Germans. Every human being that perishes innocently deserves the compassion of his fellow human beings. All who know of his martyrdom and do not prevent it are guilty. Today German martyrs heap coals of fire on their tormentors' heads. Yesterday it was the Jews. Tomorrow it might be the Negroes, or the Arabs. Should one individual concern us more than another? Shouldn't it mean the same to our sense of justice when a human being is being hurt, an innocent person persecuted or a defenseless person abandoned, whether in this part of the world or in any other?

Fifty-three frozen bodies were pulled from Polish refugee trains during Christmas week. That is only a tiny fraction of the thousands and thousands who died fleeing their homeland in the past twenty years.

"The greatest migration of all times," an English newspaper writes. Frank wrote down the figures.

"It's true. If you add it all together . . . ," he says and, depressed, he stares at his piece of paper full of numbers.

"Read it to us," I urge him. He draws the candle closer—for the past forty minutes we've been waiting for the electricity to be turned on again—and begins to read.

"Stop it!" Heike calls out, covering her ears with her hands. Frank falls silent. Depressed, we all just stare ahead.

The refugees on the highway to Frankfurt come to mind. "It hurts," cried the child from Silesia who turned his bleeding feet up, trying to balance himself on his bare heels. "It hurts!" Maybe he has died by now.

No water, no electricity, no heat, no potatoes. Freezing cold, day and night. Soon the theaters will be closed and the auditoriums will be turned into public warm-up centers. "The supply of coal is near total exhaustion," write the papers. Streetcar lines have been taken out of service, the number of trains reduced, businesses are closed, public agencies cut back on their services. The drafty stations are crowded with people waiting for trains. They storm the trains. Packed like sardines, they are crowded into unheated compartments. Icicles hang from the ceilings, and all the door handles are white with frost.

"I'm stuck," grumbled a passenger next to me yesterday as he angrily tried to pull off his woolen glove that had frozen to the brass handle.

Power shortage . . . power shortage. The price of coal on the black market has risen to a hundred and fifty marks. For countless Berliners their beds are their only sources of heat. If only the weather were kinder or the occupying power that is supposedly behind in its share of coal deliveries to Berlin by thousands of tons.

"The refugees from Poland will not be the only ones to have frozen to death," sighs Frank.

• • •

SUNDAY, JANUARY 12, 1947

"Look at that," says Heike, handing me a page from the newspaper. "The rats are deserting the sinking ship."

I look at the personal announcement section. "We announce our engagement: Eva Schmidt—Lester Stone, New York . . . Renate Hoffmann—Charles Miller . . . Clare Frank—Edward Grey, Chicago . . . Detroit . . . Los Angeles." "Hmm," I say. "There seems little demand for German men."

"That's what I mean," Heike replies. "Of twelve personal announcements, ten announce engagements with Americans. And that in a Berlin paper."

"Maybe they love each other," I say.

Heike looks doubtful. "Maybe."

In the evening I discuss it with Frank. He laughs at me. "Why do you take it so seriously? For heaven's sake, let them fraternize. There's a lot to be said for it if it makes American mothers-in-law realize that not all German girls are shrews, and if it lets American soldiers know how bourgeois families here endure cold and hunger with dignity. And as far as cigarettes and cocktails are concerned . . ." He smiles indulgently. "Not everybody's conscience is a precision balance. And you can't expect it to be, either."

"But . . . ," I object.

"There's no but," Frank interrupts me, looking more serious now. "Can you blame hungry children for chasing after a piece of sugar? For trying to make their miserable life a little happier? What can you offer to them except ruins and tears, shattered hopes and scant promises? We were scarcely born when Hitler came into power, they will tell you. We didn't vote for him. You voted for him. You brought us up in his spirit. Now you want us to take the consequences. We don't give a damn about your consequences. We claim the right to enjoy our own lives."

"But not this way," I protest. "Not so importunately materialistic, so painfully selfish."

"How else?" Frank asks. "How can you reap idealism where you haven't sown it? In order to feel enthusiastic about freedom of thought, you first must learn that freedom of thought is something to be cherished. And not be brought up to regard it as a crime. We theorize about democracy, freedom and pacifism as if we were writing in Chinese for illiterates. We must turn the soil if we want anything new to grow out of it, and not just trim the branches. We shouldn't be surprised if these branches end up bearing rotten fruit."

"You're right," I admit meekly. "As of tomorrow I will become a farmer."

"Or a missionary," Frank jokes, amused. "Missionaries are said to have the greatest talent for that sort of farming."

• • •

MONDAY, JANUARY 13, 1947

The cold has let up. And in some mysterious way, the Klingenberg power station has received new supplies of coal in time to forestall the ultimate power catastrophe. We wrap one less scarf around our necks and breathe a sigh of relief.

This afternoon at five o'clock a man is supposed to come who, for ten cigarettes and one pound of flour, will thaw our water pipes with two liters of black market gasoline.

• • •

THURSDAY, JANUARY 16, 1947

We have no water, or to be precise, we had some. But only for twenty-four hours. Then the pipes froze again. From the cellar to the attic. So much for two liters of black market gasoline, ten cigarettes and the pound of flour we had saved up.

Again we carry our bodily wastes out of the house in little packages —like most Berliners—and, shamefully, dump them in the nearest ruin. Again we carry water from three blocks away, knock it out of the bucket in the morning, and get angry when the electricity is shut off before our ersatz coffee is ready.

But the *Tägliche Rundschau* boasts: "There is reason for hope in Germany. Representatives of the Socialist Unity Party met with General Sokolovsky. No more grade five food ration cards in the Soviet zone. No more dismantlement. A considerable reduction in the withdrawal of manufactured goods. Return of seventy-four large-scale enterprises to the people. Tripling or quadrupling of production."

It sounds as if the Golden Age were upon us. But on closer inspection you find out that the two hundred large-scale enterprises that were exempted from dismantling have instead been turned into Soviets corporations.

Indeed, a substantial gain! Now German workers work for Russian interests in Germany instead of in Russia. But whether they will still do so tomorrow is questionable. "All laborers and clerks will be employed wherever they are needed," the usual employment contract states. "The management reserves the right to assign tasks outside the company."

We still remember last fall's "voluntary compulsory transfers." How do we know whether the two hundred enterprises now owned by the Russians do not have just as many subsidiaries in Simbirsk or Archangelsk? Or whether next week factory worker Schulze will be needed more urgently there than here? If only we could find out when they are tricking us and when they really mean well by us.

"Mean well?" people sneer. "None of them means well. Neither the English, nor the Americans, nor the Russians. They're all letting us perish. They're all doing us in."

• • •

FRIDAY, JANUARY 31, 1947

Again temperatures are falling. One cold wave after another. Power outages of eight to ten hours a day. Those who still can, heat with fuel obtained on the black market. The number of those who can afford it is dwindling. Equipped with knapsacks, baskets and shopping bags, people set out for the Grunewald forest, jammed together in overcrowded trains, and waste hour upon hour searching for one day's worth of firewood.

In plain terms the papers report: "Found in their beds starved and frozen to death . . . Gerhard Z., seventy-three years old . . . Anna K., sixty-four years old . . . Bertha O., fifty-nine years old . . . Joachim D., one year old . . ." The lower the temperatures drop the more ghastly the rise in the number of victims of the cold.

I return from downtown. A scanty fire is burning in the fireplace. In front of it sits Frank reading the latest news, a pile of papers scattered around him.

"The number of victors has increased," he greets me.

"Post festum? I thought the war was over."

"So did I," Frank replies. "But not Mr. Figl. At least he seems intent on revising its outcome."

"Let me see," I say, sitting down next to him in front of the fire.

". . . to be treated as a nation that has been oppressed by Hitler and has been liberated only now," I read. "Austria, the first country to fall prey to Hilter's aggression . . . to be exempted from reparation payments as a nonhostile nation . . . to claim reparation payments from Germany . . ."

"What rubbish," I stammer in disbelief. "Of all people, our sister nation in the Axis. The eager yes-men and enthusiasts of 1938!"

Frank grins. "That must have escaped their memory. Together with the fact that Hitler wasn't German but Austrian."

"Do you think they mean it seriously? I still can't believe it. My ears still are resounding with their 'Heil Hitler' shouts on that terrible twelfth of March when Andrik and I were listening to the radio and just couldn't believe that the rebellion we had expected had turned into a National Socialist triumph. 'Austria is part of the German Reich. Seyss-Inquart is its governor. Its army incorporated into the Wehrmacht of the Reich. Its army, police and public servants are under oath to Hitler,' German stations broadcast on March 13, 1938, to the sound of trumpets and the blare of military marches. Did anybody refuse to take the oath? Did a single person get up to throw a bomb at the head of the conquering hero as he marched in?

"In 1933 people had no idea of the extent of crimes this man was capable of. In 1938 people knew—they must have known from emigrants' reports, from the laws regarding the Jews, the persecution of Communists, the concentration camps. Why didn't they draw the consequences? Why do they only dare so now after Hitler is dead?

"Nazism began in Austria, found support in Bavaria and ended in Prussia. Prussia is now being punished by being dissolved. The Bavarians claim it wasn't their doing. And Austria claims reparations. Has the world gone completely mad?"

"It appears that way," Frank grumbles. "And if it should really be possible that one day the earth might be blown up by accidentally released nuclear energy, I must say not much will be lost . . . If in the

thousands of years of his existence man hasn't come up with anything
better . . ."

• • •

A publishing company has asked me to a meeting in Hamburg. It
is very urgent, they cabled. Urgent! How can anyone these days travel
on short notice from Berlin to Hamburg? With an interzonal transit
permit? I applied for it five months ago. The American and English
authorities approved it. "Reason enough to be turned down by the
Russians," mock the authorities who approved it. It seems to be an
unspoken law. An approval of an interzonal transit permit by the
Western Allies results in rejection by the Russians. And vice versa, if
approved by the Russians.

In two days I am supposed to be in Hamburg. In two days I will
have to have performed the miracle of having obtained a permit by the
ration card issuing office, a travel permit, an interzonal transit permit
and a train ticket. For ordinary people that means waiting in line for
at least four times twenty-four hours. About sixteen applications and
forms have to be filled out. Between twenty and sixty questions to be
answered on each of them. Bribe coefficient: impossible to calculate
beforehand.

• • •

WEDNESDAY, FEBRUARY 5, 1947

An English travel order spares me all the trouble. Within five hours,
a ticket for the English military train from Berlin to Hanover is procured. Getting from Hanover to Hamburg should be easy. Tomorrow
evening I will depart. It is seventeen degrees below zero. But since it
is an English military train, I can count on intact windows, light and
even heat.

155

Ruth Andreas-Friedrich

• • •

"In the West they're better off than we are," people in Berlin say.

"In Berlin they're better off than we are," people in Hamburg say.

"The Russians are the most discredited among the occupying powers," a Russian officer told me recently.

"We hate the English more than you hate the Russians," three Hamburg citizens tell me today.

No doubt: I have come to a foreign country. Between Helmstedt and Marienborn runs a border that separates two worlds.

The train from Hanover to Hamburg is overcrowded. I stand squeezed between suitcases and people. A one-and-a-half-hour delay in getting to Hanover. The train to Hamburg is three and a half hours late. From seven to half past nine in the morning I wait on the uncovered platform, shivering with cold. Nobody announces anything. Nobody knows how long the train will be delayed.

People wait. As the day dawns at fifteen degrees below zero, they wait for the train to Hamburg. "It's the same every day," grumbles a malcontent trudging past me. "Since the damned . . ." He looks around and falls silent.

Slowly and joltingly the train moves across the snow-covered countryside. Dozing off, I listen with half an ear to the conversations around me. They do not sound good.

". . . these days all of Germany is a concentration camp with Allied flags flying over it . . ."

". . . as I told my son, if only one Pole stays alive . . ."

". . . there certainly was more food to eat back then. And in general . . ."

There it is, the new solidarity! The front against the occupying power. And if once in a while a positive word reaches my ear, it is uttered in remembrance of things past.

"when we were stationed in France . . ."

"and then my commander said . . ."

"and suddenly I was hit . . ."

156

The eyes shine. The mouth, a moment ago twisted with bitterness, widens into a broad grin. Soldierly romanticizing. Soldiers' talk. Precisely that kind of mentality we had abjured forever in May 1945.

. . .

I walk around the city exploring people's opinions. "Why do you complain so much? Why do you hate the English?"

"Because everything they do is wrong," people answer.

"And where do they go wrong?"

"They made a police state out of their zone. They harass people through German police. They interfere with every detail. Whatever initiatives we manage to come up with, they suppress with red tape, and they practically control the entire economy."

"Well, aren't they the victors?"

"The victors?" I am met with a wall of ice and derision. "Fine victors they are! If they hadn't stolen our atomic bomb . . ."

"*Our* atomic bomb?"

They nod with an air of superiority. "Of course ours. It was all ready. Except that those saboteurs, those . . . ," an abusive word interrupts the angry torrent of words, "kept it away from the Führer."

"But that's . . . ," insane, I want to say but they do not let me finish.

"Think of it," they interrupt me in a triumphant manner, "when did the Americans get here? In April 1945. And when did they drop the atomic bomb on Japan? In August. Well?" A look of satisfaction underscores this astounding logic. They are Nazis, I think, horrified.

They are Nazis, I cannot help thinking as I become aware of the eagerness with which former Party members here give each other a leg up. And even the latest popular joke—best is to become a Party member because it assures you a job—only reinforces my dismay. Is that what the English accomplished in two years of democratic education? So that people condemn them blindly and out of their disappointment escape into new and frightening nationalism.

I see the number 88 written in chalk on a wall. There it is again— and then again. In the course of an afternoon, I read the same number

157

six times. Coincidence, I think at first. "Intentional," people inform me with a wink. The letter *H* is the eighth letter in the alphabet. HH —88—Heil Hitler. I am speechless. I feel as if I have stepped back in time.

Like a stranger I walk through streets lined with ruins. I find it odd that I feel attached only to ruins whose coming into being I have witnessed, while others—I am looking with indifference at the ruins of St. Pauli—leave me unconcerned. At most I feel indignant that they still are there. No question about it: Hamburg does not look very cleaned up. No women doing construction work can be seen either. But still, everything somehow smells of peace. A somewhat scant peace, but nevertheless peace.

Here, no Makar Ivanovs disappear. Here, there is no fear at all. "88!"—Heil Hitler, people write on the walls. How ungrateful they are. Don't they realize that freedom from fear is an advantage too? These are the rewards from Nazis who fled to the West during the last weeks of the war, and of the continous illegal influx of Nazis to the English zone since 1945. "In the English zone they're more lenient toward Nazis," it was said back then. So the English zone became a Nazi paradise. Denazification—child's play! The number of arrests— hardly worth mentioning. Treatment in the internment camp— gentlemanly. Until the Nazis forgot that they had been Nazis, and the English decided to tighten the belt of occupation measures. Confiscation of apartments, coal shortages, food shortages. People are outraged. "How come? Two years after the war? And this is supposed to be democracy?"

What is considered a cause for grievances in the Eastern zone—the classification of food ration cards into five grades—is being praised here as an enviable advantage.

"It entices your women to do construction work and your workers to work in the factories," employers in Hamburg say. "We can't find workers. Our women don't do construction work. Black marketeering is easier, they think. Having the time to procure supplies is more profitable than hourly wages. So what choice do we have if we don't want the factories to lie idle? We bribe them with scarce goods. We offer premiums in order to make the work more attractive. Official black marketeering, so to speak. Each month something that is in short supply. In bartering terms this particular item is worth four pounds of bacon. Your premium is a food ration card grade one. How infinitely simple! How enviably easy!"

Looking at things from this perspective undeniably changes them entirely. For the first time I see the "hunger card" in a different light. As a lever to boost the economy. As a remedy for that missing sense of responsibility for reconstruction. Here the boosting of the economy for the most part takes place behind closed doors. Being sure of his standard food ration card, the unemployed citizen goes bartering. Half a box of soap powder equals 5 marks, equals three beers, equals 30 marks. A quarter pound of tea equals 100 marks, equals a pound of butter, equals 240 marks.

The important thing is to match up supplier and consumer. A house is being repaired. The starting capital: 15 liters of alcohol. From 15 liters of alcohol, 38 bottles of liquor are made. Three bottles of liquor equals an elegant rug, equals half a ton of potatoes, equals 30 bags of cement. To repair a house you need 15 bags of cement. The rest is exchanged for a Christmas goose, equals 2 pounds of coffee, equals 2 iron girders. Ten bottles of liquor will bring 6 cubic meters of lumber. One cubic meter goes as payment to the carpenter, the second is exchanged for window glass, the third for 2,000 bricks. The fourth, fifth and sixth are needed for the reconstruction of the house. A complicated puzzle that only insiders know how to solve. I feel dizzy from figures and objects of exchange.

• • •

HAMBURG, WEDNESDAY, FEBRUARY 12, 1947

The only thing here reminiscent of Berlin is the cold. In Hamburg just as many people die miserably of cold as in Berlin.

Coal . . . coal! A kingdom—a crime—murder if necessary for a single bucket of coal! The depots are looted, the freight trains plundered. Like a swarm of locusts a mob of women and children descends upon every arriving freight car. Teeming and scurrying. More and still more. They fill their bags and pockets with coals and briquettes. In no time the heaps of coal have melted away. In the distance the sound of a whistle. For a moment the coal car looks like a petrified anthill. Then a fidgeting about, and they are off in a flash. The hubbub is over. The emptied freight car stands alone on frosty tracks.

"Coal pilferage," people in Hamburg say with indifference. "There isn't a train that isn't plundered."

"What about the police?"

"They always get there too late. As far as coal pilferage is concerned, they're on the side of the vanquished."

• • •

FRIDAY, FEBRUARY 14, 1947

Freezing, I head back to Berlin.

I get to the station one and a half hours before departure. I climb through the window to get on the train. Then for six hours I stand in the unlit corridor, squeezed between boxes and bags of potatoes. The only way to cope is by reciting poems to myself that I remember spasmodically. The car smells of onions, fish and unwashed people. It seems a relief when occasionally the pungent smell of a homemade cigarette blends in with the foul stench. Four people are jammed into the bathroom. And then the so-called "bread cough." This awful effect of food that is hard to digest, which these days fouls the air in all public transportation.

Engine problems. A stopover among snowdrifts in the middle of nowhere. By the time the train arrives in Hanover at three in the morning, the military train to Berlin has left an hour before. "It happens frequently," the man in the red cap says indifferently. "The next train leaves tomorrow night at one o'clock." A twenty-two hour wait at fifteen degrees below zero.

The covered platform is crowded with people lying on the wet stone floor. They look pale and tired. They too are waiting for a train. And until it arrives the platform's stone floor serves as a bed.

"Is there anyplace around here to spend the night?" I ask. People just stare at me. On stiff legs I stumble through the gate. My throat is parched. If at least I could find something to drink. A kindly soul points to the stairs on the left leading to the bunker. Waiting in line

160

for twenty-five minutes I struggle down the stairs. A low cellar. The air is suffocating. People sit on tables and chairs, overcome by exhaustion, as if sleep has mowed them down. Pushing and shoving in front of the bar. Coffee is being offered there. A ten-mark deposit is required if you take the tin cup in which it is served to one of the tables. A ten-mark deposit for a drink that tastes like dishwater. I swallow the hot liquid as if it were bad-tasting medicine. The main thing is that it is hot. Then I make way for the next person. "Drink faster, comrade!" the Russian satirist Soshtchenko would say. He does not say it, because what he says Soviet Russia does not like to hear.

By the time I leave the bunker it has turned four o'clock. The coldest hour of the night. Still nineteen and a half hours to go. To me it seems as if time has stopped and eternity has begun. A desolate eternity illuminated by the glaring light of two arc lamps. If it were dark at least, I wish, as I reluctantly mingle with the masses of people inside the station. People huddle in every corner. They are swarming all over the place, crowding in front of the gates and pouring in from who knows where. Ragged, tattered and torn, uprooted, and stranded here by fate. The flotsam of the German collapse. An inferno of misery. I stumble over something soft. A man lies in front of me, snoring. Grunting, he turns over. His pants are torn. Instead of shoes he wears rags tied with string around his feet. If he moves his head another inch it will lie in a filthy puddle. The station lavatory is his dressing room. The floor is his bed, the drafty entrance hall his living room, kitchen and market. Two cigarette butts—one mark forty. A salvaged woolen glove—fifteen marks. You subsist on whatever you can get hold of. Today it's this—tomorrow that. And when your time has come you will die wretchedly wherever you just happen to be. Perhaps on the stairs of the station in Hanover. Perhaps in the waiting room in Braunschweig. Or curled up on the straw mattress of a random twenty-pfennig bed.

The city supplies transients with food for three days. Three-day ration cards make "passing through" an end in itself—a permanent occupation—a purpose in life.

I wend my way through the crowd, the suitcases, baskets and knapsacks. Never before have I heard so many different languages and dialects within such a small area.

161

"American soap at fifty marks a piece," a woman whispers. The hand that offers it to me is so dirty that I feel like suggesting she should wash herself with it. But I don't. Who knows when she ate her last piece of bread.

At five in the morning I end up in front of the Red Cross bunker. Again a long line of people on the grimy descending stairs. I am handed a gray slip of paper. "Mission Shelter, Hanover Central Station" is printed on it. Checking of identity papers. Half the people waiting with me slink away with a bad conscience. The rest of us enter through a gate. I have to pay twenty pfennigs and am asked whether I want a bed. The bed card is yellow and costs fifty pfennigs. As it is handed to me five girls are being led away. They are screaming like hell. None of them looks older than sixteen.

"For heaven's sake, what's going on?" I inquire, feeling alarmed.

The woman checking identity papers looks indifferently after them. "No papers," she says as if it were the most boring routine. "Runaways. Tramping about infecting men."

The people pushing and shoving behind me grumble. "Move along! Don't just stand there."

As if through a sieve I am being squeezed into the bottleneck at the gate to the Hanover Central Station Shelter.

Wooden benches standing in rows, one after another. People, half-sitting and half-lying down, huddle on them. Sleeping or dozing, mouths agape, heads dropping to their chests. The next room is the men's dormitory. Triple-tiered bunks. Wheezing and snoring on every straw mattress at fifty pfennigs apiece. I tiptoe through to the women's dormitory. A sullen-looking young woman assigns me a straw mattress. Second row to the left, fifth bunk, third level.

"I'd suggest you use your suitcase for a pillow," she peevishly advises. "And everybody's got to clear out by eight o'clock."

By eight o'clock? Already it's a quarter past five. Time-lapse sleep, I try to cheer myself up as I haul myself and my suitcase up to the third level of the fifth bunk in the second row to the left.

Below me a woman is whimpering. She is whimpering so desperately that I cannot sleep. "Is there something wrong with you?" I finally ask her.

Moaning, she turns around. The smell of blood blended with some other nauseating stench assails me. "Ra . . . ra . . . raped," she utters

gaspingly. "To . . . to . . . torn up . . . eight . . . times . . . at . . ."
She is unable to finish. The rest is drowned by pitiful moaning.

I tear at my suitcase. "Cotton wool," I think. "Handkerchiefs." But
what good are cotton wool or handkerchiefs for the unforgettable shock
of having been raped eight times while trying to cross the border
illegally? For the next two hours and forty-five minutes the unknown
woman below me moans and groans miserably into a filthy straw
mattress.

At eight o'clock the night is over. The lone fact that it is getting
light outside comforts me. You can go to the movies, sit in a café, try
and find a warm place somewhere away from the ruins. Anything to
get away from the area around the station, that breeding place of
horror.

Between ten A.M. and seven P.M., I twice view a film entitled *Rendezvous at Midnight* in an unheated theater. Three times I stop in
dreary bars to have a little glass of beer, a cup of broth and some hot
beverage. The shelter opens at eight o'clock. A straw mattress on the
third level of the fifth bunk in the second row to the left is better than
a fourth little glass of beer, I decide, and I sink into leaden sleep till a
quarter to midnight. For eighteen hours now I, too, have belonged to
the flotsam of Hanover.

• • •

SUNDAY, FEBRUARY 16, 1947

Frank awaits me at the Charlottenburg Station. "Good to have you
back," he greets me, with nary a complaint that both yesterday and
today he had to wait on the platform for three hours. It occurs to me
that home is where they love you, and gratefully I return home to my
life with Frank and Heike.

• • •

MONDAY, FEBRUARY 24, 1947

A new cold wave. I've already lost count of them this winter. "Increasing number of casualties . . . coal shortage . . . shortage of electricity . . . limited train service. Nearly three thousand businesses are closed . . . Disasters all over the world."

The fact that other people are cold too offers little comfort when you're chilled to the bone in your own bed. The papers demand drastic relief measures. How can the city council take drastic measures when of the seventy-five resolutions passed by the council since November 1946 only three have been approved by the Control Council. The others have either been defeated or, after having been "tabled" for four months, have still not been decided on. We now pay bitterly for the fact that the Social Democrats began their government with so little support from the Russian occupying power.

The Social Democratic functionaries meet for heated debates. "Resign," demand the independent ones. "Let the Control Council deal with the whole damned business. Why should we bother with being puppets in this chimera of a democratic government? So that the Socialist Unity Party can gloat at us and profit from it? Let's call a spade a spade! No more resolutions should be passed. The public should be informed that not we are responsible, but the discord among Control Council members."

"But what about our posts?" object the utilitarians. "We can't all lose our jobs."

The cautious and the timid, the compromisers and subordinates prevail. As they now prevail everywhere. In all public agencies, in all parties, at all conferences, all over the world. Is it really so surprising that the masses, who never look at the cause but only at the effect— the effect of failure—secretly long for a savior?

"Don't forget," Frank was saying only yesterday, "that in comparative world history we, at this moment, are only at about the period of the Napoleonic "Hundred Days." Until March 20, 1815, the Congress of Vienna debated endlessly, and the allies in the Napoleonic Wars just couldn't agree on a postwar Europe. Then people were ripe for a new Napoleon.

"And today? Just try it! Let the Americans broadcast over the radio that Hitler has landed at Tempelhof Airport along with a thousand aircraft. Let his double storm over Kurfürstendamm tomorrow with all pomp, including motorcade, cordons, shouts of Sieg Heil and whatever else it takes. And then see what happens. And how far the German people have gotten in learning about democracy."

I believe he is right. In between times, there has been too much cold and hunger. There has been too much fighting and too little consideration of human imperfection. Why should what happened to the French people a hundred and twenty years ago not happen to us too? We who, due to our loss of leading personalities in the course of the past thirty-three years, are represented on the world stage only by second-raters or even third-raters. If things won't get settled in Moscow . . . On March 10 the foreign ministers of the four victorious nations—Molotov, Marshall, Bevin and Bidault—are supposed to meet in order to settle the matter. This time in Moscow, so at least there will be a difference in the place where they meet. The world is optimistic and once more expects everything from this new conference. Unity, the removal of zonal boundaries, order in Europe, the settlement of all conflicts, and peace—the peace which for two years we have ardently and desperately longed for. The Biedermeier tailcoats of the Vienna Congress have been exchanged for tuxedos. Let's hope the tuxedos will prevent another "Hundred Days."

• • •

TUESDAY, MARCH 4, 1947

The Moscow Conference temporarily upstages even the problems of hunger, cold and coal shortages. In the same way that a drowning person clutches at a straw, the people of Berlin put all their hopes in it, confident that "things will come out all right." As if Marshall, Bevin, Bidault and Molotov could suddenly make coal drop from the sky, as if they could conjure apartments out of ruins, raise the temperature by twenty degrees, or make a wheat field grow as if by magic.

So many illusions. As long as man can still take comfort in illusions he is not completely lost.

• • •

MONDAY, MARCH 10, 1947

Today the foreign ministers arrived at their destination. It's up to four men to decide the fate of millions of desperate people.

165

"If at least they would negotiate the release of our prisoners of war," people say.

"Negotiate their release?" others reply scornfully. "When, after two years of great effort, we still haven't succeeded in finding out their exact number, no less their names."

Two to three million German men are still missing. Some have not been heard of again since Stalingrad. Others were missing in action after the battle of Orel, the defeat of Warsaw, the retreat from Poland, the battle for Berlin. Are they alive? Did they die? Have they been wounded, captured, deported, killed, or starved to death?

For two years all inquiries about the fate of the German prisoners of war have been met with persistent silence on the part of the Russian military government. Letters seem to get nowhere. Petitions remain unanswered. Letters from all over Germany pile up in the offices of political parties and newspapers. "Help us get our men back. Appeal to their humaneness. Ask for their names! Ask for their number! Move heaven and earth so we can find out the number of survivors." All efforts are futile. It is like running up against a wall made of cotton wool. Why do they want to torture us? Why have they remained silent?

For sure, Russian mothers, too, didn't know for four years whether or not their sons survived the war far away from home. Under Hitler millions of Soviet prisoners of war died in Germany, succumbed to epidemics, starved or were tortured to death. We—in particular we—are in no position to judge them if they now pay us back with suffering for suffering, with reprisals for reprisals. But there has been an armistice for twenty-three months. And in Nuremberg an international tribunal is passing judgment on behalf of France, England, America and Russia on the crimes against humanity committed by the Nazis.

"They don't mean reprisal," people say. "They're interested in an additional labor force. As an advance payment of reparations." Sneering, they come up with the following calculation: "Two million men equals eight million marks in labor per day. At sixty pfennigs an hour. Minus eighty pfennigs a day to feed them. Eight million marks a day equals five billion marks in two years." They grin derisively. "Five billion marks in labor. It's quite a sum to be discreetly pocketed as reparation payments. And that the Western Allies let them do it . . ."

There is a lot of shrugging of shoulders and head shaking in Berlin about this manner of settling accounts. So much so that our own guilt is almost forgotten.

• • •

SUNDAY, MARCH 16, 1947

Molotov has announced the number of the prisoners of war. At least that much the Moscow Conference yielded so far. But instead of relief, disappointment and desperation spread among the population. Eight hundred and ninety thousand, five hundred and thirty-two. It almost makes you want to ask whether it isn't perhaps thirty-two and a half or three quarters. Less than a million. What about all the others? Mr. Molotov's announcement has wiped them out. Has blown them away like chaff in the wind. Has made them vanish into thin air. For a million mothers, for millions of sisters, children and wives, their son, father, husband or friend has been killed in action only today, two years after the war. Killed in action with Molotov's words: "Eight hundred ninety thousand, five hundred thirty-two men remain in Russian captivity." Set the flag to half mast over Germany! Oh weep, Hecuba!

"That, too, is a lie," the mourning are being comforted. "They didn't count the skilled workers among them. Skilled workers are valuable. Not prisoners of war anymore but tovarish candidates. Including them you can add at least another five hundred thousand to the total." A straw of hope. But there are thousands who blindly and desperately clutch at that straw.

• • •

WEDNESDAY, MARCH 26, 1947

The foreign ministers gathered in Moscow are not the only ones to decide. Nature, too, tries in its own way to solve the problem of German overpopulation. Like ancient Egypt, the whole country seems to be afflicted by seven plagues. As soon as the plague of war was over, there came the plague of rape. Followed by the plague afflicting refu-

167

gees. And while this one is still going on, a new plague, the cold, sets in with biting frost. The dying continues. On March 14, within three hours, a sudden twenty-five degree rise in temperatures, such as Europe has not experienced in a hundred years. Slush, ice, power outages. People slip on the icy streets as if walking on glass. Every step in the darkness beomes a Saint Vitus's dance. A Saint Vitus's dance which overnight fills all hospitals in Berlin with casualties. People with fractured bones or bad sprains. Many suffer fatal skull fractures.

After the fourth plague has done its damage, the fifth one is already approaching. As the great thaw sets in, an awful smell pervades the ruins, remindful of the consequences of last winter's pipe bursts. While Berliners open their windows to let the spring sun warm up their cold rooms, the Oder bursts its banks. Its waters flood seventy thousand hectares of farmland and wash away villages, cattle, houses and people. People escape by boat with only their lives. Again thousands are rendered homeless and countless others die a sudden death.

"There are four hundred seventy-five new cases of tuberculosis in one week . . . every sixty-seventh Berliner is suffering from venereal disease," the statistics report. "The average age of people suffering from venereal disease is between seventeen and twenty-eight." So death takes its toll even among unborn children. If the Moscow Conference does not now put a stop to the apocalypse . . .

• • •

TUESDAY, APRIL 1, 1947

"Bad news, bad news," our Allied friends say. The Moscow "dispute" is not getting anywhere. Every topic that is taken up is put aside without result. The four "Allies" cannot agree on a single issue. That is what happens when opposed world views meet in pretended solidarity. What we experience daily in microcosm is repeated here on the grand scale.

As long as Mr. Hitler was the world's number-one enemy, the worldviews of his adversaries made no difference. Neither for those inside Germany nor outside. But as soon as the world's enemy was defeated, this question of worldviews came immediately to the fore.

And it was found that they were opposed. More and more opposed with each new day. For the German adversaries of the world's number-one enemy, the stages leading to this insight have been the strike vote, the bickering in the press, the discord in the city council and everyone's merciless feuding with everyone else. Tensions in the Control Council, the ineffectiveness of the conferences, the banning of Western occupation forces from the Russian zone, George Marshall's appointment as the American secretary of state, Truman's recent speech against Communism, increasing anti-Soviet feeling in the United States, more and more open aggression between the Western and the Eastern victors—these have been the stages leading to this insight among his adversaries outside Germany.

The victors seem almost resentful toward us Germans because we too have only gradually come to realize that the initial course of rapprochement has changed in the interim. And again it looks as if the politicians are expecting the average German to show more political insight, more prudence and foresight, than they themselves are capable of. Expecting the average German during the Hitler regime to decide against Nazism five years before Godesberg. Expecting the average German in postwar Germany to retroactively decide against Communism, from the time of the Frankfurt friendship, the United Nations Organization and the Potsdam Agreement.

In the Ruhr District and in the English zone people have been demonstrating for weeks against the rapidly deteriorating food situation. Strikes alternate with marches against hunger. In the French zone people receive eight hundred calories a day. On paper they are supposed to get more. But paper won't blush, nor will it mention that the respective rations might have been intended but have never been allotted. Instead of the 450 grams of fat per month, 125 grams. Instead of the 450 grams of sugar per month, none at all. Instead of the intended 1,000 grams of pasta per month, none at all. "Instead won't get us fed," people say. So they go on strike. Or try to attract attention through hunger marches. The pleasure of having the freedom to demonstrate unpunished or with only minor punishment is something they have not enjoyed for a long time.

In the Russian-occupied zone they respond with stiffer methods to the "noncooperation" of certain circles. By arresting those who dare to express opinions differing from those of the Socialist Unity Party. People who have, in one way or another, made themselves unpopular with the regime suddenly vanish into thin air. These are the methods that create the gap and make the opposing worldviews irreconcilable, that turn yesterday's friend into today's enemy. In the lives of individuals as well as among nations. What can we expect from Moscow under such auspices?

• • •

SATURDAY, APRIL 5, 1947

Nothing! Nothing at all! Neither peace nor a redrawing of the eastern boundaries, neither the removal of zonal boundaries nor a joint monetary regulation. It seems as though they have only come together in order to demonstrate to the world how to most skillfully talk at cross-purposes. "At our expense . . . on our backs," people complain, each day expecting less and less from the Moscow Conference.

• • •

WEDNESDAY, APRIL 16, 1947

At the Kremlin the negotiations drag on, while in Berlin people struggle through the tangle of new daily and hourly ordinances, forms and questionnaires. Rarely has a country been buried under as much red tape as Germany is now.

I talk with an entrepreneur from the Eastern sector. "If it goes on this way," he says, pointing at a heap of forms piled up on his desk, "any initiative on our part will soon be smothered in red tape. Twenty-eight questionnaires a month. For four weeks a special secretary has been busy solely with filling out official forms. Industrial summary. Report on the fulfillment of production quotas. Productivity report. Inventories every five days. Biweekly reports, monthly reports, quarterly reports. Tell me, how are we supposed to find time for productive work?"

In the afternoon I visit one of Heike's colleagues.

"It's intolerable," she complains, pointing at her swollen feet. "If things go on this way I might as well give up my profession. For three days my kids have been down with the measles. At noon I have to leave to pick up the food allotment for the baby. One hour traveling time for half a liter of food. At two o'clock I have to leave to pick up the school meal for my older girl. One hour traveling time for half a liter of food. At four o'clock I leave to get my own meal at the theater. One and a half hours' traveling time for half a liter of food. At seven I put it all into one pot and thank fate and the Allies for presenting me with meals for the baby, from the school and the theater, and imagine how wonderful life would be if one could have all three meals at the same time at home."

However, you cannot have them at home all at the same time. And if it does not take three and half hours of traveling time, it takes three hours of waiting in line, three hours of struggling against inadequately organized distribution, three hours of racking one's brain about what, in heaven's name, one is supposed to serve one's family today. Hours are wasted with running in place. Not only in one's professional life but in one's personal life as well. And in the Kremlin, are they wasting any less time with running in place?

• • •

FRIDAY, APRIL 25, 1947

The foreign ministers departed yesterday. The outcome: the prospects for peace, friendship and the opening of the zones have become dimmer and dimmer, and we have one million men less than we had hoped.

• • •

MONDAY, MAY 5, 1947

A leaden restlessness has seized the people of Berlin since the end of the Moscow Conference. "Should one stay?" "Should one leave?" "Will there be war?" Our instincts have become insecure since we feel like mere pawns in the game of world politics. When Hitler was in power everybody had an unchanging goal: for the Nazi it was the victory of Adolf Hitler, for the anti-Nazi, the end of Nazism. What is the goal now? Rapprochement? Separation of the zones? War?

Rumors abound. "All of Bavaria is one huge arsenal. Every night Russian troop transports roll westward. The Western Allies will be lucky if they manage to stop the Russian advance at the Atlantic." They make you want to duck and stop your ears.

"War," says the newspaper vendor. "War," says the streetcar conductor. "War," say the mailman, the grocer and the butcher's wife at the corner. The same people who just three years ago would have preferred to chew on shoe leather rather than endure the misery of bomb attacks for one more day now talk of a new war as the only possible way out. Out of the drudgery of waiting in line, the monotony of eating grits, the inequity of denazification, the senselessness of the questionnaires, the disappointment with the Allies, and the whole hopeless mess of our postwar situation. People have long since ceased asking themselves how we got into this situation or reminding themselves of what Germany looked like before Hitler came to power and after.

Today, May 5, 1947, Hitler has been dead for two years. And what has come after him appears so unbearable to the heirs of his collapse that they would almost prefer a calamitous end to an endless calamity. "Rather war. Rather to be chewing on shoe leather than to endure this senseless mess any longer."

What good does it do that in the West the English and American zones are unified. The Western unity renders the East-West disunity all the more obvious. "We expect the positive economic effects of the bizonal union to be fully felt by the year 1950," an American economist declares. And what about the hunger demonstrations? The strikes? The dismantling and slackening, due to bureaucratism, of any initiative, and likewise of any projective planning, due to the incessant rumors of war? Nobody feels like rebuilding his house for new bombs. Nobody can be expected to save his money for the revenue office or the currency reform. What for? Why? Having to ask "Why?" or "What for?" in every area of daily life drives one near to losing one's mind.

• • •

THURSDAY, MAY 8, 1947

In Bavaria, too, people seem not far from that state. Except that they seem to be losing their minds in a different way than people in Berlin. Dr. Hundhammer, the Bavarian minister of culture, advocates the reintroduction of corporal punishment in the schools. The district leader of the Bavarian farmers' union, Dr. Fischbacher, demands that all Prussians should be driven out of Bavaria and that miscegenation between Bavarians and non-Bavarians should be declared "blood defilement." Instead of a brotherly unity to pull out the wedge that the antagonism between the Allies has driven between East and West Germany, people are deliberately forcing it deeper and deeper.

"There will be war," people in Munich say. "But since the fallout from the atomic bomb that will be dropped on Berlin won't spread beyond Hof, we needn't worry much about it."

Bavaria to the Bavarians. Baden to the Badeners. And for Berlin? The next atomic bomb that will be dropped. A sad way for the Fatherland to show its gratitude for two years of "bridge building."

• • •

SUNDAY, MAY 11, 1947

"Don't forget to reset your watch," Frank reminded me last night. There is no way to forget it. For days my ears have been ringing with everybody's ccomplaints about the "new harassment." As of Sunday, Moscow summer time. In the summer of 1945, too, we set our clocks two hours ahead. And we didn't suspect any evil intent. Saving of electric power, simplification of the transport of occupation forces, or God knows what other reason might have been behind it.

"Even our sleep they cheat us out of," people are now complaining left and right. "They begrudge us even a few miserable hours of sleep."

It is disturbing when a man loses the capacity to see the positive

173

side of things. Disturbing not only for himself, but even more so for those who undertake to rule over him. Reaction, reaction. From all sides increasing signs indicate that there will be a third world war. No matter against what. No matter against whom . . .

• • •

". . . against Bolshevism," some say. "More and more threateningly the hand reaches for the rest of Europe. The Communist International, sacrificed for the Western Allies during the war, has now come back to life through the Cominform, the Communist information bureau. The Fifth Column is on the march. And once it has reached its goal . . ."

". . . against Fascism," others say. "Don't you see how it is gaining all over the world? In France de Gaulle's influence is stronger every day. All it will take is a little coup d'état and dictatorship will be firmly established. Not only in France but also in Spain."

America? "In ten years there will be Fascism in America," an American claimed recently. "Except that over there they will call it antifascism." Bitter words. But what if there is some truth behind them?

". . . against the reaction," the next ones say. "What should we come to if the priests—as in Bavaria—demand proof of their parishioners that they went to confession, if, in moral outrage, the sexes are prohibited from swimming together, corporal punishment is reintroduced and bigotry prevails. Back to the Inquisition. Back to the burning of witches. Is this the reality of our democratic dreams?"

Neither this nor that. But it appears that there is little room at the moment for the Social Democratic ideal among red, brown and black dictatorships. Almost too little to keep hoping for their realization in practice.

Battleground Berlin

• • •

Whenever one thinks that nothing works anymore, a glimmer of hope appears from somewhere. This time it comes from the auditorium at Harvard University where Marshall, the American secretary of state, yesterday announced to an assembly of students an extensive relief plan for the reconstruction of Europe. Finally a constructive proposal. Doubly constructive in that it serves East and West equally.

The Germans, too, seem to remember that they have things in common. Yesterday, for the first time since the end of the war, the heads of all four zones met in Munich to discuss measures necessary to prevent another miserable winter in Germany. If one sets a good example . . .

• • •

SATURDAY, JUNE 7, 1947

. . . the others don't necessarily follow. Before the last of the Eastern zone's chiefs had entered the Bavarian state chancellery, his Eastern colleagues had already left the conference room. The delegates of the Eastern zone have returned to Berlin. They could not even agree on an agenda. Another hope turns to disillusionment. What if the relief plan for Europe suffers a similar fate?

• • •

SUNDAY, JUNE 22, 1947

Not yet. Thank God, not yet. This time they seem intent on losing no time turning theory into practice. A new invitation to all Allied foreign ministers to meet in Paris on June 27. The topic of the conference: the Marshall Plan. Russia accepted the invitation. Almost before it had even received it.

"The Americans will extend them credit, and in exchange they will retreat to the Oder," people rejoice. Disillusionment turns into hope again!

• • •

THURSDAY, JUNE 26, 1947

We are not cheerful. The American government banned the import of cigarettes. And that to a country where now for years Chesterfields are used as the standard currency.

"What do you think is the most effective way to combat the black market?" an American finance specialist asked me recently.

"By giving us cigarettes," I replied.

He looked at me disapprovingly. "Might a vanquished people be so addicted to intoxicants?" I interpreted his look. A hundred times I have asked myself the same question. Why do people who never touched a cigarette before suddenly smoke? Why do they sell their food ration cards just to buy a pack of cigarettes on the black market at an incredible price? Why at a time when the monthly cigarette allotment is twelve cigarettes per person? That is per every male person. Women get only half as many. Why don't we draw the conclusions from this lack of supply and stop smoking altogether? Because we are unable to. Daily, if not hourly, fate presents us with new shocks. The shock of a night of bombs, the fear of being raped, the insecurity of life in Berlin, the whole misery of our life in the ruins—all that cannot be compensated with oatmeal. Or with grits or ersatz coffee. It is the discrepancy between the intensity of our fate and the drabness of our daily life that makes us addicted to cigarettes. For a few happier moments they offer escape from an unbearable reality. This is the secret that made Chesterfields into the standard currency. And as long as we are condemned to cope with so much more than our strength permits, they will remain a focus of our desire.

Now the importation of tobacco has been banned. What an illusion to expect that stopping the supply will stop the demand. If only the occupying powers could show a little more compassion for our personal needs. What do the sated know of the hungry? Or people who throw away half-smoked butts about those who eagerly sacrifice three and a half marks for one of those butts. On the black market or wherever they can get it.

• • •

Tuesday, July 1, 1947

America proposes and Russia disposes. In this case the black market for tobacco. Directly into its own pocket.

Returning home from a rehearsal Heike holds a white cigarette under my nose. "Do you know what this is?" she asks, and without waiting for my response she continues in a pompous manner, *"Droog,* friend of the poor, hope and comfort to all nicotine addicts." She raises her hand holding the cigarette. "The victory of the East over the West—at least as far as cigarettes are concerned. As many of them as you want. They've managed it."

"What?" I ask, a little alarmed.

"Well," Heike says cheerfully, "putting the profit into their own pocket." She lights her cigarette and sits down next to me on the armchair. "Now, listen to that. What does the clever American say? Tobacco is the soul of the black market. So we ban its import. What does the clever smoker say? I cannot live without tobacco. The Americans ban its import, so I must be prepared for the prices to double. What does the clever Pole say? The Germans cannot live without tobacco. The Americans ban its import. So let's invest thirty thousand dollars to buy American cigarettes and pump them into the black market. One pack equals twenty cents. One pack equals a hundred and twenty marks. That means six hundred marks per dollar. Hurrah, that's a bargain for us! So, what does the clever Russian say? Without tobacco the Germans cannot live. Six marks per cigarette is too much in the long run. So let's get into mass production. 'Droog' brand instead of Chesterfield. At two marks instead of six. What a deal!"

"And how does it taste?"

"Not bad. Certainly better than other people's butts."

I shake my head. "What a racket! They always seem to find a way to outsmart the others."

Ruth Andreas-Friedrich

Heike laughs. And for the first time she carelessly lets her cigarette burn up in the ashtray.

• • •

FRIDAY, JULY 4, 1947

Panic! The Paris Conference has failed. "No agreement could be reached between the foreign ministers of France, England and Russia," writes the *Tägliche Rundschau.*

"The intention of the Marshall Plan is to rob independent European countries of their self-reliance and place them under American control," Molotov declares in Paris. "Russia opposes the Marshall Plan because it splits Europe in two." Having said that he bows politely, says goodbye, and leaves. Bidault accompanies him to the door. *"C'est fini!"* he sighs as he turns around. That's the end of hope, the end of an indivisible Europe.

Without any mention of the fact, the curtain between East and West has begun to drop at the Elbe. People just don't know it yet. At most they suspect it because of the first indirect consequences.

Panic! The black market price of food and household necessities is shooting up feverishly. There's no gasoline to be had. Incredible sums are being paid for cars and motorcycles. Separation is imminent, all these measures suggest. Save yourself if you can! To the West . . . to the West . . . We feel as if we are standing on melting ice that is about to give way at any moment. Will we manage to reach the shore? But which shore?

France is in a tremendous crisis. Strikes, disclosure of subversive plots, the radical parties of the left and the right are gaining constantly and threaten to crush the small moderate center between them. In Spain, the Fascist Franco. Italy is about to go Communist. Wherever one looks: collectivism, catastrophe or near catastrophe.

Perhaps it is ourselves who err. Individualists against the world trend, standing in the way of the twentieth century's collectivist destiny. What remains of a democratic Europe if France turns Gaullist, if Spain marches under Franco, Italy under Togliatti, and Poland and East Germany—which means Russia—under Stalin?

178

Battleground Berlin

A grotesque situation in which the narrow strip between Elbe and Rhine, West Germany, together with England is defending democracy in Europe. Against Fascism from the West and Communism from the East. One day they might even call Mr. Hitler back from the dead in order to close the collectivist gap. Save yourself if you can! But where to? And why?

. . .

Agitated, Frank comes into my room. "There's reliable news that the Western Allies will be getting out of Berlin within the next three months. Get the suitcases out of the cellar. It's time to pack."

I'm terrified. The prospect of having to evacuate bag and baggage again after barely two years of peace seems more than miserable to me.

"Think of our Jewish friends," Frank warns. "Those who leave last fare the worst, glad in the end to escape with just their lives."

"What about Berlin? What about the bridge? Who will stay if we set a bad example."

Comfortingly, Frank pulls me to him. "We're not leaving right away," he tries to reassure me. "However, slowly we ought to come to understand that someday we will have to leave. And then we don't want to be on the other side of the curtain 'totally bombed out.' With a handkerchief in our hands as our only remaining possession."

Three hours later the first suitcase goes into the mail. A little of everything, following the pattern of air-raid shelter bags.

In the evening I am at a reception for the Allied press. "What would you do if you were in our shoes?" I ask an American journalist.

"If I were under eighteen, I would join the Communist Party. If I were over eighteen, I would leave Europe."

"Why join the Communist Party?"

"Because in ten years at the latest, Europe will be Communist," he replies, "and because it isn't worthwhile for a young person to be in opposition all his life."

Fine prospects! The cocktail I was about to drink has lost its flavor

179

now. "But wouldn't you take us along . . . I mean when you leave?" I dare to ask.

He looks impenetrable. "In such an emergency . . ." The rest of the sentence remains open. Tacitly I conclude that in such an emergency too, God will help only those who help themselves.

. . .

TUESDAY, JULY 8, 1947

It's bound to go wrong. Every day new facts make it clear just how inexorably the countries east and west of the Elbe are evolving in different directions. Already the city treasury of Berlin, substituting for the banks that have remained closed since the end of the war, issues scarcely any German banknotes anymore, but almost solely Russian-Allied notes. People call them "minus bills" because a minus sign before the identification number makes them different from those printed by the Western powers. Minus bills are not, or only reluctantly, accepted by West German banks. Here too, a gulf divides us. "It will be to no avail," I remember the words of our Communist acquaintances after the strike vote. "On May first there will be unity . . . and in six months we'll call for a merger." The six months have passed. But their goal remains the same. And imperceptibly, with stubborn perseverance, they are getting closer and closer to it. Woe to the opponent who is not yet prepared for this mentality. Who unsuspectingly falls for it again and again.

. . .

WEDNESDAY, JULY 9, 1947

England and France have not given up hope. They have sent invitations to twenty-two nations to meet on July 12 in order to discuss the Marshall Plan. West Germany is supposed to be represented by its military governors. Sixteen nations have already agreed to come. Czechoslovakia is among them too. Its prime minister, however, has gone on a suspiciously sudden trip to Moscow. Yugoslavia, Romania, Bulgaria, Poland and Albania have declined.

"Thank you, we don't need anything," they declared about the American offer of help, and ducked deeper under the shadow of "big brother." In Paris they are talking a lot about a door that "stands open." We will have to wait and see who will pass through it, after all.

• • •

FRIDAY, JULY 11, 1947

Neither Hungary nor Finland. Instead, at the last minute, one of the guests sneaked out again. Mr. Gottwald, the prime minister of Czechoslovakia. "Boy, what a talking-to they must have given him in Moscow," Heike says, displaying more shrewdness than respect.

Sooner than we anticipated, the fronts on either side of the "curtain" have been consolidated. Eastern bloc against Western bloc. Satellite states of the Soviet Union, say the Western Allies, against satellite states of U.S. capital, say the Eastern Allies. One thing is sure: The dividing line runs through the middle of Germany . . . "Pack the bags!" Frank urges.

• • •

MONDAY, JULY 21, 1947

In Paris an agreement has been reached surprisingly quickly. Amazing, how easy it is to negotiate when there is no one around who always says no when the others say yes, and always says yes when the others say no. Sometimes one wonders whether the Western Allies are still at all interested in coming to an understanding with Russia. Already in June it seemed as if Molotov's consent to come to Paris, rather than pleasing his Allies, had taken them aback. A defective limb should be cut off. An infected country, isolated. Perhaps the founding of the Cominform has evoked this insight among the Western Allies, has finally made them see through the tactics of their Eastern Allies. The Soviet tactics are to create disorder. Where chaos prevails, where hunger and discontent are ruling, people automatically turn to Communism. So they foment the strikes, interfere with reconstruction, water the currency, pursue a dilatory policy in every way conceivable.

Each month of stalling benefits rearmament—a precious gain of time for completing the atomic bomb. America has the bomb. And since Marshall's speech at Harvard they also seem to have come to the conclusion that only an economically sound Europe can form the solid bloc capable of stopping the Soviet advance toward the West.

And what is Germany's role in this program? We criticize foolish parents who treat their adolescent son as a little child, while at the same time they want to see him celebrated as a hero. He is supposed to be, simultaneously, their "good little boy" and an outstanding person whose brilliance reflects back on them. Two irreconcilable opposites in one person. "To eat the cake and have it too" is how an American would see such a conflict. Applied to our situation this saying could be altered into "Germany as a bulwark against Bolshevism, while dismantling all factories that enable Germany to be competitive." Is the bulwark supposed to begin at the Oder, the Elbe or the Rhine? Perhaps fate is assigning the task to the Western Allies to keep pulling imperceptibly at the Iron Curtain until it drops lower and lower.

• • •

SATURDAY, AUGUST 2, 1947

A sigh of relief! Vacating Berlin has been postponed. Actually it is questionable whether it has ever been seriously considered. Among authoritative circles in the military government, it has been pointed out that America has never given up an outpost.

And what about the rumor? It only came up because England did not want, or was perhaps unable, to any longer assume the cost of the occupation of Berlin. No reason to worry. America would step into the breach and in the future would cover eighty percent of the occupation costs. Berliners will get used to talking even less than before about the English and French occupying powers. The new arrangement only follows an inner truth. There are just the two opponents in the world: Russia and America.

Does that make us feel safer in Berlin? The constant up-and-down

182

of hope and fear has taught us to see the problem of our situation from a different point of view. Certainly, the Western Allies will not surrender Berlin. But they will not be able to prevent Berlin from becoming a fortress. In a fortress there is no room for cultural activity. A fortress means a front. And only those who consider themselves combatants should remain. "O Heaven," we pray, "give us a sign." The more clearly we realize that one day we will have to leave Berlin, the weaker becomes our determination to actually do so. Are we hoping for an underground passage that will lead us outside of the fortress at the very last moment? One single train a day runs from Berlin across the demarcation line. Traveling for twelve hours, one has to stand all the way to Hanover. The inspection of baggage and identity papers at the Marienborn checkpoint takes four hours. If you have eyes to see with, you hardly need a more convincing sign of how meager the communication is between Berlin and the West.

· · ·

SUNDAY, AUGUST 17, 1947

Fate has decided it for Frank, summoning him to Munich. On September 1 he will leave Berlin. It chills me to think about it. To be separated! To no longer be able to say to each other: I don't feel very happy today.

Mail from Berlin to Munich takes five days. Sometimes ten. More often fifteen or even twenty. You write into a void and out of the void, some time or other, comes an answer. Or else none. As chance will have it.

Two years ago Andrik died. Fabian is gone, and Dagmar has moved away. Jo Thäler lives in the hospital. At the end of the war we were a community. What has driven us apart? It chills me. Stay here, Frank, I want to say. But I don't. I know it would be unreasonable to do so. You don't hold back someone who has the chance to escape the fortress.

For the last two days there have been rumors that shipping furniture to the West has been banned. The interzonal train is still running. It takes about four weeks to get an interzonal transit permit, a registration card and a ticket. At the Charlottenburg Station every day, between nine and one, people fight each other for a seat on it.

"Stay here, Frank," I call out, standing at Andrik's grave. But the earth is silent and from the grave rises the smell of decay.

• • •

WEDNESDAY, AUGUST 20, 1947

"Frank is going to Munich . . . Frank is going to Munich." The phrase runs through my mind constantly. I walk the streets, and every tree, every smoke-blackened ruin, reminds me: "You were here together." How can one live when one is separated. By the fourteen days the mail takes, by four weeks of standing in line for stamps and permits and a questionable—more than questionable—interzonal train.

We pack two hundred parcels. Each weighing sixteen pounds. This is the limit by which, according to the newest ordinances, one may bring one's belongings to the Western zones. For freight transports so many permits are required that one might die before getting all of them. The post is uncertain. Those who want to be on the safe side arrange their move through registered parcels. Each weighing four pounds. In little installments, so to speak. One wary person brought it to more than a thousand parcels. We take the risk. Three times sixteen pounds of bicycle parts, at least, are a bicycle.

Only one a half weeks to go . . .

• • •

FRIDAY, AUGUST 22, 1947

. . . only nine days to go. What is more important? To remain faithful to a city or to remain faithful to a person?

"You still have me," Heike comforts.

"Sure," I smile, looking at her with gratitude.

Battleground Berlin

· · ·

Pack the knapsack, make sandwiches, fill a whiskey bottle with coffee. Frank will be traveling for thirty-five hours.

We are having a farewell breakfast at home in the housing complex at the water tower. On the table stands Andrik's photograph. Each of us lost in his own thoughts. One turns silent when there is so much to say to one another.

Yesterday we heard a rumor that Makar Ivanov was in Siberia. How quickly one gets to Siberia. And how far it is to Munich. Looking at his watch Frank gets up from the table. He lets his eyes wander over the room. This is where we forged identity papers, hid our illegals, trembled with fear of the English bombs and where, for nine years, we have hoped, risked, struggled and doubted.

We were a team. Berlin was a team, the victors were a team. At this moment—I can feel it—the resistance group "Uncle Emil" ceases to exist, the miracle of that community definitely and irretrievably sinks into the shadows of the past. To live means to adapt. It took us sixteen months to understand that to adapt to the postwar situation means to separate.

· · ·

Wednesday, September 10, 1947

A "displaced person" is a person out of place. Gradually, one almost gets the impression that half the world is out of place. When consulting a history book two hundred years from now, perhaps they will read that "the second European migration began around the year 1900 and ended around 1960, after the Third World War." Three lines in an encyclopedia under *M* for migration, and behind it an ocean of tears, hecatombs of dead, and an endless hither and thither of masses of refugees.

Where did it start? With the Greeks who were driven out of Asia

185

Minor, with the Armenians whom the Turks expelled, with the Russian emigrants, the Spanish, the Italians or the Germans? Will the refugees from the East be the last ones or the illegal emigrants to Palestine? No one is where he wants to be, no one is where he belongs.

"Displaced persons are the Fascist scum of Europe," says the Russian-licenced magazine *Neue Berliner Illustrierte*. "In their own countries they are wanted as war criminals and they prefer a nomadic life in Germany to a return." But where should they go, these unfortunates?

Yesterday, in the harbor of Hamburg, four thousand five hundred Jewish refugees were disembarked from the three *Exodus* ships and taken to two internment camps near Lübeck. "We want to be at home somewhere," they had decided and in mid-July had embarked for Haifa without official authorization. The English immigration authorities are outraged. The ship was boarded, the illegal immigrants forced to change to three English transports and return to Europe. "We want to be at home somewhere," they insist, and go on a twenty-four-day hunger strike. The ships sail to France. The passengers refuse to disembark. "Take us back to Palestine," they demand. One month goes by. The transports head for Gibraltar and from there to Hamburg. In the English occupied zone, passengers may be forcibly disembarked, if necessary. Displaced persons!

England doesn't want them, America doesn't want them. America has been chewing for a year on their offer to admit ten thousand people. At the same time they wonder why it shouldn't be possible to relocate a few million people in the ruined rest of Germany.

A group of deportees from Königsberg arrives in Berlin. Their hollow-eyed faces look dead. Of two hundred thousand Germans, six thousand are still alive, they report. In cellars, in holes, like moles under the ground. Subsisting on garbage, sometimes dead bodies, they look like animals rather than humans, corpses rather than living people. Those who recount it also bear little resemblance to living people. Displaced persons!

A freight trains rolls through the Russian zone. Overflowing with tattered figures. Children and women, a few old men among them. "Who are you, where do you come from?" people on a train running in the opposite direction call out at them. "We're the last Breslauers," cries a feeble, toothless old woman.

Battleground Berlin

Displaced persons! The lowest rank in the hierarchy of mankind. The papers complain about immorality in the relocation camps, the black marketeering in the barracks of the UNRRA.* "Asocial elements," they criticize, and most likely they would like to add: There you are, it's the Jews again!

How is one supposed to integrate if one is out of place? For two thousand years the majority of the Jews have been out of place. For twenty years some Europeans, for two years a majority of the Germans. Once uprooted it is hard to take root again. Emigrants almost never do. If everything goes well, perhaps their children will. It must be a terrible fate to be like the Wandering Jew, without a home, without an objective, to be lumped with the displaced persons.

• • •

THURSDAY, SEPTEMBER 18, 1947

News from Frank. Southern Germany is suffering its worst drought in a hundred years. Rivers dried up, numerous districts without water, power outages, transport breakdowns, dust, heat and deep, very deep, depression. The sixth of the Egyptian plagues is visited upon us. The plague of war, the plague of rape, the plague of miseries of refugees, the plague of cold, the plague of flood, the plague of drought. What will the seventh be like?

For many weeks now the sky has been relentlessly blue. Crops have withered, the cattle are lowing in the stables. One wonders what Heaven will come up with next in order to try mankind.

• • •

WEDNESDAY, SEPTEMBER 24, 1947

In Nuremberg one trial follows another. The nineteen who were sentenced last October have been followed by many others. The Nazi lawyers and prosecutors, the Nazi doctors, the accountable directors of I.G. Farben, high-ranking officers, high-ranking Party officials. For

* United Nations Relief and Rehabilitation Administration.

187

the past year and a half a day doesn't go by without the newspapers running at least one front-page column full of accounts of the Nuremberg trials. One doesn't even look at them anymore. A world tribunal in permanent session ceases to appeal to feelings of remorse. The prominent and the most prominent in the limelight of journalistic sensationalism. Heinrich Himmler's bedside rug goes to America at a top price. An awful silver goblet that someone was smart enough to engrave with "Adolf Hitler—to his beloved Reich's gamekeeper" earns its owner four cartons of Chesterfields. Justice covers her face.

And who emerges as the winner of the snail's race in the courts? He who can prove that he was "coerced" into joining the Party. He who can convince the court that he helped one or even several Jews during the Nazi regime. When one reads the reports on the exoneration of defendants by the trial courts, one gets the impression that for every persecuted Jew there are about sixty Party members who claim to have tried to ease his terrible lot, if only by occasionally donating potatoes. Not to mention the fifty million nonparty members whom one could more easily believe capable of such courageous love of their fellow man. In some districts of Berlin, for one thousand Reichsmarks may be obtained documents and eyewitness accounts that prove "one was coerced into it" or that one helped out a Jew with some potatoes.

"The basic concept is wrong," say the reasonable ones. "He who lets himself be coerced into something is not a courageous man. And certainly not a democrat. If our judges want to teach us democracy they must not reward 'having been coerced into it,' but rather confession. They are unleashing a host of irresponsibles upon the future Germany."

Each denazification procedure takes about ten months. Three months to get a trial date, two months for the confirmation of the verdict by the German authorities, and about six months for the final confirmation by the appropriate occupation authority. In the meantime one is kept in a vacuum. Neither fish nor fowl, neither citizen nor criminal. Out of place—a displaced person, a DP.

Battleground Berlin

• • •

MONDAY, SEPTEMBER 29, 1947

Sometimes I wonder how things could have gotten so miserably stuck. And it seems to me that all misfortune comes from the fact that nobody is able to put himself in another's place. Neither the non-Nazis in the place of the Nazis, nor the DPs into that of the non-DPs, nor the victors in the place of the vanquished. Everyone thinks he would have acted differently had he been in the other's position. Better, more ethical, more responsible. Has he tried it out? Everyone criticizes everyone else. No one is critical of himself. And over the constant give-and-take of accusing each other, people forget about the one thing we do need—to set a good example.

• • •

WEDNESDAY, OCTOBER 5, 1947

The fear of the coming winter weighs heavily on all Berliners. Of having to freeze through another winter . . . Heike manages to get hold of two tiled stoves. On the black market, because the ration coupons won't get you very far. Just recently a coupon-issuing office closed because it hadn't been able to procure more than a handkerchief in the course of six months. The stoves cost four hundred cigarettes, their installation fifty. Payable in "Droog," friend to the poor.

"And what do you plan to use for fuel?" I inquire.

Heike smiles encouragingly. "Time will provide and answer."

As if she had foreseen the future, within twenty-four hours the "answer" arrives. In the form of a man who toward evening rings our doorbell. Humbly he plucks at his coat, mumbles something about a good opportunity that requires quick action. From all his stammering only one word hits my ears like an electric shock: Coal!

"How much?" I hastily ask.

"Two thousand pounds."

"And what's the price?"

189

Again his answer is drowned in mumbling. "Thirty-five marks or three pounds of bread for one hundred pounds," I manage to catch. "Worker . . . unloading . . . hunger . . . ," he continues mumbling.

A miracle! My conscience, which does not approve of black marketeering, tries vaguely to resist the temptation. In vain. Perhaps if it had been warmer. In a jiffy I calculate our supplies. We have plenty of bread. The ration for an entire week is in the kitchen. So it will be bread! The man receives four loaves of bread as a deposit. In two hours he will deliver . . .

"In two hours?" Heike asks doubtingly, smiling maliciously.

We wait until midnight. We wait until three o'clock in the morning. The stove is cold and our stomachs are rumbling with hunger. Not a crumb of bread is left in the house. Heike tiptoes around me as if I were seriously ill. Slightly mad, her look tells me. Four loaves of bread! To a man at the door!

"He seemed so friendly," I weakly attempt to justify myself.

• • •

FRIDAY, OCTOBER 17, 1947

From cautious inquiries we gather that the hungry coal deliverers must have died of indigestion. Seventeen loaves of bread fell into their hands. For weeks they have been making a business out of their fellows' fear of winter. I fell for it! What a fool I am! Goodbye coal. Goodbye to a warm stove. And the worst of it is that you can't even report them to the police. Because people who live in glass houses . . .

• • •

MONDAY, OCTOBER 20, 1947

The victors still cannot make up their minds whether they want to eat their cake or have it. Eat it, their—especially the French—fear of new German aggression advises. Have it, their—especially the American—fear of Soviet aggression advises. Four days ago Marshall demanded "immediate measures to prevent a political, economic and

190

psychological collapse in Europe." At the same time, the papers published a list of industrial plants to be dismantled in the united Western zones: 682 factories, among them 302 arms-manufacturing plants. One cannot imagine what will be left after that.

A year ago today, the first elections took place in Berlin. Following the administration installed in 1945 by the Soviet commander, they were supposed to result in a free city government. What's become of it?

Reuter, who was elected mayor, has not been recognized by the Russians. Arbitrarily the Russian occupying power interferes with the work of the city council. Quarreling at every city council session. Passive resistance on the part of the Socialist Unity Party against all bourgeois measures. Because every important act of the city government requires a unanimous authorization by the Control Council, very little ever gets done. "No," the Russians say with a polite smile, if it regards a motion by the Social Democrats. "No," the Western Allies say, smiling just as politely, if it regards a motion filed by the Socialist Unity Party. One step forward, two steps back. The city council of Berlin steps warily. Foreigners who visit us claim Berlin is the most interesting city in the world. We would be more at ease if we were a little less interesting. We are hardly more than the mat on which two wrestlers are fighting for the world championship. Had they chosen Kötzschenbroda as the place to hold their duel, then perhaps Kötzschenbroda would have been the focus of interest. Of Marienborn nobody knew anything either before it became a chink in the Iron Curtain. Fate decided in favor of Berlin and it fell to it to be a four-power city. Berliners struggle earnestly to live up to their destiny. They understood it as being a "bridge" in '45. As a "bridgehead" they came to understand it in '46 and '47. In 1948 will it be a "doormat," and in 1949 perhaps even a "battlefield"?

. . .

FRIDAY, OCTOBER 31, 1947

The hostile Allies begin to drop their masks. America announces an extensive propaganda campaign against Communism. All American-oriented papers and magazines in Germany are supposed to take part in it. The ugly sound of saber rattling arises over Germany. And because Berlin is the focal point, it is loudest here.

At the same time they are getting ready for another conference of foreign ministers in London. Amazing is the patience of diplomats in continuing to look for a way out in a situation where the possibilities of communication have long since been exhausted.

• • •

TUESDAY, NOVEMBER 4, 1947

By chance a clipping from the *Neue Zeitung* falls into my hands. Its title is "The Zone Situation."

"The French," its author says, "believe that the Germans have no right to be in politics. In domestic politics as well. They encourage neither the parties nor the unions. They cool the functionaries' ambitions, they bridle all zeal in parliament. They believe that by itself a poor administration is better than good policy. The mentality of their zone is determined by a kind of political discontent.

"The Russians think differently. Politics are necessary: their politics: Socialist Unity Party politics. They support its functionaries, they sponsor its propagandists. They believe that bad policy is still better than a good administration. And because they are consistent they do everything to realize this idea. That's why the Socialist Unity Party is thriving. But the mentality of their zone is one of fear.

"The English believe that what proved successful with them should prove successful in Germany too: a majority voting system, social democracy, planned economy, total freedom to criticize. In reality only the criticism is functioning. The Germans of the British zone are masters at it. The mentality of their zone is one of frustrated know-it-alls.

"The Americans believe that a democratic attitude is preferable to any party dogma. Consequently their attitude toward German domestic politics is the least fixed. And the attitude of German domestic politics toward them is the least resentful. Paradoxically the American zone's mentality of calculated expectation is the most European."

Intelligent observations to which I have little to add. Except perhaps a characterization of the mentality of the fifth zone—the four-power city Berlin. This may best be summarized in one phrase: a dance on the edge of a volcano.

. . .

FRIDAY, NOVEMBER 14, 1947

From time to time the crater opens up and swallows one dancer or another. Now it has seized the journalist Dieter Friede. A few days ago he received a telephone call at his apartment in Wilmersdorf and was asked to come and see a friend in Friedrichshagen who had had an accident. Friede left and did not return. More and more leave and never return. They disappear—vanish into thin air. The police pretend not to know. Mr. Margraf, the chief of police, is a member of the "National Committee for a Free Germany" and does not like to see Soviet interests interfered with.

"Where is Dieter Friede?" his colleagues and friends ask, alarmed.

"Where is Dieter Friede?" the Western press picks up the question, and carries it from door to door, from ear to ear, until all Berliners are frightened and join in: "Where is Dieter Friede?"

At a city council meeting the case is argued. The Eastern press jeers: He was seen in a bar! Drunk in the Western sector! But he has been spotted there as little as the other 5,413 Berliners who, according to data compiled by the Social Democratic Party, have vanished from our city since 1945.

What good does it do to stage Sartre and Shostakovich, Thornton Wilder and Benjamin Britten. Or that we can see films in four languages and that ours is the most interesting city in the world, if we can be taken from our apartments, not knowing whether our end will come in Siberia or at the hands of GPU interrogators. In Nuremberg people are being sentenced to death for this kind of thing. But Nuremberg is in the Western zone and Berlin . . .

Poor Dieter Friede! The fact that he reported on the Eastern zone is no reason to lure him into a trap and let him vanish. Oh Andrik, dear Andrik! Perhaps you died at the right time. Frank is in Munich. Jo Thäler rarely comes by. He too has been forced into isolation by the march of events.

In the evening, when Heike and I sit huddled close together in front of the cold fireplace, it seems as if we'll never get warm again. Swing is coming over the radio. We turn the dial and the five-beat rhythm of a Russian church choir reaches our ears. Gentle, good and devout. "If only they always were like this," Heike sighs, resignedly waving her hand.

• • •

WEDNESDAY, NOVEMBER 26, 1947

The conference in London began yesterday. As usual we are informed, for the time being, only of the fact that all the important people have arrived. Accompanied by his bodyguard and a police escort, Mr. Molotov's first "No" came even before the conference had begun.

The Austrian foreign minister has arrived as well. To be there in case of need. Our "victorious brother in the Axis" dreams of an "honorable peace." To then be even better able to forget his former Nazism.

"It's sure to turn out badly," prophesies the man on the street. "It's got to fail because it just can't succeed!"

• • •

FRIDAY, DECEMBER 12, 1947

Patiently, the Austrian foreign minister waits in his hotel room. It is not an easy task to stand idly by. Little progress is being made at the London conference. Instead something else comes to the fore, stealthily, like a panther, and dangerous as an epidemic. A general strike in France. A general strike in Rome. Increasing unrest in the Balkans.

While Mr. Molotov is in London saying no with a polite smile, his fifth column tries to render Europe ripe for attack. Please, no catastrophe now, we silently pray. Not now when it is so cold and so dark.

Battleground Berlin

. . .

SATURDAY, DECEMBER 13, 1947

A song is going around the city. It's being sung in the cabarets; people whistle the tune on the street.

> If you know little Gustav,
> Don't let the Bewag* know,
> Back he quickly turns,
> And still he's always right;
> Let your meter churn,
> And on comes your light.

Hearing it people smile knowingly. "Of course, there's little Gustav! But you can also . . ." And moving their hand as if they were loosening a screw, their smile turns even slyer.

"What is it all about?" asks the uninitiated.

It is about the power supply allotment. Once again it's just barely enough to stay alive. And because necessity is the mother of invention, she invented little Gustav, a miraculous device which, when put on the electric meter, makes it run backward.

But you also can . . . Oh yes, you are capable of many illegalities when your teeth are chattering with cold. Without heat you are only half a person. With heat a meter cheater, who hardly dares to open the door when the doorbell rings. Because it could be . . . oh God, it could be the meter man!

If a law is broken by such a large percentage of the population, something must be wrong with it. Or with the people. In England, they say, there are no meter cheaters. And certainly no little Gustav. But in England people do not just vanish either. And nobody there need fear punishment for something he has not done.

---

* The Berlin utilities company.

Ruth Andreas-Friedrich

• • •

TUESDAY, DECEMBER 16, 1947

After three inconclusive weeks the London conference of foreign ministers has been adjourned. "There's no point in continuing the debate," Marshall declared.

We thought as much even before the conference began. Again they are talking about "open doors" and "still possible communication." It's odd how each era seems to need a slogan. In the Nazi period they were constantly "unmasking" their adversary; now they're always "holding open the door."

"There is a draft," one feels like calling out. The question is who will catch cold first.

• • •

SATURDAY, DECEMBER 20, 1947

Again rumors circulate that a currency reform is imminent. With time one becomes impervious to such forecasts. You just can't constantly have your rent paid five months in advance. In daily transactions money is no longer an important factor anyway. If you go to the hairdresser to have your hair washed, you must bring soap, a towel and five pieces of wood. Two pounds of rags gets you a scouring cloth. A hundred pounds of rags gets you a suit. For six pounds of bones you get a piece of soap, for four pounds of waste paper a book. With luck, four pounds of the *Völkischer Beobachter* might even get you Homer, or other favorites from Pushkin to Goethe, Shakespeare and Racine. Four pounds of Nazi newspapers wondrously obtain for you the company of the world's greatest minds.

Battleground Berlin

· · ·

WEDNESDAY, DECEMBER 24, 1947

For the first time in many years, Heike and I are spending Christmas Eve alone. Frank sent a telegram. Jo celebrates in the hospital.

As we do on every holiday, at night we climb over the cemetery fence. At least Andrik shall not feel alone. The grave mounds are frosted with snow. Suddenly Heike stops still. "Listen," she whispers, "there's somebody there."

Holding our breath we listen to the darkness. An uneasy feeling. You hear only your own heart beating, but you know somebody is out there. That eyes you can't see are looking at you, that thoughts are directed at you that you can't size up. A drop falls from the tree next to us, landing on the tombstone beneath. It makes us flinch. I reach for matches. "Are you crazy?" whispers Heike. "They'll see us!"

Slowly our eyes get used to the darkness. "It's nothing, it's nothing at all," I attempt to reassure us both while trying to pierce the darkness.

Heike bends down to pick something up. A sprig of everlasting flower. It looks familiar. But that's . . . now I know. Only yesterday I put it on Andrik's grave. "Thieves!" With one leap I am at his grave. Thieves! Gone are the flowers, gone the little Christmas tree. Gone are the boards of the bench next to the grave.

"On Christmas Eve of all days," Heike stammers and, aghast, she stares at the muddy blend of snow and earth. This is not the first time they have plundered the cemetery. Why should the dead need flowers when the living have nothing to eat? Why should they need benches when he who needs the wood freezes in front of a cold stove? Behind the hedge something crunches in the snow. We do not turn around.

· · ·

FRIDAY, JANUARY 2, 1948

Happy New Year! King Michael of Rumania abdicated. In Bucharest a people's republic has been proclaimed. The king should

197

consider himself lucky that they let him leave the country un-harmed.

Here the Eastern Bloc—there the Western Bloc. Although the embargo on interzonal shipments of personal belongings has been lifted, its enforcement is so complicated that, practically speaking, nothing has changed. A relocation permit to the Western zones, an exemption order, a statutory declaration accompanying the customs declaration, authorization by the local military commander and a waybill of the German interzonal transport authority, authorized by the Russian military administration. But what would the Russian military administration authorize anyway? Certainly not shipments for the sake of a person with Western sympathies. We feel powerless in the face of approaching disaster, and even more powerless to try and prevent it.

• • •

SATURDAY, JANUARY 10, 1948

"Have you heard?" my newspaper vendor whispers, confidentially leaning over the counter. "Stalin is dead."

Taken aback I recoil. "Since when?"

"Since the day before yesterday." He purses his lips and winks meaningfully. "Revolution!" he whispers prophetically.

"Stalin is supposed to be dead," Heike greets me.

"You don't believe that, do you?" I reply.

"Why can't something like that be true for a change?" she counters. "Sooner or later even dictators die."

But not the right ones and not at the right time, I think dejectedly. Almost always years too late.

• • •

MONDAY, JANUARY 19, 1948

Is Stalin dead? Does he lie seriously ill at the Kremlin? We do not know. Three days ago the Soviet military government revoked all frontier-crossing permits, that is, they revoked all permits to leave Berlin by car.

"It's just temporary," the competent authorities try to reassure us. "New ones are coming. It's still business as usual."

Well, they may issue new permits someday. The only question is to whom, or better even, to whom they will deny them. For the time being all traffic over the border is stopped. Strict controls on all major roads. Secondary routes are sealed off with roadblocks. People whisper to each other: "If this isn't a dress rehearsal . . ." And more doggedly than ever they struggle for a seat on the interzonal train.

• • •

THURSDAY, JANUARY 29, 1948

We hang on General Clay's every word, weighing every possible interpretation. Will he stay in Berlin? Are the Americans going to leave the city?

"If the Russians were to block the railway, we would supply our troops by air, and the Russians would have no choice but to take over the food supply of the Western sectors as well," he is supposed to have said recently.

Well and good! But how will we fare then? The example of the Russian zone is not very reassuring. The example of the prisoners of war returning from the Soviet Union almost prompts you to turn on the gas.

Heike adds up what's left on our monthly ration card. Four kilos of bread, one kilo of pasta. "We should set up an emergency supply," she suggests. "Rye flour soup is still better than grass spinach and bark stew."

• • •

MONDAY, FEBRUARY 2, 1948

Finally, after nine months of applications, questionnaires and political investigations, the publishing house I work for has been licensed by the appropriate military authorities. At the same time the procurement of paper has become more and more difficult due to increasing transport restrictions. We fight for every ton. One cannot print without paper. The Russians have paper. Understandably, they only give it to those who are willing to sing their song on it. To us their propaganda rings more and more dissonant. Not because it means Communism but because it means compulsion to accept it. Coercion, through unwelcome means, to dance to Moscow's tune. We do not want happiness after the Moscow fashion.

• • •

WEDNESDAY, FEBRUARY 18, 1948

Biting cold. On my way to the publishing house nipping frost nearly cuts my ears. Gruff people hurry past. In the editorial office everybody sits huddled together around the only stove.

"No paper again," the editor-in-chief greets me. On the black market it has risen to three thousand marks a ton. "The Soviets make us pay dearly for their ideology." He doodles on the blotting paper in front of him. "If they keep making it so difficult to obtain transit permits, we might as well give up before we've even gotten started."

"Or try to get a Russian licence," our apprentice grumbles from the corner where, his fingers numb with cold, he is writing some kind of list.

I take a look at what he is doing over there. "Mr. David Smith, 119 West Avenue, Chicago," I make out. "Mrs. Gladys Brown, 7740 Bradford Street, Lost Angeles."

"But what are you up to?"

He looks up from his work. "I'm copying addresses for CARE* packages," he mumbles.

I'm taken aback. "For CARE packages?"

"Well," he replies obstinately, "if they don't get the idea themselves . . ."

I feel my blood freeze. "So you copy just any addresses?"

"Out of *Who's Who,*" he nods, not appearing to understand why I am getting so angry.

The editor-in-chief clears his throat. Without a word he points at

---

* Cooperative for American Relief Everywhere.

two newspaper clippings in front of him. I glance over one of them: "Only today I received the sad news that my dear mother, Mrs. Rosa X., my three sisters, Hanna, Clara and Käthe, as well as my nephew Franz K. and my nieces Esther and Miriam have died in Auschwitz." A black edge, a name and an address in California. Deeply moved I put the paper aside. Seven people! Out of one family! I glance at the second clipping. Three lines. Underlined with blue pencil. ". . . because of this announcement I received forty letters from Germans unknown to me, of which thirty-seven asked me for relief packages."

I look at the editor-in-chief. He grins. I look at the apprentice. I feel like slapping him in the face. "They just want to starve us," he growls rebelliously.

I am speechless with rage. "And how many packages did you send when millions of Chinese starved in China?"

"Or in India, or Greece," our secretary suddenly joins in.

An awkward silence. Everybody looks embarrassed. Then our apprentice grabs his list and crumples it up. I didn't send one either, I think. How great and admirable are people who send relief packages to unknown fellow men. No matter whether these fellow men live in China, India or . . . in Germany.

• • •

THURSDAY, FEBRUARY 19, 1948

Irritated, Heike turns off the radio. "That beats all," I hear her say angrily. "Do you know whom they've just arrested? The Scholtz-Klink woman! Our dear Reich women's leader."

"I thought she was dead."

"Not at all. She has been hiding in a castle. Under a false name. She supposedly has even been denazified. Next thing you know, they will have awarded her a prize." Heike shudders. "Again typical. The little guys are being hanged and the big shots walk away."

"We were already firmly aware of that in 1945," I try to soothe her anger.

"All the worse then," Heike complains.

• • •

SUNDAY, FEBRUARY 22, 1948

The differences intensify. A governmental crisis in Prague. Take-over by the Communist minority. Czechoslovakia too seems to be going Soviet. Check to the West! smiles Stalin.

• • •

MONDAY, FEBRUARY 23, 1948

In London representatives of England, France and America are meeting to discuss the economic reconstruction of Western Europe. Check to the East! smiles Truman.

• • •

WEDNESDAY, FEBRUARY 25, 1948

Moscow offers Finland a military pact like those with Rumania and Hungary. If it is ratified, Finland's independence will be done for. Check to the West, smiles . . .

• • •

THURSDAY, FEBRUARY 26, 1948

Belgium, Holland and Luxembourg too are being consulted at the three-power conference in London. They plan to create a preliminary stage for an all-German government by expanding the bizonal economic council. Check to the East, smiles . . .

Battleground Berlin

. . .

In Czechoslovakia action committees have been formed to purge the entire country of politically unreliable elements. Woe to him who thinks differently! Check . . . , smiles Stalin.

. . .

SATURDAY, MARCH 6, 1948

Two days ago negotiations started in Brussels for a Western European pact. Check . . . , smiles Truman.

. . .

TUESDAY, MARCH 9, 1948

Russia protests against the resolutions of the three-power conference in London, and, under the title of "German Economic Commission," proposes the formation of an Eastern zone government. Check—but not checkmate!

. . .

FRIDAY, MARCH 19, 1948

While the Western and Eastern power barometers are rising alternately, the parties in Berlin are preparing for a public rally on March 18, the anniversary of the 1848 revolution.

"Freedom, peace, democracy," shout fifty thousand demonstrators gathered on the Platz der Republik in the Western sector. Rain is pouring down on them. Wind tears the words from the speakers' lips and carries them flutteringly over the surging crowd. Revolutionary songs are sung.

Ruth Andreas-Friedrich

"We don't want another dictatorship! We demand the return of our deportees," shouts Franz Neumann, chairman of the Social Democratic Party in Berlin, shaking his fist toward the Eastern sector.

"Freedom . . . freedom . . . freedom," applauds the crowd.

Two Soviet officers stand silent in their midst. They do not flinch, and their eyes look dull as iron.

"Warmongers, Nazis, reactionaries, secessionists," shouts the speaker, shaking his fist toward the Western sector.

"Unity . . . unity . . . unity," applauds the crowd.

A few American journalists stand silent in their midst. They do not flinch, and their eyes look as cold as steel.

• • •

SUNDAY, MARCH 21, 1948

The Western and the Eastern press outdo each other in describing their own rally as gigantically as possible, while belittling the one of the other side. Each side accuses the other of being a lackey, while the onlooker wonders doubtingly which of the two demonstrations might have found the approval of the 1848 revolutionaries.

Yesterday a Finnish delegation went to Moscow to conclude the negotiations on the pact with Russia. "If Finland falls we will be next," predicts the man on the street.

And signs are increasingly pointing that way. Nearly every hour brings more alarming news. On Saturday the Soviets left the Control Council after a heated debate. The Socialist Unity Party—imitating the Czech example—has formed action committees for purging unreliable elements. Again, masses of people flee toward the West. A few weeks ago, after their district leaders had passed some time in Karlshorst, the Eastern zone party districts of the Christian Democratic Party and the Liberal Democratic Party, the only parties permitted in the Soviet-occupied zone besides the Socialist Unity Party, were unexpectedly streamlined. A witch hunt has begun against the party districts in the Eastern sector of Berlin that have not followed suit. Almost daily people disappear under mysterious circumstances.

"Do what you can to get out of Berlin," writes Frank. "If you wait much longer it may be too late."

But where shall we go? My publishing house is based in Berlin, and when I talk to the licensing authority about a possible evacuation, they look at me in surprise. "But why? *We* are staying in Berlin."

And we? For the hundredth time we discuss this question at the editorial office. Will they really stay?

"Of course not," says one.

"Of course they will," says another.

"It's very simple," says a third. "Berlin will be exchanged for Thuringia and the status quo of 1945 will be reestablished." This formulation, so considerate of Western prestige, is spoken with such glibness that one may readily assume this isn't the first time he's expressed it.

To me the whole affair does not seem simple at all. And when looking at the gloomy faces of my fellows it doesn't seem to me that they think it's that simple either.

• • •

THURSDAY, MARCH 25, 1948

Dieter Friede. Dieter Friede! The mystery of his disappearance has been cleared up, meanwhile, in a dreadful manner.

On November 1, at two o'clock in the afternoon, three GPU officials in civilian clothes showed up at the house of one Dr. Dau, a physician in East Berlin.

"Write," they say politely, "that a man by the name of Seiler is lying in your apartment suffering a serious knee injury."

"But I don't know anyone by the name of Seiler," the physician objects.

"Write," the officials repeat. Their tone is polite but very firm. Dr. Dau writes.

"Now call Mr. Friede and ask him to come to the injured man in your apartment."

"But there is no injured person in my apartment," the physician protests.

One of the officials pulls a piece of paper out of his pocket. "Here is Mr. Friede's telephone number. And now will you please . . ." His tone is polite but very firm.

Dr. Dau telephones. He asks Mr. Friede to come to his apartment.

The evening passes, the night and the next morning. In the doctor's waiting room sit three GPU officials. They are polite but very firm. At last Dieter Friede arrives. And shortly thereafter a wine-red limousine drives away with him and his captors.

Somewhere in the West lives his daughter, Christiane, a child barely ten years old. "I hope Papa had a chance to kill himself before they killed him," the child says, weeping upon hearing the news. Something is very wrong when ten-year-old children talk about "killing oneself." The world order should not let it happen. But the world order . . .

• • •

WEDNESDAY, MARCH 31, 1948

. . . is coming apart in a more and more alarming way. Along the demarcation line dramatic events seem to be under way. There are rumors of barbed-wire fences, troop concentrations and increasing numbers of police. The illegal shipment to the West of the contents of a two-room apartment costs twenty thousand marks. Save our souls, sigh millions of Berliners.

General Clay, speaking in Washington, is quoted as saying that the demarcation line between Eastern and Western ideology runs along the Elbe. "We believe that we have established a border there that we shall hold," he added.

And what about Berlin? Or Thuringia? And the status quo of 1945? If only one could penetrate the future with X-rays! But perhaps then one might pray like Dieter Friede's daughter: Here's hoping we manage to kill ourselves first.

• • •

FRIDAY, APRIL 2, 1948

Here's the picture! The Soviets have pushed the button and the already meager communication between East and West has been reduced to a minimum. "To stop irregularities and to guarantee orderly

206

interzonal transit" is their official explanation, and effective immediately they impose a rigorous surveillance of all shipments to and from Berlin, as well as strict controls on all travelers from the West who pass through their zone.

News from the border areas follows in rapid succession. "Police, military and civilian, being deployed in force around Helmstedt . . . the two regularly scheduled official American trains halted at Marienborn . . . the official English trains denied permission to pass through . . . sixty-seven travelers on the official French train detained by Russian officials."

At the Brandenburg Gate and other checkpoints between the Russian and the Western sectors, Soviet soldiers and German police are stopping every vehicle that crosses the sector boundary. The city is feverish with anxiety. Never before has war seemed so imminent.

As soon as I get home I rush to the radio. RIAS—the American station. "General Clay has been authorized to take all necessary steps. We are prepared for anything." A great weight is lifted off my heart. So they will do something!

The Berlin station—the voice of Soviet Russia. "Expansion of interzonal traffic." What? Did I hear it right? "Some border crossings have been temporarily closed in order to make repairs necessitated by the uncommon strain to the railroad tracks." So there we have it: bridge repairs, defective railroad tracks and technical difficulties. Appearing like ministering spirits as soon as Aladdin Sokolovski rubs the magic lamp. Temporarily! Temporarily, just for the fun of it, the railroad tracks of Marienborn will be repaired in the Ural Mountains. The Americans had better act now!

• • •

SUNDAY, APRIL 4, 1948

And they have. So it says in bold letters in the paper this morning. "General Clay is authorized to open fire if necessary."

". . . to open fire," the words spread by word of mouth across the city within an hour. People tell it to one another, whisper it or say it over the telephone, and then smile with relief. It's been weeks since

207

any words have had such a comforting effect as these. But do we really want another war?

"It's the only way out," many say. "As long as the power struggle between Russia and America has not been settled, there will be no peace."

"It's madness," reply the reasonable ones. "But experience has shown that dictators always go as far as the democrats let them. Move for move. Why can't the Americans think up some bridge repairs too? Why don't they come up with the idea to require a service area every two hundred meters along the highway from Helmstedt to Berlin. Composed of tanks, for example. There won't be a war if the Americans are prepared for one."

Could their reasoning be right? For the time being, however, all traffic at border crossings has come to a standstill, and General Clay is authorized "to open fire if necessary."

• • •

MONDAY, APRIL 5, 1948

Now the Allied military authorities too seem to dissolve. "In order to facilitate and expedite their work," the Soviet commander has proposed the suspension of several working committees, and at the same time he announced that Soviet representatives would no longer participate in them. We take notice of the fact and keep waiting for the "American service stations." And for the time being, West Berlin receives by air what it can't get overland. Three days ago a so-called airlift was established by the English and the Americans and it has been reported that already twenty-five tons of food have been flown into the city. Twenty-five tons is twenty-five thousand kilograms. Since the population of the Western sectors is about two million people, that means twelve and a half grams per person. Not including members of the occupying forces. May Heaven preserve us from having to depend permanently on this means of supply.

Battleground Berlin

. . .

THURSDAY, APRIL 8, 1948

Just as unexpectedly as it began, the blockade has been lifted. Nobody talks about defective railroad tracks anymore, and the bridges seem to have been repaired overnight. Letters arrive from the Western zones. "Get ready to leave. Seize the opportunity. The next time the door slams shut it won't open up again so soon."

Once more I try my luck with the licensing authority. They shake their heads. "It's a matter of pride," they tell me. "*We* stay here."

"Of course," I stammer, feeling like a traitor.

. . .

SATURDAY, APRIL 17, 1948

The appearance of normality is deceptive. Beneath the cover of alleged order, there is feverish activity. On April 7 the post offices in Berlin were notified that from now on all shipments to the West must receive Russian authorization. Despite all efforts they have still not succeeded in obtaining the necessary forms for filing an application for authorization. Parcels keep piling up at the post offices. One hundred thousand, two hundred thousand, three hundred thousand. In vain the postal authorities request the right to refuse any more of them. As in the fairy tale about the gruel that wouldn't stop rising over the edge of the pot, the warehouses are overflowing with parcels. And there are still no American tanks on the highway between Helmstedt and Berlin. "We can't start a war over parcels in Berlin," the Americans say. Certainly not. Not because of the interzonal corridor either. *One* corridor as a cause for a world war certainly should suffice.

Tomorrow there will be elections in Italy. There is the possibility that the Communists will attempt a coup d'état. It is generally assumed that the Americans will intervene militarily in such a case. We hope it won't come to that. Finland has proven that it is possible to hold one's ground without getting into a war. After six weeks of negotiations,

209

they've managed to avoid getting swallowed up by Russia. Never would we have imagined that Finland would offer inspiration to us.

• • •

THURSDAY, APRIL 22, 1948

To hold out. Not to lose one's head. To clench one's teeth and take courage from the fact that sooner or later things will change.

Three of our acquaintances have disappeared in the past couple of days. One a journalist, another a Social Democrat, and the third was employed by an American office. He was bringing files from one office to another and never returned. He has been missing now for thirty-eight hours. It is of no avail that week after week the courts convict kidnappers. The theft of living flesh continues unabated. The list of men and women who have disappeared in Berlin since 1945, published in the *Tagesspiegel,* grows longer every day. "Let's hope they managed to kill themselves first," one fervently prays at every name.

Because Police Chief Margraf keeps silent, the press has taken matters into its own hands by instructing people how they may best protect themselves against kidnapping and illegal arrest. "Make them identify themselves . . . Remember their badge numbers, start screaming in case they use force, resist, fight back, and attract as much attention as possible so your next-door neighbors, family members and people in the neighborhood notice," it warns. And this going on in the twentieth century!

• • •

FRIDAY, APRIL 23, 1948

Italy held out too. No coup d' état, no overthrow, no need to intervene militarily. Perhaps slowly the Soviets will realize that, with the coming of the Second World War, they let slip the chances for their plan to bolshevize Europe. Perhaps they will still reach an agreement in Berlin. Heike and I celebrate this glimmer of hope on the horizon with a holiday schnapps. At eight marks fifty a glass.

"Damned expensive," I say.

But Heike laughs. "Currency reform evasion," she says and cheerfully downs her glass.

• • •

SATURDAY, MAY 1, 1948

Posters, demonstrations, festive May Day rallies. Again the fraternal parties demonstrate, going in opposite directions. At the post offices the number of parcels increases by another hundred thousand, and since yesterday five railroad cars full of letters from the West are standing in Marienborn, waiting in vain to be cleared. I am afraid we drank our schnapps too soon. So much for that glimmer of hope.

• • •

WEDNESDAY, MAY 12, 1948

Radio Moscow: "Exchange of diplomatic notes between America and the Soviet Union. Mutual desire to discuss and settle outstanding differences."

Radio London: "The English government has learned of the renewed contacts between the United States and Russia only through the newspaper."

Radio Paris: "Isn't the Moscow dove of peace rather a bomb of peace?"

Radio Stockholm: "In case of conflict the Scandinavian states must try to stay out of it."

Radio Berlin: "The United States and the Soviet Union agree to further negotiations."

"Attempts to settle affairs. Exchange of opinions. The United States harbors no hostile or aggressive intentions toward the Soviet Union." Like wildfire it shoots across the world. Inflaming people, arousing passionate discussions. America negotiates with Russia! If they negotiate, there won't be war. If they negotiate . . . Oh, hope, oh, glimmer of hope. Oh, what a wondrous dawning of renewed hope.

But why didn't the Allies know about it? Why, we wonder, were the Russians in such a hurry to announce this new attempt at peacemaking.

・ ・ ・

THURSDAY, MAY 13, 1948

Because again it failed. A clarification of positions but not of the problem. What remains of the "glimmer of hope" is the "door" that "still stands open." Russia talks about it. America talks about it, while at the Control Council and the demarcation line one door after the other slams shut.

・ ・ ・

MONDAY, MAY 24, 1948

On the door of our building a sign is posted: "If you want to avert misery in Germany sign the petition for a plebiscite."

On the building next door a sign is posted: "A partitioned Germany will prolong our misery. A united Germany will ensure our daily bread."

On all doors on our street, signs are posted. Sidewalks and streets are littered with handbills. "Berlin fights for a plebiscite. Big campaign by the Socialist Unity Party from May 23 to June 13. Plebiscite on German unity."

The message sounds tempting. But behind the plebiscite is the People's Committee. Behind the People's Committee is the government of the Eastern zone. Behind the government of the Eastern zone is the SMA, that is, the Soviet Military Administration.

"For the plebiscite to prevent the partition of Germany," says the Socialist Unity Party.

"Against the plebiscite as a matter of Soviet foreign politics," says the Social Democratic Party.

So one side says yes, the other says no. If you are not sure what to

212

do, you can count your buttons to decide. One must admit that, judging by outward appearances, the moral justification rests on the side of the Soviet Union. They demand what we should desire. Unity, joint currency reform, withdrawal of occupation forces and peace with Germany. So why do we resist? Because we are afraid. We have been afraid since 1933. First of the Gestapo, the concentration camps, and of running risks to express anti-Nazi opinions in Hitler's Germany. Then of the GPU, the concentration camps, and of running risks to express anti-Soviet opinions in Soviet-occupied Germany. We distrust this new call for peace because in it we discern the fatal future refrain of annexation. Intimations of lock and key. The tiny dot of Berlin locked in by the vast Soviet zone. All those countries under Soviet influence have been cut off from the Western world since 1917. And in those countries, anyone who does not conform to the will of the rulers disappears behind bars.

Since 1945, two hundred thousand people from the Eastern zone are presumed to have been transported to Russia. About thirty thousand people are wasting away in the concentration camps of Sachsenhausen and Buchenwald. Maybe Makar Ivanov is among them. And Count X., or our next-door neighbor, or Dieter Friede, or that Social Democratic Party official who two weeks ago, when he went to his niece's confirmation in the Russian zone, was taken away at night by soldiers and police and disappeared.

The list of people we are mourning becomes longer and longer. This may be no criterion. It may be there are circles in Berlin or even in the Eastern zone who are missing none of their friends. Under the Nazis too there were many who didn't miss anybody, who knew nothing of concentration camps and arrests, who didn't know any Jews or politically persecuted persons, and who swore by all that's holy that everything to this effect was nothing but a concocted horror story. Maybe then as now we've been too one-sided in our choice of friends, too rigid in our condemnation of certain behavior. How is one to make sense of it all?

On May 15 the State of Israel was proclaimed in Palestine. On the same day the Arabs flew four air raids against Tel Aviv. Yesterday the Jewish capital, Jerusalem, was about to capitulate. How is one to make sense of it all?

Ruth Andreas-Friedrich

• • •

Prices are rising. One scarce commodity after another disappears from the black market. Currency reform seems certain now. "Devaluation ten to one . . . The Russians go along with it . . . the Russians don't go along with it . . . Berlin will have Eastern currency . . . Berlin will have Western currency . . . Berlin will have its own special currency." We may choose which solution we want to prepare ourselves for.

"I think for a starter we should assume it will be the Reichsmark," Heike says resolutely, and emptying the contents of her purse onto the table she begins to count. She counts fervently for a long time. At last she looks at the pile of paper and says: "Today's junk, tomorrow's wallpaper. I opt for junk."

"What do you mean?" I ask with interest.

"I mean that today this pile of paper will still buy us some kind of junk, while tomorrow it might be worth no more than some scraps of paper barely worth using for wallpaper."

In the afternoon we set out to "invest Reichsmarks." The investment opportunities are limited. Toys, household goods, lamps, cosmetics, baking essences, costume jewelry. "Junk" is the correct term for most of what is on the market. Heike has made up a list: toys to give away, household articles for our own use, one or two lamps—provided they are not too ugly, and certainly no baking essences, no handicrafts, and of the cosmetics only those that may be assumed not too harmful to health and beauty. "Which means none of them," I conclude, remembering our past experiences with toothpastes that turned into cement, with crumbling lipsticks, with evil-smelling lotions and hair tonics consisting of water and some unidentified coloring agent.

The stores are crowded as they are in peaceful times. Apparently we are not the only ones, these days, who are inclined to stockpile toys, bulky kitchen utensils and ugly lamps.

"What are we going to do with all this junk?" I grimly inquire as we walk along Steglitzer Hauptstrasse loaded down with our pur-

214

chases. Six kitchen knives that do not cut, six tin spoons with edges that do, a useless soap dish, four wooden ladles full of cracks, two lamps without sockets or switches, but with nightmarishly patterned lampshades, and in spite of all, six tubes of cement toothpaste, six crumbling tubes of lipstick, and toys—enough toys to open a toy store.

"Don't worry," Heike tries to comfort me, "at least we skimmed the cream. Those who come after us will fare worse."

• • •

FRIDAY, JUNE 11, 1948

Buying fever, fear of currency devaluation, crowds in every store. The investment frenzy is spreading like an epidemic, enticing people to spend their money, driving them through the stores, up and down the streets, not permitting them to rest until they have spent their last hundred-mark bill. Incredible prices are paid for scarce commodities. One pound of strawberries for twenty-five marks, one pound of cherries for twelve marks.

"We're not selling any," the cherry tree owners of the western suburbs demur. "We're waiting for the currency reform."

"Then you can wait until you are blue in the face," prospective buyers retort angrily and hurry after the next opportunity.

To invest, to invest . . . just to avoid ruin! From hour to hour, the Reichsmark's value drops. Banknotes fly about. A tip of five marks, a tip of ten, twenty marks to a beggar. Hundreds of marks are spent in bars that serve spirits, thousands are spent in illegal pubs. The topic of conversation in the subway: where to invest money. The topic of conversation at the publishing house: where to invest money. The topic of conversation at home, on the street, to the left and to the right, inside and outside: where to invest money.

"I buy coffee," someone says. "One can always use coffee." And he goes and buys twelve pounds of coffee at twelve hundred marks a pound. His savings from three years of work. Devaluation: one for ten. It's going to be expensive coffee this man will be drinking after the currency reform.

This person buys a hundred chisels, another buys two thousand test

215

tubes, someone else spends three hundred marks on laxatives, and the next one, ninety marks on health tea. At the municipal railroad stations discreet briefcase carriers make profits like never before selling American chocolate, candy and caramels. They disappear as soon as the police show up, only to return all the more numerous as soon as the coast is clear again. Berlin is selling out. Berlin is in a panic. To invest . . . to invest, just to avoid ruin.

• • •

MONDAY, JUNE 14, 1948

And yet we still do not know what our currency will be and whether the Soviets will go along or not. According to press reports there is "a door always standing open" in this matter too. However, inquiring among Allied circles one is dismayed to learn that a "temporary closing of the border" is expected soon. What sort of door is it that remains open when this one slams shut again. At least for us, who do not live in front, but rather behind it.

• • •

TUESDAY, JUNE 15, 1948

The prices go up every hour. One pound of coffee, two thousand marks. One cigarette, thirty marks. You are lucky to find one at all because the black marketeers too are beginning to feather their nests. Hoarding . . . hoarding, rather than selling at all for Reichsmarks.

The last useless products and decorative articles disappear from the shop windows. "Closed due to illness . . . temporarily closed due to lack of supply." "Sold out" signs posted on the glass doors of the stores are spreading like typhus.

I enter my favorite bar. Three days ago it was crowded with customers and the waiters were sweating running from table to table with loaded trays and stuffed wallets. Now the chairs are empty. Only at the bar stands one solitary customer drinking a modest seltzer. Beer —sold out, spirits—sold out, matches, cigarettes, tobacco—entirely out of the question! I ask. I beg. I implore the waiter, the porter, the owner. With great effort and distress, the latter struggles with himself, finally letting me have a crushed Chesterfield. "Because it's you! My last one!" he says, and without the slightest scruple he charges me forty marks for it. Those who come last pay the highest prices, I tell myself, feeling rather immoral about it.

With all the time spent feverishly investing one's money one hardly finds a moment to read the paper. Supposedly, Sokolovsky is still talking about a joint currency reform, while pretending not to notice what is going on around him. Between purchases one finds out about detained mail trains and freight shipments, about new trenches being dug along the border, about travelers being arrested and—oh, that familiar excuse—that the bridge on the highway between Helmstedt and Berlin has had to be closed for an indefinite period due to "urgently needed construction work."

• • •

WEDNESDAY, JUNE 16, 1948

The throng turns into panic, the fever into frenzy. To invest, to hoard, to pocket, to divest again. The price of coffee climbs to twenty-four hundred marks. Heike and I stay home and contentedly inspect our toys, kitchen utensils, lamps and cosmetics. Compared with the junk one finds now, we really did skim the cream. Now, the cracked wooden ladles and the kitchen knives that do not cut seem high-quality products to us.

"And furthermore, we didn't have our clothes torn off," Heike says, gratified. "It strengthens one's self-esteem to be able to celebrate while others are running themselves ragged." She turns on the radio and, with an air of leisurely enjoyment, she listens to the news.

No definite date for the announcement of the currency reform. Instead, a row at Allied military headquarters. And—disgrace upon disgrace—the court in Marburg has declared Major Herber, accused of "having forced his way into the room of General Olbricht on July 20, 1944, together with a troop of heavily armed officers, arresting him and shooting at Count von Stauffenberg, and thus having dealt a fatal

217

blow to the July 20 operation," as "not accountable." Then the radio falls silent . . . And then . . . it comes out with the truth about Dieter Friede. Frank Howley, head of the American military government in Berlin, publicizes his correspondence in this matter with General Kotikov, the Soviet commander of the city.

On November 7, the U.S. government formally requests an explanation from the appropriate Soviet authorities. On November 17, General Kotikov replies: "Your letter requesting an investigation concerning the missing journalist Dieter Friede has unfortunately reached me only this morning. At this point I can inform you that neither I nor my staff know anything concerning this matter." He concludes his letter with the obliging promise: "I will take all necessary steps in my sector in order to thoroughly investigate the matter, and shall immediately notify you of the results."

Exactly a month later, on December 18, this "immediate notification" arrives. "I'd like to inform you that after a thorough investigation of the case of Dieter Friede, conducted by the Russian military headquarters, we have established that the Russian authorities have not taken a German by this name into custody, neither on the day you mentioned nor on any day since. Nobody by this name could be found in hospitals or other institutions within the Russian sector. If Friede has really disappeared, we advise you to question the other commanders of the Allied occupying powers."

All this happened seven months ago. Now the Russians announce that they arrested Dieter Friede on November 2 and that he has been in their custody since. "He was a spy. He admitted it himself," they say to justify their actions. But why did they deny it for seven months? Why do they lie and claim what they themselves do not believe. We listen to the report and the blood freezes in our veins. Makar Ivanov too was supposed to have admitted something. "They smashed their clubs on him" in order to make him do it. What matter property and investment, what good are all the words about unity, peace, people's government, as long as the reality is such as it is? So brutal, mendacious and unfathomable.

Battleground Berlin

· · ·

THURSDAY, JUNE 17, 1948

Every mark bill burns like fire in one's hands or pockets. Buying, buying, no matter whether one can use the stuff or not. A rumor flies across the city. "Stamps are supposed to keep their value." Greedily the mob of buyers storms the windows for stamps at the post offices. Long lines of people, screaming and pushing. "Ten sheets of twenty-four-pfennig stamps. Five hundred local postcards, five hundred international postcards." People stock up on stamps enough to supply their great-grandchildren.

Municipal railroad tickets good for ten rides are supposed to keep their value. And the five-ride tickets for the streetcars. There is hardly anyone who still buys single tickets. If this madness goes on much longer we will all end up in the insane asylum. And still nobody knows yet whether Berlin will be included in the currency reform. East mark, West mark, Berlin mark. People act on suspicions. "Come what may, we're already broke anyway."

A special announcement on the radio. Tomorrow evening at six the date of the currency change will be announced in the Western zones. Tonight the Russians demonstratively left the meeting of the Allied commanders. Which means they will not be going along with it.

· · ·

FRIDAY, JUNE 18, 1948

Two more hours to go. We are glued to the radio. People are rushing about on the street. Hardly a store is still open. Fifteen minutes, ten minutes . . . Silence! Is it the calm before the storm or after? Who knows. Now it comes! The announcer clears his throat. We hear him breathe and the rustling of paper. "The first law enacted by the military governments of the United States, Great Britain and France to reform the German currency takes effect on June 20. Devaluation ten to one. The new currency is called the Deutsche Mark. The old

219

currency will be withdrawn from circulation as of June 21. Coins and notes with a nominal value of no more than one mark, as well as stamps, remain temporarily legal tender at a tenth of their nominal value." And then: ". . . At first Berlin will remain unaffected by the monetary reform. For the time being Berlin as a four-power city retains its old monetary system. No economic barriers between Berlin and the Western zones."

The storm's wind blows at force eleven. Over the demarcation lines, the sector boundaries and the newspapers' printing presses.

• • •

SATURDAY, JUNE 19, 1948

The Soviet Military Administration, the SMA, protests. The Socialist Unity Party protests. The People's Council, the Soviet-inspired parliament of the Eastern zone, summoned to a special meeting, protests. Marshall Sokolovsky appeals to the citizens of Germany: "The separate Western currency is illegal. Berlin is part of the Eastern zone. Circulation of the notes issued in the Western zones is illegal in the Soviet-occupied zone and in Berlin, which is part of the Soviet zone. Importing them is punishable by law." Damn it, that sounds quite clear!

"If they're clever they will close the border," says Heike. "Otherwise they'll be up to their necks in Reichsmarks. In two days a lot can be transferred from over there . . ."

The border is already closed. With rattling noise the Iron Curtain finally came down between Helmstedt and Marienborn at midnight last night. Just now the SMA announced: "In connection with the separate currency reform the Soviet Military Administration has been forced to take the following measures in order to protect the interests of the population and the economy:

"All travel to and from the Soviet-occupied zone of Germany is suspended.

"Entry is refused to vehicle traffic of every sort coming from the Western zones, including all traffic on the highway between Helmstedt and Berlin.

Battleground Berlin

"Passage of pedestrians from the Western zones into the Soviet-occupied zone via the checkpoints along the demarcation line is suspended."

Now we're in for it! Snap, said the mouse finding herself trapped! We poor little mice of Berlin!

. . .

Sunday, June 20, 1948

"What now?" I ask Heike. "What now?" Heike asks me. "What now?" all Berliners wonder on this Sunday of the Western currency reform.

The papers offer little new information. Only that feverish activity had set in at the printing presses of the press licensed in the East, and many rumors are circulating as to its purpose and intent. People talk about a new currency for the Eastern zone. About notes being stamped, about perforation and production of so-called stickers that, stuck onto the old money, are supposed to form an improvised emergency currency. In any case, it seems that up to the very last moment the Russians neither believed it nor were they in any way prepared for the West to take this step.

We have no more money to spend, and even if we had it there is hardly any possibilty to spend it. The tension of the last days suddenly has given way to a vacuum. The issue of currency reform seems to have left all Berliners with an upset stomach. A morning-after feeling is in the air. One feels like having been left standing in the cold.

"The best thing to do is to go for a walk," Heike recommends. "Some fresh air might eliminate the whole mess from our minds."

No sooner said than done, and in the afternoon we stroll along the Havel toward Kladow Beach. It is hot and summery.

"Would you like to take out a boat?" I ask, looking longingly at the cool waves of the Havel.

Heike nods in agreement. We rent a canoe at a boat rental place. It is called *Small But Mine* and does not look very seaworthy. Soon we are floating along in the middle of the river. Left and right the riverbanks are moving by. Rushes and pines. Somewhere shots are fired.

"Are we, properly speaking, in the English or the American sector?" I ask Heike.

She laughs. "Neither nor. But if you'd like to familiarize yourself with the geography let me present it to you"—she points to the riverbank on the right—"British occupied zone"—she points to the riverbank on the left—"American occupied zone"—with an all-embracing gesture she points forward—"Russian-occupied zone."

"And what about the Havel?"

"A trizonal enclave. In case of doubt . . ." She pauses and points at the dim brass letters depicting the name of our canoe.

I'm a bit overwhelmed by the symbolism of it. I see the narrow arm of the Havel. The fragile canoe in which we are floating along. Rocking pitifully between the world powers. *Small But Mine,* a nutshell in the current. If a storm came up, we would capsize. We can only hope that the weather holds.

. . .

MONDAY, JUNE 21, 1948

The Eastern papers report: "Immense amounts of Reichsmarks being smuggled into the Soviet-occupied zone." Increased controls at the borders. Increased tension between East and West. At the publishing house the mood is dejected. The paper factories supplying the Western licensees are on the other side of the demarcation line. Today they've supposedly demolished the bridge across the Elbe near Magdeburg via which, till now, all automobile traffic between Helmstedt and Berlin had run, due to "urgent repair work." Farewell to our hopes of a breakthrough by a Western Allied convoy that would force open the interzonal corridor.

The power struggle is being carried out on our backs. There is less and less paper for printing, and less and less electricity for operating the printing presses. Which means our chances of practicing our profession are decreasing from week to week—perhaps even from hour to hour. Well, if at least we were a militant paper. But as a simple cultural magazine, trapped in the fortress of Berlin, licensed by the West and with no chance of Soviet support . . .

"Not very pleasant prospects," our publisher sums it up.

Two hours later the licensing authority informs us that effective immediately we have permission to print a part of the magazine in West Germany. But how will it get there? And how will it get back?

"Let's wait and see," our editor-in-chief says, beaming with optimism. "In any case, they're not leaving us in the lurch. So ways and means will be found . . ."

So the day that began with worrying ends once again with new hope.

• • •

TUESDAY, JUNE 22, 1948

The price for a pound of coffee is three thousand marks. A loaf of bread, two hundred marks. One Chesterfield, seventy-five marks. One wonders where the goods are still coming from. There is a buzzing in the air as in the time of bombs. On short notice, the American military government has increased air traffic to Berlin several times over.

"We're able," says General Clay, "to supply the ten thousand Americans in Berlin via airlift for an indefinite period of time." And again he adds optimistically: "The Russian occupation authorities will not let the German population of the Western sectors starve."

We are less hopeful. Although they say that Sokolovsky supposedly accepted the invitation by the Western Allies for a four-power conference on the currency reform, at the same time he supposedly ordered the mysterious activities taking place at the printshop of the *Tägliche Rundschau* to be speeded up. What can we do? Mark time and wait to see what they decide for us. Heads or tails—Reichsmark, East mark or Berlin mark.

"In the West they're now eating cherry tarts," Heike says dreamily as we go to bed beneath the drone of airplanes.

"And smoke Chesterfields at ten pfennigs apiece," I complete the information we obtained through the RIAS station, meanwhile wistfully putting out in the ashtray the few millimeters that remain of my cigarette.

"I wonder whether it might happen here too that a currency miracle will overnight conjure all the merchandise in short supply into the stores," Heike meditates. Then I hear her pull the blanket over her head and mumble sleepily: "Cherry tarts!"

An hour later I wake up. I feel restless. I step to the open window and look out into the night. The trees are rustling sleepily. From the cemetery comes a smell of earth and wilted flowers. Andrik lies there, very alone. "Andrik," I call, wishing he could answer. He does not answer. The trees stop rustling. Not a sound can be heard, no breeze. The silence that offers no echo seems so unbearable that I run to the radio and tune in a late program.

News: "The conference of the financial experts of the four occupying powers ended at ten-thirty P.M. without having achieved an agreement. No date has been set for another conference."

• • •

WEDNESDAY, JUNE 23, 1948

Extra edition of the *Tägliche Rundschau:* "Decree number 111 by the commander of the Soviet Military Administration in Germany. Democratic currency reform in the Soviet-occupied zone and Berlin. As of June 24, 1948, new notes will be introduced for the entire territory of the Soviet-occupied zone in Germany and the greater Berlin area: the Reichsmark and Rentenmark, as formerly, with special coupons stuck on. Coins remain in circulation at their nominal value. The only legal tender in the Soviet-occupied zone and the area of greater Berlin are the Reichsmark and Rentenmark with special coupons stuck on, as well as coinage already in circulation. As of June 28, 1948, the circulation of marks issued by the Allied military authorities, as well as of the Reichsmark and Rentenmark without special coupons, is to be discontinued. Signed: W. Sokolovsky, Marshal of the Soviet Union."

Special edition of the *Telegraph*, the English-licensed Berlin daily: "The Soviet orders to change the currency in the greater Berlin area are in contradiction to the four-power agreement on a four-power administration of greater Berlin. In the French, British and American sectors these orders are null and void and do not apply to the inhabitants of these sectors. Contraveners will be prosecuted. The necessary steps will be taken to introduce the new currency of the Western zones into the three Western sectors of greater Berlin."

There we go. Instead of one new currency we have two. And as of the day after tomorrow, the Iron Curtain along the Elbe will be met by the Iron Curtain right across Berlin. Something dangerous is brewing. Strangers talk to each other on the street, worriedly discussing the precarious situation. At four o'clock the city council is supposed to hold a special meeting. "There's going to be a row," sighs everyone with whom we speak.

At three o'clock Heike and I head for City Hall. The closer we get to it the more alarmingly the streets are congested. Trucks, bicyclists, pedestrians. All the followers of the Socialist Unity Party seem to have been ordered to join in. Red flags are fluttering. Above the heads banners are flying: "We want only one currency." In front of the gate to City Hall the crowd is swelling dangerously.

Somebody shouts: "Down with the secessionists!"

Somebody answers: "Damned Soviets!"

People are yelling. Their faces twisted as if they're suffering convulsions. The crowd surges forward. Trampling, pressing and pushing ahead like a stream of lava. There! Shoving, pushing, a flood of people surges forward. "They're storming City Hall," screams a woman.

The stream carries us away. "They broke in the door," I hear someone shout. "They're taking over the assembly hall."

Bastille! I think, alarmed. It's do-or-die now. We have entered City Hall. The surge sweeps us over stairs and hallways. In vain Suhr, the Social Democratic chairman of the city council, tries to make himself heard. "We shall not begin the session before the spectator stands have been cleared," he shouts into the crowd.

People shout him down. "Hit him in the eye . . . we want to see the secessionists." They shout in chorus. "Get started . . . get started."

Then Louise Schröder, the deputy mayor, appears. "Be reasonable. Go home. You can listen to the debate tonight on the RIAS station." Her words are met with scorn and derision. She calls out, she begs, she implores. In vain.

Two hours pass. The uninvited guests hold firm as iron. At last Chvalek, a city council member of the Socialist Unity Party, takes the speaker's stand. "Comrades," he calls out. "Wait outside. Our faction will keep you informed on the course of the debate."

His words pour oil on troubled waters. When you are used to maintaining party discipline, you listen to your leader. For another five minutes the mood vacillates between uproar and order, until it settles for order. The "storming of the Bastille" is over. To the sounds of "The Internationale" the demonstrators clear the hall.

"In France they wouldn't have given in," Heike says as we find ourselves outside again, breathless and looking rather frazzled. "Being a revolutionary obviously takes some talent, too."

We are lucky we don't have it, I think, rubbing my shin, which hurts. Or is it perhaps rather our misfortune?

• • •

THURSDAY, JUNE 24, 1948

The reprisals have begun. In diplomatic language they call them sanctions. "Sanctions" sounds nicer and less brutal. As of this morning the Soviets have cut the supply of electricity to the Western sectors. No radio, no light, no electricity for cooking, which means—like so many times before—no way of heating up a little water for coffee. Our brick stove, from 1945, has been dismantled. Heike prepares a breakfast of bread and soaked prunes. By tonight we definitely have to find some candles. But with what are we to pay for the candles? How does one pay for anything without rendering oneself liable to prosecution?

Today the currency exchange begins in the Eastern sector. On presentation of the coupon for sugar from June's food ration card, every citizen receives seventy coupon marks at an exchange rate of one to one. Up to five thousand marks of the old money may be exchanged immediately into five hundred marks of coupon money. Anything exceeding that amount will be checked. Assets held by parties, unions and state-owned companies will not be devalued.

Coupon marks are valid in the Western sectors too. But only to buy rationed food, to pay one's rent, one's fare on public transportation,

226

for postal and telephone charges, and one's electric, gas and tax bills. Coins retain their old value.

Tomorrow begins the exchange of money in the three Western sectors. On presentaiton and stamping of one's identity card, every citizen receives a per capita quota of sixty Deutsche Marks at an exchange rate of one for one. Anything exceeding that amount must be registered. Coins retain one-tenth their former value. The Deutsche Mark is prohibited in the Eastern sector. Any instance of putting it in circulation there is considered "detrimental to the economy" and will be punished in accordance with General Sokolovsky's decree 111.

At Zoo Station and the corner of Potsdamerstrasse and Kurfürstenstrasse, the former black market center for white bread and rolls, entire sheets of coupons are already being traded against Reichsmarks with a fifty percent surcharge. Thousand-mark bills are jumping from pockets. Everybody becomes his own manufacturer of new money. Ten steps away from the crowd, behind the nearest wall in the ruins, one sticks the coupons oneself onto one's remaining Reichsmarks. This kind of business requires speed. Lick and stick, lick and stick. As a capitalist in coupon money one emerges from the ruins. "Look out! Police raid!" A police car comes rushing around the corner. Everybody scatters. Like mice, the fleeing black market bankers disappear into the nearest holes. The street lies deserted before the police have even found the time to look around. Shrugging their shoulders, they climb back into their jeep and drive away. Sooner or later they'll be back. Maybe in an hour, maybe in two. And the people will scatter once again. Only to reappear a few minutes later at the same place, with the same greediness, crowding around the sheets of coupons. Money, money! At whatever cost. Hoard it, grab it, take as much as you can.

• • •

FRIDAY, JUNE 25, 1948

The last day for the old currency. Last-minute panic. Half of the people in the Eastern sector haven't exchanged their per capita quotas yet. They chase from one exchange place to the next. Everywhere the same kind of crowd, everywhere the same question: Where can you get the most? How do you get the best rate?

"First in the East, then in the West," the sly ones advise. "You have to show your identity card in the East, but not your sugar card in the West."

A capital idea, think the slyest ones, and procuring an entire collection of sugar coupons, they collect their per capita quota wholesale. One coupon at each exchange place.

"Penny-pinchers," the Reichsmark millionaires gibe. They hire a few people to work for them, offer them a share of the profits, and send them to do the waiting in line. Three people waiting in line at each exchange place. The seventy marks per capita quota plus five thousand marks in immediate exchange at the rate of one to ten. After paying fifty percent for every successful transaction to the person who waited in line, they still are left with a sizable sum. Not too bad for a fresh start.

However, it is difficult to get started! The stores are empty, and it doesn't look as though they will be filling up overnight, as in the West, with wonderful goods. In order to sell merchandise, one first must have it. But the Soviet Military Administration has ordered an immediate suspension of regular supplies of goods to the Western sectors from the Eastern zone or the Eastern sector. As of yesterday too, there is no more freight traffic across the demarcation line. The Russian military government is sorry. "After the suspension of all passenger traffic the transport administration had to temporarily suspend all freight traffic, too, due to technical problems on the railroad line. Measures are being taken to repair the line as soon as possible."

If you don't want to believe it, don't believe it. As long as there is nobody to seriously protest it, it doesn't matter whether you believe it or not.

In leading American circles they call it the most serious crisis to have developed between the Western Allies and the Soviet Union since the end of the war. We are the battleground of this crisis. Its object, its subject, its involuntary protagonist. And that's what they call currency reform. We have no light, we have no radio. And by candlelight we can think at leisure about how we may cope with our questionable distinction.

Battleground Berlin

• • •

For the time being we have enough to do trying to cope with our double currency. As of today the new mark is in effect. We just haven't figured out yet where it is in effect and what it is worth. In the Eastern sector there have been the first arrests of people carrying Western money. For "fraud and in violation of decree 111." At the newspaper stand one pays for a newspaper with a ten-pfennig coin or with one Rentenmark note. At the grocery store one pays for ten grams of margarine with a fifty-pfennig coin or with five Reichsmarks without coupon stickers. The exchange rate of "wallpaper money" drops hourly. This morning the rate was eight to one against Western currency. This afternoon it is eighteen to one. In the Western sectors, stamps are worth ten percent of their nominal value. However, since you can pay for them with Eastern money too, you have the choice of whether you would rather sacrifice two ten-pfennig pieces or two Reichsmark notes without coupon sticker for two ten-pfennig stamps. All of Berlin is going crazy. And the racketeers are the ones who profit from these wild exchange excesses.

The military governments issue one decree after another in order to get the situation under control. But due to the fact that every decree issued in the West is followed by a counterdecree in the East, there's no less confusion. The *Tägliche Rundschau* reports that unfortunately the Berlin-Helmstedt railroad line's technical problems are much more serious than originally assumed, and that the severe power shortages in the Western sectors have been due to some malfunction at the power station of Golpa-Tschornewitz, which supplies Berlin with electricity.

As a consolation, Colonel Howley, the American commander of Berlin, has assured us that despite the fact that the delivery of goods from the Eastern zone has been suspended, despite the suspension of interzonal traffic, despite the suspension of the milk supply from the Eastern zone to infants in the Western sectors, we should not despair. Food reserves in the American sector are enough to last for another

229

thirty days. And then . . . "We shall not let the people of Berlin starve," he affirms loudly and clearly. We are relieved. So it is not just the occupying forces, but we too who have reason to hope . . . We hope again! Because so far Colonel Howley has always kept his promises.

• • •

SUNDAY, JUNE 27, 1948

Electricity for two hours a day. On Sundays only one. For the sake of equal treatment, supply schedule groups have been established. So that everybody has the prospect of getting his quota of electric power at a reasonable time. The hours we are supplied with electric power are from midnight to two in the morning. Before and after, we have to do without electricity, without lights, without radio.

Recently loudspeaker vans from RIAS have been driving through the streets of the Western sector, substituting for the news service. It's quite annoying to be at the focus of world affairs and to be informed about them only between midnight and two in the morning. So we run outside when the RIAS van appears. It reports the latest and most important news: "The airlift has increased to one hundred flights daily. Swimming prohibited in lakes and rivers because they are likely to be polluted with sewage due to the power cuts. More people arrested in the Eastern sector for possession of Deutsche Marks. Exchange rate of wallpaper money for Deutsche Marks—thirty to one."

The RIAS van moves on. We are dismayed at the news. It doesn't look as if things will be getting any better very soon.

• • •

TUESDAY, JUNE 29, 1948

On the contrary. Once more the commentaries of the press on the political situation go from "grave" to "very good" to "extremely grave." As if by chance, the American deputy defense secretary, the head of the U.S. Army planning department, the commander of the British

230

troops along the Rhine, and a special commissioner sent by Truman arrived in Berlin at the same time.

"Decisions are about to be taken," the *Tagesspiegel* reports in large print. "With this latest series of violations of the agreements, Russian expansionism has created in Berlin a situation about whose gravity the United States entertains no illusions. In the government, talks are in progress in order to decide what measures need to be taken or will need to be taken, due to acts by the Russians. The decisions will be announced soon."

"Not a second Munich," one hears from all sides.

The Moscow station announces the resolutions agreed upon in Warsaw by the foreign ministers of the Russian satellite states to solve the conflict in Germany: "Formation of an all-German government. Peace with Germany. Withdrawal of all occupying forces one year after the peace agreement. The Oder-Neisse border will be maintained. The Ruhr to be controlled by the four powers."

If we really would have peace . . . What if after the occupation troops have been withdrawn there is another call for fusion, the long-aimed-for "call for a merger" . . . Who will then say no? Who will say yes? Who will make sure that we will be able to say yes or no without coercion? America is far away and Russia is near. Just a day's march away from being on hand as our guardian. Why have we become so suspicious that we look for a catch in every Russian proposal? Perhaps this time they really mean it.

Blockade, as another airlift plane drones by overhead every eight minutes. Blockade, we are reminded by the hours without electricity, the RIAS vans, the deserted highway to Helmstedt, the rusty railroad tracks of the interzonal line, the cancelled streetcars, the idle factories, and the streets and houses without light in the Western sector of the fortress of Berlin.

"We will dry out the Western sectors like a tied-off wart," the Soviets have supposedly said. And *this* time they no doubt mean it.

Ruth Andreas-Friedrich

• • •

At the Zoo Station currency is being traded. One need only mingle with the people crowding the streets from the railroad underpass all the way to the Memorial Church, and hold one's Eastern or Western bills visibly in one's hand. In less than two minutes the exchange transaction is under way. "Do you need East marks . . . ?" "Do you need West marks . . ." One slowly passes by and a person whispers something into his ear. A furtive glance around . . . he reaches into his wallet . . . and as if by magic the six West marks in his hand change into fifteen wallpaper notes. Four days ago the exchange rate dropped from thirty or even forty to two and a half. Why? We know as little about that as we know about everything else affecting the ups and downs of our life under the blockade.

"Try to figure this one out," Heike complains. "Matches, only Western money. Onions, half East and half West. Raisin allotment, Western money. Sugar coupons, Eastern money. A small bunch of chives, half and half. Soap, Eastern currency. The matching soaking agents, Western currency. Are we mathematical acrobats, or what?"

"Try to figure this one out," says our publisher. "Newspapers are paid for only with Eastern money. To print them requires Western money. Our employees are entitled to twenty-five percent Western currency, but the money we make is one hundred percent Eastern currency."

• • •

"It is amazing how everything here has changed in the past three weeks," writes Frank from Munich. "Nobody talks about calories anymore, because there is enough to eat. The stores are full of goods, there are plenty of papers and magazines to be had. The only thing we don't have is money . . . The news reaching us from Berlin is alarming. I worry about you. Come to the West!"

Battleground Berlin

Should we leave? Should we stay? I look at the empty stores. I convert Eastern money into Western money and Western money into Eastern money. In the *Tagesspiegel* I read that the gas allocation has had to be cut and that the present allocation of electric power supply can not be maintained any longer, that already fifty percent of all West Berlin enterprises have had to close due to power shortages, and that subways and streetcars are running only until six P.M. I hear that the Soviet Military Administration has submitted thirty notes protesting violations of air traffic regulations in the air corridor and that, as of today, they have also suspended all waterway traffic between Berlin and the Western zones, due to "repair work at the lock at Rathenow." And I think: We should leave.

Then I sit in the streetcar to Moabit. Next to me sits a woman. Carefully, as if afraid of spilling something, she looks at her shopping bag. We start talking.

"I am on my way to see some friends," she says. "The Russians supposedly cut off the water supply in Moabit. I want to go over there and bring them some water. So at least they will be able to make some coffee."

Water to Moabit. In empty vinegar and seltzer bottles. I look at the woman and think: We must stay. We must not desert people who carry water for coffee from Charlottenburg to Moabit.

• • •

TUESDAY, JULY 20, 1948

Now we stay—now we go. Now we go—now we stay. If only one knew how things will develop. We still cannot make up our minds. The airlift stabilizes. Every three minutes there is an airplane. As of recently they supposedly are even flying in coal. "We shall stay," the Americans assure us daily. But what's their reason for staying?

"Because the airlift gives them a great chance to train pilots for an eventual war," gibe those who are anti-West. "And because by expanding the Berlin airports they are building the best air bases right under the Russians' noses. Or did you believe they were staying because of you?"

Bridge—bridgehead—doormat, I quietly recapitulate the stations

233

of our decline. Could it really be that we are only a doormat? . . .
"Berlin is fighting for the freedom of Europe. The courage of the
people in West Berlin is saving democracy in Europe," one Western-
zone politician after another assures us. Telegrams expressing support
arrive from all countries. In Lower Saxony people donate one day's
food ration for Berlin. Eggs are being collected, butter, meat, cheese,
milk powder and medical supplies. "With thanks to our brave capital!"

The cases are piling up at the airports. The only thing lacking is
the cargo space to transport them. The world's compassion moves us
quite a bit. So we aren't just a doormat after all. And if we can hold
out a little while longer . . .

• • •

FRIDAY, JULY 23, 1948

No light, no radio, no electricity to cook. Fortunately it is summer,
we think every day. The days are longer, and it doesn't matter so much
that for days on end one eats nothing but bread with margarine and
chives. One could drink water too. But since the water purification
plants have stopped functioning it is advisable to drink only water that
has been boiled. One can boil it at night. Between midnight and two
in the morning, when ration group C—as in Caesar—receives its
power supply for the week. Sometimes we get it as early as eleven-
thirty. So we sit around waiting. We grope our way around the apartment as if blind. We yawn and talk about the blockade. Whether the
airlift will work and whether Berlin will be able to hold out.

"Berlin will hold out," we say as we light our evening candle. "It's
a matter of energy and nerves."

"Berlin cannot hold out," we sigh as the candle burns down and
the minutes pass at a snail's pace. Our conversation becomes slower
and slower. All we want to do is sleep. If it continues this way much
longer we shall break down . . . It is a question of nerves. Heike begins
to weep out of weariness.

"Ah," we suddenly call out as if with one voice, "light!" We start
running about laughing, as noisy as if we had been drinking wine. To
the light switch, to the stove, to the radio. To cook, to wash some

234

stockings, to iron a blouse, to listen to the news. More than anything: to listen to the news. The RIAS station broadcasts news every hour throughout the night. We listen to the Eastern station, we listen to the Western stations. Above us the droning sound of airplanes. Every three minutes . . . It is a question of nerves. Between midnight and two in the morning, we feel our nerves are very strong. Not doormats but heroes. Called upon to defend freedom in Europe. At two o'clock our day is over. At seven the new one begins. Without light, without radio, without the possibility of cooking.

• • •

SUNDAY, JULY 25, 1948

It is a question of nerves. A month ago today the wallpaper mark was born. Today is its death day. In accordance with a decree by the head of the Soviet Military Administration, the coupon mark in the Eastern sector and the Eastern zone will be exchanged into German marks issued by the German Central Bank. The exchange rate is one to one. The per capita quota is seventy marks. Anything exceeding this amount will be credited to a savings account that the owner may supposedly dispose of freely as of August 15, after the "authenticity and validity" of the notes submitted have been checked. After tomorrow coupon marks will no longer be accepted. The exchange places for the per capita quota as well as the savings accounts are in the Eastern sector. Once again we are running to exchange our money. Endless lines. People shoving, bickering and shouting. An application by the city council to establish exchange places in the Western sectors as well has been rejected by the Soviet Military Administration. So now we rush to Köpenick or Lichtenberg, to Weissensee or Hoppegarten, to get rid of our coupon marks. At six o'clock streetcars and subways stop running. "They must think they can do anything with us," people grouse, doggedly pushing their way into overcrowded trains. Hero or doormat. What is happening here today is nothing but the struggle to survive.

Ruth Andreas-Friedrich

· · ·

More and more it looks as if the blockade is here to stay. Our experiences with Nazism and post-Nazism have already taught us that of all possible outcomes, it's almost always the worst possible that results: an unbearable situation becomes permanent.

On July 6 the three Western powers protested in Moscow against the blockade of Berlin, but agreed to negotiations as soon as it was lifted. On July 15 the Soviet Union informed its Western Allies that they too would agree to negotiations on a four-power basis but they were not willing to lift the blockade as a precondition for further talks. Two "open doors" and nobody enters. The day before yesterday it was announced that the ambassadors of the three Western Allies in Moscow were supposed to personally hand their governments' responses to the latest Soviet note to the foreign minister. "Mr. Molotov is out of town," a press release by the Soviet foreign ministry stated today. It was uncertain when he would return.

Everything seems uncertain. The "open doors" are creaking, and beset by this disagreeable sound, we slowly prepare ourselves for being a city on the front lines for life. Maybe one ought to go West after all. I inquire at the American air travel agency. I am told that all seats on sale for Deutsche Marks have been sold out for the next two weeks. Unless—they look at me furtively—I could pay the fare in dollars. The possession of dollars is illegal. On the black market they are sold for twenty-eight West marks apiece. Discreetly, because a German caught with dollars goes to prison. At best, you can arrange to have someone entitled to possess dollars buy the ticket for you as a gift, and reimburse him at the black market exchange rate . . . But that is something that's being done and not talked about, people tell me, discreetly making me understand that they "have done it already." Air passage from Berlin to Frankfurt costs twenty-eight dollars. Twenty-eight times twenty-eight. Who has 784 West marks to pay for just one flight from Berlin to Frankfurt? Not to mention the possibility of ending up in prison if caught.

"Come! Come!" Frank urges in every letter. But even if he were dying and I should never see him again—I still could not come. The flight tickets available for Deutsche Marks are sold out for the next two weeks. My "coupon marks" are in a "savings account" in the Eastern sector. Our publishing house earns only Eastern money. And because our magazine is not militant but merely a cultural one, we are last when it comes to paper distribution via the airlift. So we should consider ourselves fortunate if the sale of the tiny edition covers at least the greater part of our East mark expenses. Berlin is a prison from which only a few lucky ones, once in a while, obtain permission for a limited leave. Loyalty toward a city—or loyalty toward a person? I hate being in a prison.

• • •

TUESDAY, AUGUST 3, 1948

Last night the three Western ambassadors in Moscow went directly to Stalin. "They entered the gate to the Kremlin at five to nine, Moscow time," it is reported today. Other than that—no comment.

• • •

WEDNESDAY, AUGUST 4, 1948

All Russian papers publish the official Soviet communiqué on Stalin's meeting with the diplomats of the three Western powers. It is thirty-four words long and says: "On August 2 J.V. Stalin, President of the Council of Ministers of the Soviet Union, received the American ambassador W. Smith, the French ambassador Chataigneau, and F. Roberts, the personal representative of British Foreign Minister Bevin. The Foreign Minister of the Soviet Union, V. Molotov, attended the meeting." Period, close. And we know just as little as before. Journalists from all over the world engage in speculation. The fact that the three ambassadors left the Kremlin "smiling and in a good mood" and that upon their return to the American embassy they "did not even wait for the elevator but ran up the three flights of stairs to

Smith's office" is interpreted as a favorable sign. And, in addition, that it was "the longest discussion" Stalin has granted in years.

•   •   •

THURSDAY, AUGUST 5, 1948

"No comment," Secretary of State Marshall says in Washington.
"No comment," Foreign Minister Bevin says in London.
"No comment," Foreign Minister Schuman says in Paris.

•   •   •

WEDNESDAY, AUGUST 11, 1948

No comment. However, on the ninth the three ambassadors conferred with Molotov, and it is expected that this first meeting will be followed by many more long meetings . . . It is a question of nerves!

•   •   •

SATURDAY, AUGUST 14, 1948

Proposals and counterproposals. Their contents have not been made public. One day it looks favorable, the next day it looks unfavorable again. The East says: Four-power negotiations and then comes the lifting of the blockade. The West says: Lifting of the blockade and then come four-power negotiations.

"It's disgraceful when four parties live in a house and one of them forces the other three to enter the house through the chimney instead of the door," they say in England.

We vacillate between hope and despair. But vacillating slowly gets to be quite strenuous too, if one isn't the dog that fights for the bone, but the bone the dogs are fighting for.

• • •

At Herrenchiemsee in Bavaria a convention is held in preparation for the new German constitution. A West German constitution! The borders between the Western zones are removed. The sector boundaries in Berlin are growing higher and higher. "Lifting of the blockade and then come four-power negotiations."

"No, four-power negotiations and then comes the lifting of the blockade," they keep arguing in Moscow.

And while in Moscow they argue "without comment," while at Herrenchiemsee they are getting ready for the West German state, we sit here without electricity and without radio, eating dehydrated potatoes and vegetables, prunes and canned meat, pondering our situation. Hero or doormat.

"It's very simple," Heike says. "The only difference is, the West has a chance and Berlin doesn't. Except to be swallowed up by the Eastern zone in the end."

"But the Americans are staying," I object.

"Sure, they're staying. Like the guard on the lifeguard's stand in the surf. But whatever is going on, Herrenchiemsee will concern us only as onlookers and not . . . and not as beneficiaries," she finishes her sentence with a sigh.

Onlookers! The more I think about it the more I have to agree with her. "The demarcation line between Eastern and Western ideologies runs along the Elbe," Clay said half a year ago. "We have erected a border here that we intend to hold."

We are east of that border. A watchtower in the Soviet surf. The problem of the "foolish parents," the problem of "eating one's cake and having it"; these have been solved in a surprisingly simple way. The border runs along the Elbe. What lies on the other side is Germany, will be Germany. A small Germany but a friendly Germany. Without Prussian aggression, not threatening to claim world power status, not Soviet infected, in short, suitable and worthy of being integrated into the big family of European nations. The only protec-

239

tion against the advance of Bolshevism is an economically stable Western Europe. The Marshall Plan helps to achieve that. West Germany gets a government. West Germany becomes the German state. Economically stable and small enough not to pose a potential threat. A solid bulwark against the advance of Bolshevism. The good and non-aggressive child in the family of European nations. As to what is on this side of the Elbe . . . forget it! The less one talks about it, the easier it is to forget. It is a bitter truth and yet—probably the only one that might save Europe.

Since my childhood I have been a fan of the United States of Europe. Now that it is getting closer, I am standing on a watchtower in the surf and three hundred kilometers of "Eastern ideology" separate me from its border. From it—and from Frank. What good is a pacifist on a watchtower in the surf? What's the cultural magazine with little paper doing in the fortress of Berlin?

"Holding the position," I am being told. "Making the impossible possible!"

"No," I balk at the fatally familiar way of phrasing it.

"You should not forsake the community of fate," I am being urged, reproachfully.

"Yes," I must contritely concede. And once again I am torn between yes and no.

• • •

SUNDAY, AUGUST 22, 1948

At Potsdamer Platz, where the American, British and Soviet sector boundaries meet, runs the demarcation line between Eastern and Western ideologies. It is here that three days ago, for the first time, Germans shot at Germans. Berliners at Berliners. Already sometime ago Margraf, the chief of police, had declared that he would take orders only from the Soviet occupying power, and in response to that the Western Allies sanctioned a separate police force for their sectors. The police in the East call it "the illegal Western police," while the police in the West call *them* "the illegal Eastern police," and so began an edgy skirmishing from both sides.

Kidnapping across the border. Police raids. People being dragged into the other sector. People protest. Shots are fired, stones are hurled. People are arrested. People are wounded. Who is the enemy?

In Moscow they are negotiating—without comment. At Herren-chiemsee they are working on drafting a West German constitution. Between three and four thousand tons of supplies are flown into Berlin every day via airlift. And the suicide rate in Berlin, normally one and a half per day, has risen to about seven a day. A question of nerves!

• • •

WEDNESDAY, SEPTEMBER 1, 1948

The blockade will be lifted. One hardly dares to believe it, but they say it is true. Yesterday afternoon, for the first time in five months, all four military governors met in the building of the Control Council to discuss the lifting of the blockade and the introduction of a uniform currency for all Berlin. Only after the technical preconditions regarding these two issues had been clarified would a communiqué on the state of the negotiations in Moscow be published. At Helmstedt trains carrying coal and food were already waiting to roll eastward the moment the border was opened. Berliners are jubilant. No more dehydrated potatoes and canned meat. No more power cuts, no tiresome conversion acrobatics between East marks and West marks. Paper for the magazines and, what is most important, no more enmity and unrestrained hatred between Berliners.

Today the first postwar German parliament in Bonn began its constituent work. Now we also shall benefit from it. At night Heike and I illuminate our apartment with four candles instead of one. Who knows, perhaps already by tomorrow we shall have light again by just switching it on.

• • •

THURSDAY, SEPTEMBER 2, 1948

The talks between the military governors continue. The rumors that the blockade would be lifted have not been confirmed. We sit around one candle waiting for the power to be turned on.

241

Ruth Andreas-Friedrich

• • •

Soviet antiaircraft exercises in the air corridor. The East mark has dropped to three point two, and at the Control Council they are still meeting behind closed doors. For the third time a city council assembly had to be postponed because of demonstrations by the Socialist Unity Party in front of City Hall.

"Come to Munich," writes Frank. His letter took twenty-one days to reach me.

• • •

Heike comes rushing into the room. "Putsch in the city," she exclaims. "The Socialist Unity Party is staging a coup d'état."

I jump up. "Where?"

"In Parochialstrasse. They've taken over City Hall. The Eastern police have cordoned off all streets leading to it. If they manage now . . ." She wrings her hands.

For God's sake, let's listen to the news! I turn on the radio. Dead. I remind myself that this week section C—as in Caesar—has power from ten P.M. to midnight. I look at my watch. It's twenty-five minutes to nine o'clock. Another hour and a half. I run to the window, lean out far and listen into the night. All is quiet. On Bismarckstrasse two women are leisurely pulling a handcart. I strain my ears. No noise, no shots can be heard. "If it had succeeded, they would already be here," I reassure myself. They can't have succeeded.

At last, ten o'clock comes. RIAS: Toward eleven o'clock in the morning groups of people, marching columns and trucks carrying Communist demonstrators, appeared in front of the new City Hall. They shattered the glass of the entrance door, overpowered the ushers who tried to resist, and occupied the assembly hall and the spectator stand. Around two o'clock a member of the Socialist Unity Party's

242

executive committee opened a city council assembly attended only by Socialist Unity Party representatives and the leaders of the Eastern zone's Christian Democratic Party unions. At about three o'clock the demonstrators left the City Hall. At a quarter past eight, it was occupied by Eastern police and all access roads were cordoned off. At six-thirty P.M., all city councilors, with the exception of the Socialist Unity Party representatives, assembled for an emergency meeting at the Taberna Academica on Steinplatz in the British sector. They decided to meet in the Western sectors until the situation had normalized again, and to set the date of November 14 for the election of a new city parliament.

So, they failed! Or at least they didn't succeed in pulling off a coup d'état. As of today we not only have two city police forces, but also two city parliaments. Perhaps by tomorrow we will have two city governments and along the sector boundary a Chinese wall with battlements and watchtowers. Perhaps then one will need a visa to go from Charlottenburg to Unter den Linden. Just as we thought back then in July 1945 when the four-power occupation began. Perhaps.

Today at the Control Council the four military governors held their longest meeting so far. It lasted five hours and forty-five minutes. It is a question of nerves.

• • •

MONDAY, SEPTEMBER 13, 1948

On Thursday a hundred thousand Berliners demonstrated on the Platz der Republik for democratic liberties and against the scandalous events that have taken place at City Hall. They acted with righteous anger and for a just cause. Housewives ran away from their stoves, the hairdresser abandoned his customer under the drying hood, the news vendor closed his newsstand. Everybody came running, thinking: I must demonstrate. We belong to the West. We are Berliners. We are a community of fate. It is a great thing to feel a part of a community of fate . . .

After the demonstration was over, dangerous incidents took place at the Brandenburg Gate. They tore the Soviet flag off the gate, and

243

started shouting and making threats. The Russian police interfered. They fired shots. One person was left dead and several were injured. Five demonstrators were arrested. Yesterday the Soviet military court sentenced each of them to twenty-five years in a labor camp. That means death. Sooner or later, in a concentration camp or a uranium mine.

At a demonstration organized by the Socialist Unity Party at the Lustgarten last Sunday, a hundred thousand inhabitants of the Eastern zone and the Eastern sector commemorated the "victims of Fascism of all political views and religions." Is it possible that there too the housewives ran away from their stoves, the hairdressers abandoned their customers and the newspaper vendors closed their kiosks in order to "demonstrate"? Running and thinking: We are Berliners. We are a community of fate.

It appears uncanny from such a perspective. As if we were all deeming ourselves chosen for a task that is beyond our power. Is it within *our* power whether the Allies stand united or at odds with each other? Is it within *our* power whether we will be part of West Germany or not? Is it within *our* power whether the blockade hangs over Berlin or is lifted? We demonstrate for or we demonstrate against it. With childish overzealousness always three steps ahead of our respective occupying power.

"The Berliners are like the cocks in Spanish cockfights," somebody "neutral" recently said. "Each occupying power puts its fighting cock in front of it. Then the two keep pecking at each other until one of them is carried away dead and the other is dying. And even while he is dying, the victorious cock cranes his neck and lets out a triumphant cock-a-doodle-doo."

. . .

THURSDAY, SEPTEMBER 16, 1948

The Control Council building stands empty. The conference of the military governors has failed, and new steps are being prepared in Moscow. It is said that they want to try a second time to appeal directly to Stalin. Generalissimo Stalin is away on vacation, the Soviet press reports. He left the city several days ago and would be spending a month vacationing on the Black Sea.

The Soviets are astonishingly conservative in their excuses. Repairs of bridges or sluice gates, defective railroad tracks, and vacation trips. Now, supposedly, the Berlin matter will be passed on to the United Nations Security Council. For the third time since the war's end, the adjectives in the commentaries on the political situation have gone from "bad," to "worse," to "well-nigh the worst."

• • •

MONDAY, SEPTEMBER 20, 1948

We are using up our last paper. "For the foreseeable future no paper for magazines can be flown in via the airlift," the licensing authority has declared.

It is understandable. Before paper is flown in for magazines unconcerned with daily politics, coal must be flown in for those companies that print daily papers that report on what is happening politically. And before coal is flown in for those companies, dehydrated potatoes and fruit, fat, protein and carbohydrates must be flown in to keep those alive who work in those companies. The chance of illegal supplies from the Eastern sector or the Eastern zone becomes smaller and smaller. At the border crossing points, even the smallest quantities of food are confiscated by the Eastern police. Controls on the subway, controls on the trains of the municipal railroad system. Police raids on the street, inspection of luggage, and confiscation of all Western money found on those subject to these controls.

It is not impossible to obtain paper illegally. Because, in spite of all, the Soviets are interested in Western currency. But where can one get Western currency if one does not have it? The exchange rate lies between three and a half and four and a half marks. Any item on the black market requires Western currency at a rate of three and a half to four and a half times that amount in East marks. It makes no sense to sell products that cost more to produce than one can sell them for. It would amount to giving away fifty thousand ten-pfennig pieces every two weeks. So we'd rather not take the opportunity to obtain paper illegally. "We have to hold the fort . . . make the impossible possible," our editor-in-chief obstinately insists.

Today the Western representatives left Moscow. Empty-handed. Now it is up to the United Nations Organization "to hold the fort" and to try to make the impossibility of an East-West agreement in the Berlin conflict possible.

• • •

TUESDAY, OCTOBER 5, 1948

Jo Thäler has left Berlin. "It's pointless to stay here," he said on parting. "Berlin is lost."

One after another gets ready to leave. With twenty kilograms of luggage if by way of the airlift. With knapsack and a small suitcase if he dares cross the border illegally. Anything more than that must be left behind. It's not for the first time we are starting a new life without furniture. One's circle of intimate friends grows smaller and smaller. It gets more and more difficult to reach them. It's impossible to get everywhere on foot, and even in a big city, a pedestrian's day has no more than twenty-four hours. That's not to even mention the problem of power outages. "Come at nine o'clock at night," one's friends say. "From nine to eleven we have electricity. So we can offer you some hot tea." "Come at midnight," the hairdresser says to his customer. "From midnight till two in the morning we have electricity. If you live nearby it shouldn't be a problem."

There are quite a few who have a different approach. For example, those who are connected to an "Allied cable." The "Allied cable" is the term for luck in West Berlin. The code word for the fact that one's electric line is connected to a cable that supplies offices or residences of the occupying powers. Although they are subject to power cuts too, they do have light from six to eleven at night. And at eleven at night a normal person can go to bed satisfied, having listened to the news undisturbed, having mended his socks, washed his laundry, cooked his dinner, served his friends, read his paper, in short to have taken care of everything one normally feels like doing after coming home from work.

We are not connected to an "Allied cable." It is a matter of luck. Living in an "electrified" area, however, one becomes painfully aware of it.

• • •

THURSDAY, OCTOBER 14, 1948

Our editor-in-chief has figured out a way of being able to stay in Berlin even without paper. "It's an inspiration," he says, beaming. "We do the typesetting in Berlin, fly the matrixes via airlift to southern Germany, print it there, and have the complete edition returned to Berlin via the mail train."

"However inspired, you seem to forget that your fourth step requires the cooperation of the Soviets," I cannot help remarking.

He looks at me reproachfully. "The mail train is running!"

His optimism touches me. I look at his emaciated face, his baggy suit. He never complains about the dehydrated potatoes or the power cuts. His fingers are yellow from smoking cigarette butts, and in his eyes everybody leaving Berlin is a traitor. Betraying the common cause of all Berliners. The cause of freedom.

For freedom's sake the Western-oriented city council has today moved out of the City Hall and taken up residence in the British sector. Two city parliaments, two police departments, two city governments and also—since a short time ago—two universities. The Chinese wall along the sector boundary is rising slowly but surely.

• • •

SATURDAY, OCTOBER 23, 1948

The nights are getting longer, the days are getting cooler. Whenever one runs into an acquaintance on the street, he asks: "Do you have coal? Do you know where there is any coal?"

Supposedly the Almanac predicts a mild winter. Since we have given up hope of the blockade being lifted, we cling to this prophecy. Anything rather than freeze again as in the winter of 1946. Without

247

light. Sitting around cold stoves in dark houses. Back then they allotted us one hundred pounds of briquettes. To last for the entire heating period. This year one hears nothing about coal allotments.

"Register your food ration cards with your household registration card in the Eastern sector," the Eastern papers advertise. "The Soviet occupying power is able to supply people sufficiently in the Western sectors too."

A tempting offer if one thinks of the possibility of an ample coal allotment. Utopian though if one considers that one will have to carry each of one's purchases across the sector boundary. On overcrowded trains and through the controls of the Eastern police, each time subjected to the risk that just that fat, soap, coal or meat ration one wants to buy is not available that day. Then rather dehydrated potatoes, decide the majority of West Berliners. Demonstrating once again— partly heroism, partly survival instinct—their solidarity against the East.

• • •

WEDNESDAY, OCTOBER 27, 1948

For a whole month now, at the U.N. Security Council, the neutral countries, headed by Argentine foreign minister Bramuglia, have tried to work out a solution to the Berlin conflict. They have worked out a detailed schedule for reaching a degree of consensus between the differing positions: lifting the blockade, then four-power conference, versus four-power conference, then lifting of the blockade. Thinking that what is not possible consecutively might perhaps be acceptable simultaneously, Bramuglia and his neutral colleagues worked out a corresponding proposal and presented it to the representatives of the two opposing parties. "Yes," voted the Western ones. "No," said Vishinsky, the Soviet delegate, vetoing the resolution on behalf of Russia. So this attempt to save Berlin seems to have failed too.

"Go West," Heike advises me now too. "Those who have no reason to stay should get out. Academia is out of place after Stalingrad, a humanist educational publication out of place on the front lines."

"What about you?" I ask.

She shrugs her shoulders. "As long as we still can do theater here . . ."

"As long as the mail train is still running . . . ," I complete her line of thought, and neither of us finishes the sentence.

• • •

FRIDAY, OCTOBER 29, 1948

Andrik's English friend has left Berlin too. Many members of the occupation forces have been replaced in the past few months. They have completed their service. New ones have replaced them. One has to get acquainted with them first. But it is difficult to get acquainted because most of them speak only English. When one asks them how long the blockade will last they answer with a philosophical smile: "Oh, about fifty years." It might be easier to imagine it for fifty years for one who, being a member of an occupying power, has electricity between five and eleven P.M., or who can just go back home if he doesn't like it here anymore. Our home is Berlin. With an Eastern and a Western currency. Supplied by airlift and separated from the rest of Germany by two hundred kilometers of Eastern ideology. A watchtower amid surging waves. Its walls eroded by these breakers more and more dangerously each week.

The People's Committee is getting ready for another meeting. They say important issues are to be discussed. Preparation for an Eastern state, elaboration of the constitution that has been drafted for the Soviet-occupied territory. General Seydlitz, cocapitulator at Stalingrad and vice-president of the national committee "Free Germany," has been traveling through the Eastern zone inspecting the People's Police. Refugees from that zone report that its force has been increased to two hundred thousand men and that it is well equipped and provided with arms. "It's highly unlikely that they received the guns just for cleaning," the refugees from the East add, hinting that one should be prepared for another attempt to overthrow the government—when the nights are the longest and winter the coldest. Under these auspices the Warsaw demand for a "withdrawal of all occupation forces one year after signing the peace agreement" sounds not at all tempting.

• • •

TUESDAY, NOVEMBER 2, 1948

Presidential elections in the United States. Most likely Dewey, the Republican candidate, will be elected. "If he wins the election, the policy toward Russia will get tougher," Berliners say, not really sure what they should prefer.

• • •

WEDNESDAY, NOVEMBER 3, 1948

He didn't win. To everybody's surprise Truman, not Dewey, won the election.

"It proves that the people do not want war," the optimists conclude.

"It proves that the blockade will continue," the pessimists say with resignation.

The black market price for coal is fifteen marks West German currency per hundred pounds. The average Berliner buys his fuel by the pound. There still hasn't been any mention of a coal allotment. However, it is rumored that for the time being it won't be more than twenty-five pounds. Subways and streetcars are crowded with brush-wood gatherers. Every passenger carries a bundle. One is lucky if one manages to stay clear of their bulky load and keep one's stockings intact. The owners of gardens cut down their trees. Holding out . . . If only we knew how much longer we still have to hold out!

• • •

FRIDAY, NOVEMBER 5, 1948

It's all over! The mail train has stopped running. "Detained at the border," the official explanation plainly states. Fifty thousand copies of our magazine are somewhere between Helmstedt and Marienborn.

250

Between Bebra and Eisenach, or wherever it was the train tried to pass the demarcation line. In plain terms that means: bankruptcy. True, it's not the first one in the course of the past four months. And most likely it won't be the last one either. However, one feels much more affected by it if it happens to oneself. It affects one more directly than it would by just reading about it in the newspaper. Frank cables: "Take the next plane out."

"Let's hold out," our editor-in-chief says stubbornly. "On December fifth there will be elections in Berlin. On December fifth it will be decided."

• • •

Monday, November 22, 1948

We are cold. Heike pokes the embers in the stove, sighing: "If only we had those fifty thousand papers. Who knows at which zonal border they have been left lying to rot."

Our reserves are depleted. When we go to bed we dress as if heading for an expedition to Greenland.

"It makes one look so ugly," Heike complains, looking at herself hidden beneath three sweaters, two pairs of woolen underwear and four differently patterned scarves.

It makes one look so ugly, I think, looking at my fellow men, their faces blue with cold, their bodies covered with layers and layers of undefinably colored garments.

Thirteen days until the election. In the Eastern sector it has been prohibited. The official explanation is that there will soon be free general elections for all Berlin. And at the same time, for the entire area of the Eastern sector, that particular Sunday has been proclaimed "a work Sunday for the reconstruction of Berlin." With special allotments and food without coupons. "Perhaps even with coal," a rumor is being spread. A hundred and ten thousand Berliners live in the Western sectors and work in the Eastern sector. They are afraid of losing their work if they do not participate in doing reconstruction work that Sunday. If they do participate, they cannot vote. It is a question of nerves!

Ruth Andreas-Friedrich

• • •

WEDNESDAY, DECEMBER 1, 1948

"The majority of city council members elected on October 20, 1946, have not carried out their duties. Therefore the city council will be unseated," the "Democratic bloc of Berlin" has decided, as was announced yesterday by Geschke, the deputy chairman of the Socialist Unity Party in the city council, at a special meeting in the Eastern sector. In preparation for general democratic elections, a temporary democratic city council has been formed. With Friedrich Ebert, the son of the former president of the Reich, heading it as mayor, effective immediately. Congratulations! Consistent with having two city councils, we now have two mayors as well. The Soviet Military Administration assures him of their support. And in front of the university—the Eastern-oriented one—ten thousand Berliners are demonstrating. For peace, unity, democracy. And against the "secessionist city council."

• • •

SUNDAY, DECEMBER 5, 1948

Elections in West Berlin. No disturbances. No attempts to interfere with it. They say the turnout is huge.

• • •

TUESDAY, DECEMBER 7, 1948

West Berlin has voted. Of about one and a half million people entitled to vote, one and a quarter million voted against the politics of the Socialist Unity Party. An admirable result considering that this decision most likely will have to be paid for with an intensification of the blockade, a winter without coal, nights without light and a permanent diet of dehydrated potatoes, dehydrated vegetables and canned meat. We feel as if we had wings. We feel it's great to be a Berliner. It is wonderful to live in a city that prefers death to slavery, that has decided to suffer more deprivations rather than dictatorship.

"Thanks to the defenders of freedom," telegrams arrive from all over the world. However, the mail train no longer runs, and the struggle for freedom, too, requires some material basis for existence.

• • •

MONDAY, DECEMBER 13, 1948

When I get to the publishing house the editor-in-chief greets me with the words: "No paper." When I go to the licensing authority the officer in charge says: "No paper."

The airlift . . . "It's the foggiest winter in eighty years," the meteorologists claim. The airlift does what it can. But neither can it do the impossible.

"You must get out of here," Heike urges me. "Once you're in the West perhaps you . . ."

"Hurry up and get out," Frank urges me. "I am sure in the West you can . . ."

Andrik, I think. How could I abandon Andrik? In the fog the tombstones in the cemetery look like ghosts. No solace comes from the damp mounds. No solace comes from Andrik. What a mistake that I am looking for him here.

In the early afternoon I go to the Overseas Airlines travel agency. I am told I can have a reservation for the twenty-ninth. A reservation isn't a decision yet. Perhaps the plane won't fly that day. There may be fog, a snowstorm, or some other incident . . .

• • •

SATURDAY, DECEMBER 18, 1948

We received the first coal allotment. Twenty-five pounds of bituminous coal. Exactly as the rumors predicted it.

Over the airlift the fog continues. Is Heaven in league with the Soviets, I wonder. My flight reservation is for eleven days from today.

253

Heike and I talk little about it. I am not preparing anything either. We act as if everything will remain the same. Getting home in the dark. Waiting for electricity. Talking about the blockade. Pondering over Eastern money and Western money. Our daily kiss good night. Oh dear little Heike!

• • •

TUESDAY, DECEMBER 21, 1948

Something dismaying has happened. The village of Stolpe, on the northern edge of Berlin, with nearly a thousand inhabitants, who had voted "for freedom" on December 5, has been ceded to the Eastern zone by the French, its previous occupying power. "Incorporated into Brandenburg, in accordance with the agreement of October 29, 1945." This morning, between one and three o'clock, Soviet troops suddenly occupied the village. Its inhabitants are desperate.

"And what will we do if one day Berlin is incorporated like Stolpe?" some cynics ask. If only we knew! People around us look stunned and upset, and everybody has the same question: "Is that the future of those who voted for freedom?"

• • •

WEDNESDAY, DECEMBER 22, 1948

The Western city council protests against the unexpected cession and the violation of human rights. It would do anything to support those inhabitants of Stolpe who did not want to remain under Soviet rule. But what about their houses? Their apartments, their jobs, their livestock, their whole daily routine? Again people are fleeing across the border. Rather dead than enslaved. Rather dispossessed in the West than under the terror at home.

Battleground Berlin

• • •

All my papers are in order. In five days I am booked for the flight to Frankfurt. I say neither yes nor no. The weather report predicts continuing fog. Who knows . . .

"By the way, I got us some fir sprigs," Heike tells me toward evening. I completely forgot. It is Christmas. When the electricity is on she prepares a punch of brandy and sugar. "Cheers," she mumbles. We do not look at each other.

• • •

SUNDAY, DECEMBER 26, 1948

Saying good-bye. Walking through the streets I feel like touching every stone. I approach strangers, asking them something. They are Berliners, I think. The affinity I feel for them, the love. Here nobody says that they stole our atomic bomb. Nobody wants to reintroduce corporal punishment or allows his judgment of someone to depend on whether he is from Bavaria, Baden or Berlin.

My editor-in-chief looks at me as if I were a deserter. But he too has no more hope. There are not many people to whom I have to say good-bye. I am walking through the streets as in a dream. Over there, in front of that overpass, Andrik died. He, too, loved Berlin and would not want me to leave. There is the house where they came for the Jacobs, the Bernsteins and little Evelyn who only once in her life had eaten a real pear. The café where Heinrich Mühsam sat putting his papers in order has long since ceased to exist, destroyed just like the villa on Ihnestrasse in Dahlem. I put some flowers on the graves of Ursula Reuber and Eva Gerichter. You willed us to be the administrators of your uncompleted life's work. Have we carried out that task, have we carried the spark across the times? I think of Count Moltke, of Trott, of Wolfgang Kühn, of Anna Lehmann, Peter Tarnovsky and Margot Rosenthal. I think of Mr. Erichsohn whom I never met, who

255

didn't want to go on and decided otherwise. And I do feel a little like a traitor. But isn't their task beyond Berlin, beyond time and place? Freya Moltke's words come to mind: "It is a grace to be allowed to carry on the spark. Sometime—at the end of the desert—it will be waiting for us too—the child."

It's late by the time I get home. Heike runs to meet me in the hallway. Her smile looks a little forced. "I have been waiting for you!"

• • •

I never realized that twenty kilos of luggage is so little. I am packing with a scale. Winter clothes. By the time summer comes, I will have been back for a long time. I just don't want to get sentimental now. Heike has procured a bottle of cognac. "Cheers!" she mumbles. And again we do not look at each other.

I must leave now. It takes two hours to get to the Tempelhof Airport. There are strict controls. All luggage is searched. A bodily search. Statutory declaration that one carries no more than three hundred West marks. Then a cordon separates those departing from those who stay behind. "Heike," I stammer. She waves. I see her childlike face in the dense fog.

"Fog," I tell myself. "The plane won't fly."

Outside, engines roar. "Passengers for the Berlin to Frankfurt flight are requested to take their seats," someone announces over a loud-speaker. Mechanically I start moving. Mechanically I sink into my seat and fasten my seat belt. "Toward freedom," the person next to me says. Toward freedom, I want to respond. But the words are stuck in my throat.

The engines roar. We are rolling down the runway, slowly at first, then faster and faster until, with a jerk, the plane rises into the air. Lawns, lights, building walls, railroad tracks, streets disappear in the fog. Somewhere down there Heike stands and cries as I do. Somewhere down there, disappearing in the fog, lies the battleground of Berlin.

AFTERWORD

Who was Ruth Andreas-Friedrich, the author of *Battleground Berlin?* Born on September 23, 1901, in Berlin-Schöneberg, she was the daughter of Privy War Councillor Dr. Max Behrens—whose title makes him sound more martial than he really was—and his wife Margarete. She spent her childhood in Berlin, Stettin, and Metz and attended a secondary school for girls in Magdeburg until 1918. From 1922 to 1923 she worked as an apprentice in a bookstore in Breslau. She moved to Berlin, and in 1924 she married Otto A. Friedrich, an industrial manager who after the Second World War became president of the West German Employers Federation. Her daughter Karin Friedrich—who is Heike in the book—was born in 1925, and in 1930 her marriage ended in divorce.

In the 1920s Andreas-Friedrich had begun working as a journalist, writing book reviews and feature articles for the *Neue Badische Zeitung* and the *Königsberger Allgemeine,* and later she wrote for various women's papers and magazines. "From the beginning of the war I was responsible for the question-and-answer column and all topics regarding human relationships at the magazine *Die Junge Dame,*" she wrote in an autobiographical statement in 1946.

After the war, Andreas-Friedrich became the licensee and copublisher of the weekly *Sie,* but in 1948 she left Berlin—as described in

Battleground Berlin—because of the increasingly difficult working conditions, and moved to West Germany where she continued working as a journalist in Munich. In 1955 she married Professor Walter Seitz, director of the University Hospital in Munich. She died in Munich on October 12, 1977.

If one takes a look at the books and articles Andreas-Friedrich published, it becomes evident that only with two books does she enter the realm of literature: *Berlin Underground*, first published in English in the United States in 1946, and its sequel, *Battleground Berlin*, which contains her diaries from 1945 until her departure from Berlin in December 1948. Both books are extremely revealing authentic personal testimonies of German history from 1938 to 1948, that is, from the eve of the war to the beginnings of the West and East German states.

Yet it was not just literary ambition that motivated her to write and publish her 1938–1945 diaries. She wanted the German people to be able to feel something other than shame vis-à-vis foreigners; to bear witness that there were those who stayed in Berlin not because they were Nazi collaborators—she herself could easily have emigrated to Sweden—but because they were willing to risk their own lives in order to help politically persecuted Jewish and non-Jewish fellow citizens—to get them abroad, as long as it was still possible, to hide them, feed them, procure for them ration cards and identification documents. Her diary entries during the war years focus on the help that she and her widespread circle of friends, under the threat of death or concentration camp, provided to opponents and victims of Hitler. Vividly she describes for us their continually tested resourcefulness in finding gaps in the surveillance system of the Gestapo, the police, and the SS and in forging documents, and their desperation when they did not succeed in hiding someone or saving the person's life. Indeed, through her dedication to this work in a city gradually falling into ruins, Ruth Andreas-Friedrich contributed to the fact that some fifteen hundred to two thousand Jews were able to survive the Third Reich in Berlin, the Nazi capital itself. It is not surprising that Alfred Frankenstein, in an obituary published in 1977 in the *Israel Nachrichten*, wrote about her: "She is one of those just Germans who saved the reputation of her people during its worst time. May her memory be blessed."

Afterword

Those interested in further details of Ruth Andreas-Friedrich's activities in the Berlin resistance group "Uncle Emil" may refer to the Appendix of the 1986 German edition of *Berlin Underground,* which lists the code names of the group's members and contains documents detailing their activities.*

After the war Andreas-Freidrich continued her diary, and in 1949, her first year in West Germany, later to become the Federal Republic, she put together a second manuscript under the title *Battleground Berlin.* Here again she proved a keen observer of the city of Berlin and its citizens. Through her eyes we see their mixture of courage and depression, of defiance yet willingness to adapt. Relieved at having survived and at the same time as if in a daze, the Berliners in her pages take up the toilsome daily struggle for survival, clearing rubble, and reconstruction.

The entries from 1945 to 1948 are moving and shattering for two reasons. First is the terse description, painful but without self-pity, of a city so pitifully bombed out, of hunger, cold, and misery so bad we can hardly imagine anything worse. And second but equally noteworthy are the writer's terrified forebodings that her hopes for a restoration of Germany, built on reason and a sense of shame, were illusory or at least would not be realized in the near future. Her notes present unerring evidence of the failure of a real new beginning in Germany, with Berlin serving as a model—a political and moral failure due to many reasons.

As Andreas-Friedrich testifies in her telegraphic yet eloquent style, even for the most reasonable Germans and those most willing to change, hunger and cold at first simply were more concrete than "collective guilt" or shame. There was little time for serious thought as people had to resort to the wildest means, including bartering and trading on the black market, in order to somehow keep their families alive. In addition, Berlin by the summer of 1945 had become a city divided into four sectors governed by the four Allied powers. In the Soviet sector, as in the Soviet-occupied zone of Germany, fear of the Gestapo and the pervasive Nazi surveillance system was now replaced by fear of the occupying Russians and of the Stalinist communism

* Der Schattenmann, Tagebuchaufzeichnungen 1938–1945. With an afterword by Jörg Drews. Frankfurt: Suhrkamp, 1986. Paperback #126.7

they imported and brutally enforced, with the aid of the German Communists.

As the eastern zone, later to become the German Democratic Republic, with East Berlin as its capital, slipped instantly from one totalitarian regime to another, its population, unlike the rest of Germany, had no chance to breathe freely or to practice democracy. And as the Russians celebrated their victory over the country that had invaded and burned down theirs from 1941 to 1945 and killed twenty million of their countrymen, anti-Russian sentiments left over from Nazi times developed anew. These feelings, reinforced by the treatment the East Germans suffered under Stalinism, could then be used by the Western powers in their Cold War propaganda.

"The Third Reich has vanished like a ghost," wrote the diarist on May 2, 1945. Yet for Ruth Andreas-Friedrich and her friends, the surprise and relief at the collapse of Hitler's regime vanished almost as quickly. As early as May 1945, during the first crisis among the Allies, the conflict between East and West that would turn Berlin into a front-line city became evident. It remains difficult today to determine which combination of misunderstandings, miscalculations, and maneuvers of power politics led to the Cold War, which first took solid shape during the spring of 1947 as the Iron Curtain began to be lowered over Europe and across Germany. *Battleground Berlin* describes some of the factors that prevented a fruitful self-reflection on the part of the Germans at the time. As refugees being transferred from the eastern territories ceded to Russia and Poland at Potsdam streamed through a Berlin choked with rubble and stinking of decay, the already miserable conditions turned into a grim struggle for survival. Equally devastating were developments in the local political sphere. In 1946 the Social Democratic party, rich in traditions and marked by courageous resistance under the Nazi regime, was forced by the East German Communists, supported by the Russians, to fuse with them into the Socialist Unity party, which thereafter ruled—and ruined—the East German state.

Also counterproductive, Andreas-Freidrich writes, was the denazification procedure devised by the Allies, and enforced in such a routine and naive manner that it failed to distinguish between harmless and truly nefarious Nazi Party members. The Nuremberg trials, although morally justified, were carried out in an equally ineffective manner. And when in 1948–49 the Soviets undertook to blockade Berlin, attempting to cut off the city's connections to the West and starve out two million people—as the Germans had tried a few years earlier with Leningrad—resentment against Russia and communism grew and West Berliners felt as if they were on the front lines of a war.

Ruth Andreas-Friedrich was also disappointed to see how the members of her small resistance cell took different directions politically after 1945, and how the "Uncle Emil" group dispersed when they no longer shared a common enemy. And with an almost prophetic vision that anticipated the events of August 13, 1961, the building of the wall straight through Berlin, she noted on September 6, 1948: "Perhaps by tomorrow we will have two city governments and along the sector boundary a Chinese wall with battlements and watchtowers. Perhaps then one will need a visa to go from Charlottenburg to Unter den Linden [the boulevard that begins at the Brandenburg Gate]."

As early as 1948 Andreas-Friedrich had had the premonition that a wall would be the last resort, the unavoidable consequence of trying to isolate Eastern Europe from Western Europe, East Germany from West Germany, East Berlin from West Berlin. I am sure she would have shared the infinitely deep emotions with which, in the fall of 1989, the Germans finally celebrated the collapse of the hated wall.

Working in Berlin in 1948, however, became increasingly frustrating for Andreas-Friedrich. The conditions of the blockade were such that, due to the lack of paper, hardly any magazines could be published. On December 29, 1948, she left her beloved Berlin. ". . . to be living here among the ruins seems equivalent to already be lying in one's own coffin," the poet Gottfried Benn wrote to a friend from the divided, blockaded, and freezing city.

Benn was able to hold out during that terrible time, but Ruth Andreas-Friedrich could no longer live in postwar Berlin. Yet she has described it for us in a way that is totally unpretentious and, precisely because of its dry and modest style, an accurate, unique, and unforgettable document.

—Jörg Drews
Bielefeld, West Germany
January, 1990